SEND ME A
SIGN

With Love
& Many
Blessings
Kellie Grill

SEND ME A
SIGN

Doug Binder
with Dave Grill
and Kellie Poulsen-Grill

Whirlwind
PUBLISHING

Whirlwind Publishing
P.O. Box 1254
Wilsonville, Oregon 97070
(503) 685-9426
whirlwindpublishing.com

Cover design art by Paul Wright @ wrightsideupdesign.com
Back cover art: John R. O'Brien
Black and White Photos by Amanda Campy
    c/o Visual Impressions Photography
Composition: William H. Brunson Typography Services

ISBN 1-932475-07-9

This book is based on an article titled "Help From Above" that was first published in *The Oregonian* newspaper.

This book printed and bound by Eagle Web Press and Your Town Press, Salem, OR.

Send Me A Sign is a non-fiction work. All events, places, and names, except in a few instances to protect the privacy of individuals, are factual and come from the memory of Dave Grill, Kellie Poulsen-Grill and others.

For Teresa,
whose enduring spirit
continues to guide our lives

PREFACE

It is almost five years since the Tualatin City Little League softball team marched through the tournaments, each one against progressively better competition, and reached the World Series. It was back then, in the August of 2000, that I was asked to go to Lynnwood, Washington to cover Western regional games.

The assignment did not inspire me. I was leery of meeting "Little League" parents, and witnessing first-hand the epidemic of boorish behavior and pushy parenting that had made headlines.

But then I met the Grills. Dave, the dad, was one of the coaches, along with Mark Wiese and Tom Re. Good guys. Good fathers. They kept a cooler of cheap beer in the hotel room, and invited me to join them after I finished my stories.

And I met Teresa Grill that weekend. She seemed to me to be the type of woman that could maintain her grace in chaos— and a hotel room full of sixth grade girls was certainly that. I wouldn't know until later that she had been a teacher and disciplinarian at Beaumont Middle School in Portland, and later Athey Creek in West Linn.

A year later, the summer of 2001, I called Mark Wiese to ask him about the girls that played in the World Series together. Were they still playing together? How had that experience affected their seventh grade years?

Mark told me then what the family had been through. I was stunned.

I wondered about calling Dave, asking him more about what he was going through. Had the other families rallied around the Grills? Were they doing OK?

Mark put me in touch with Dave, and I drove out to one of Lauren's softball games in Newberg. We drove over to an Arctic Circle and talked about the year he and his family had been through.

Back at *The Oregonian* I was ready to pitch a story. I told Sarah Smith, one of the editors, what I had learned. I wasn't sure if the story was going to be a traditional sports story, but there was an interesting tale here. And Dave thought there was some merit to telling it.

I thought I might finish it in time to coincide with the 2001 Little League World Series, but that deadline proved too difficult to meet. Every time I went back to talk with Dave, who was by then with Kellie, there was a new wrinkle to the story. I had it ready to go by September, but then the terrorist bombings on 9/11 took away all of the paper's available space.

I kept at it. Maybe I could get the latest version in by Thanksgiving? Maybe I could get it re-polished in time to run at Christmas?

I worked to improve the story, with Sarah's help, and my story got some support from editors outside of the sports department, in the newsroom.

It finally ran as the centerpiece of the Metro/Northwest page on Valentine's Day, 2002, under the headline "Help From Above."

The article elicited a response unlike any I've ever written in my newspaper job. E-mails, phone calls, even hand-written letters came in over the course of a week. Some were supportive, a few were skeptical or downright critical, but all were touched in some way.

Dave Grill and Kellie Poulsen got feedback too, and their story kept on evolving. They asked me to turn their story into a book after a Super Bowl party they hosted in early 2003. And for the next year and a half, I made it my part-time job and hobby to write it—one Wednesday evening at a time.

I set a few ground rules early. I imagined a book that was non-fiction narrative, and that's what we have. Everything in this book is the best recollection of the people involved. The dialogue has been reconstructed to move the story forward, but used sparingly in most cases, and with the words that were most probably said.

I am not sure whether I ever arrived at a clear understanding of the number 333, but for the Grills it is simply Morse code from Teresa. I imagine three words: I love you.

I can't say that I have ever experienced the presence of angels the way the Grills have, but I do now believe in them. Most of all, I believe that a spirit can transcend the body that carried it in life. And I believe that by witnessing first-hand the energy that comforts and inspires Dave, Kellie, Nikki, Lauren and Johnny.

—Doug Binder

∞

Three and a half years after our story was first told in the pages of *The Oregonian* newspaper, there is still a surreal quality about what we went through.

Today, I was on the way back from Klamath Falls and decided to stop for gas and call Kellie. I looked down at my watch and it was 3:33 P.M. Even the second hand was clicking past 33 seconds. And I heard a familiar song, one that made me think of Teresa.

It wasn't until I returned home that I was reminded that it was my 21st wedding anniversary with Teresa. Suddenly, those little signs made sense. She still sends them to us, even when we don't get their meaning right away.

The process of writing this book was gratifying for several reasons:

First, because we felt we had a story to tell and we were determined to tell it. It turned out exactly as we wanted it. It is what it is, and we're sure it will thrill some, and exasperate others.

Secondly, writing and publishing this book has been a remarkable process. It has taken us countless hours, and has given in to many sleep deprived nights, but we did it and we are so proud of the outcome.

We hope that you enjoy our story, and that you will take something away from reading it, whether it be how to cope with someone who is terminally ill, how to remain hopeful and positive when darkness is all you see, or how to believe in and be guided by angels.

This book is our treasure. It is our gift to you.

—Dave and Kellie

ACKNOWLEDGMENTS

Who to thank poses a huge problem for the limited pages we have left in this book. There are so many people to thank we could never list or name them all.

Our lives are blessed by many incredible individuals, and we owe so many of our family and friends gratitude for all they do for us, and for all of the love and support they give to us.

Everyone who we have been fortunate enough to share our existences with deserves our recognition. You all know who you are! We try constantly to convey our love, repect, and grateful hearts to each and everyone of you on a daily basis.

Thank you to everyone involved in this book project, especially Doug Binder who shared with us his brilliant gift of writing. Thanks to all of you who believe in this book and have shared your enthusiasim and kind words. It really means a lot to us to have your support.

To all of our family and friends that are involved in our lives. You make us whole. You make us happy, and you make life grand! God bless and remember—we love you all!

—Kellie and Dave

PROLOGUE I

February 9, 2001

Dave Grill saw the first of the rainbows off to the right.

The vivid colors shone bright, fueled by a column of sunlight that punched a hole through the same gray clouds that sprinkled a lazy drizzle onto the lush green meadow. Second-growth Douglas fir mixed with oak fringed the hillsides like garland. Dave saw another rainbow in his rearview mirror. Then another one appeared, to the front and right of his white Chevy Suburban. And he saw yet another one farther up ahead, high in the sky. He began to have the sensation that he was driving through a kaleidoscope.

He shook his head and blinked, disbelieving that the rainbows could be more than an extension of his daydream about Teresa, the kids, and the next step that was beginning to seem inevitable.

The rainbows seemed to dance all around him. One in particular, to his right, seemed to keep pace with his 70 miles per hour. He was moving north on Interstate 5 in the direction of home.

Dave followed the rainbow—or maybe it followed him?—about four miles, but it never faded. It was unlike anything Dave had ever seen before. It struck him as otherworldly as if he were witnessing a UFO.

"Am I crazy?" he mumbled under his breath.

That thought was gathering steam.

It had been a whirlwind couple of months. And his emotions had run the spectrum, much like these rainbows. But this light display—and its occurring so soon after thinking deeply about Teresa—seemed more than coincidence. Dave had never really been much of a religious man. But lately, he was beginning to wonder if there was a lot more to the world than he had given it credit for.

Dave passed two cars as the rainbows were at their most radiant. He made sure to look at each driver, gesturing with his hands as if to ask, "Do you see what I see?"

They, too, had astonished looks on their faces. This remote segment of interstate in Douglas County, Oregon had somehow found a way to dazzle them all. The faces of the passengers confirmed for Dave that he wasn't hallucinating.

The rainbows had come alive, or so it seemed, and enveloped his SUV.

Were they really for him? Were they confirmation from Teresa that he was doing the right thing by moving on so quickly?

Odd, Dave thought, how rainbows kept appearing just as he was feeling especially receptive to a sign from above.

He leaned back in his seat, took a deep fulfilling breath, and smiled. With all that had gone on, most of it inexplicable, Dave knew better than to analyze it too closely. He was ready to accept it.

The rainbows, he decided, were Teresa's way of saying "Thank you" to him for keeping his promise.

PROLOGUE II

Easter Sunday, April 20, 2003

Kellie playfully furrowed her eyebrows and pressed her lips together to make a mock-angry face, but couldn't hold it in place for more than a second before she joined Nikki and Wilma in a private giggle. The three of them were huddled together at a small round table inside the Old Bridge Gourmet Deli, on Lexington Avenue in the heart of Manhattan, just a couple blocks from where they were staying at the Grand Hyatt Hotel.

Kellie had her back to the cranky man on the cell phone, who was arguing with his wife in an ornery New York accent at a volume that everyone in the crowded deli was forced to hear. He was oblivious to them as he waited for his order and shouted into the phone.

On the opposite side of them, Kellie could see a couple in their mid-20s. They were obviously smitten with one another, holding hands across their table and talking softly.

Kellie, Nikki and Wilma quietly observed one table, then the next. Wilma, between bites of a spring roll from the buffet table, commented on the spotlessness of the deli as the Chinese owner sporadically swept the few visible crumbs off a gleaming tile floor.

When the loud man's order came up, he reached to grab his bag from the counter, maintained his argument on the phone, turned, and left.

The man took the noise with him, leaving the deli suddenly peaceful. Kellie paused from chewing a bite of her salad, looked to Nikki, and said, "Oh . . . do you hear that?"

Playing softly on the radio was a tune that resonated instantly in Kellie's ears. It was the country song "I Hope You Dance," by

Leann Womack. The sound was coming from a ceiling speaker located directly above their table.

All three of them shared a knowing smile.

"Can you believe that?" Kellie asked.

All three of them shook their heads, amazed.

"That is a little freaky," Nikki said.

It was the first song they had heard since leaving the Easter service they had attended an hour earlier at the Brooklyn Tabernacle. Hearing it gave Kellie goose bumps.

Later that evening, Nikki, 17, was scheduled to sing with her Wilsonville High School choir at Carnegie Hall. That was the reason for the New York City visit, and the performance would be the culmination of a school trip that included sightseeing excursions to Time Square, the Empire State Building, the Statue of Liberty, and on a more solemn note, Ground Zero—the site where the World Trade Center towers had fallen on 9/11.

"Well, I guess we better go so we can get you ready to sing at Carnegie Hall tonight," Kellie said, smiling proudly and speaking at a volume that everyone in the small deli could hear.

The three of them stood up and picked up their paper plates, plastic forks and napkins. Kellie, one step ahead of Nikki's grandmother, glanced up at a clock on the wall as she dumped her garbage.

The sight momentarily stopped her. "Oh my God," Kellie said, turning excitedly to Nikki and Wilma. "Guess what time it is?"

Nikki looked first at her grandma, and then they answered Kellie in unison: "Three thirty-three!"

PART ONE

These Boots & Me

CHAPTER ONE

The Best Summer

Wednesday, August 9, 2000

Lauren slid the toe of her left cleat across the dirt and hard against the side of the third base bag, as if it were a starting block. She crouched slightly into a ready stance, acutely aware of the situation and ready to blast off the bag in an instant. She tightened her lips over her mouthful of braces and squinted into the bright orange late afternoon sun. Lauren wore black greasepaint across her cheeks to reduce the glare, but looking into the sun she had to focus under the horizon to see home plate clearly.

Dave Grill, her dad, was just a few feet away in the third base coach's box. His body language was subtly growing more animated, too. "Loe," as her family and most of her teammates called her, didn't need his instruction here. The 12-year-old knew what to do and when to do it. The importance of this particular at-bat made her hands sweaty inside the black gloves she wore. She took a deep breath to suppress her jangling nerves.

At the plate was lefty Carlyn Re, Lauren's best friend. The way Tualatin City had been hitting this pitcher, the outcome of this softball game was becoming a foregone conclusion. The girls from the suburb south of Portland, Oregon, led 9-0 against Foothill Little League, a team from Glendale, Calif.

The first pitch was a fastball that came in a little high, a little bit inside. But Carlyn got around on it, making enough contact to chop the day-glo yellow softball down the right field line and past first base.

Lauren shoved off third base on contact, and when she saw the ball was in fair play, she bolted toward home plate.

"Go!" Dave yelled.

She was already on her way.

Thirteen steps later, Lauren's right foot stomped on the plate, and her excitement bubbled over like an uncorked bottle of champagne. She jumped into the air electrically, half a second ahead of the realization of most spectators that the game was over. The 10-run "mercy rule" was in effect.

Without stopping, Lauren swerved to her left and ran up the first base line to greet Carlyn. They caught each other in a hug, smiling so hard it was difficult to utter more than giggles.

They were Western Regional Champions.

They were headed to the World Series.

Across the diamond charged the rest of the Tualatin City Little League team, sprinting, skipping and screaming. The girls high-fived, hugged and danced. Lauren let go of Carlyn and approached her dad, near the pitching rubber. She leapt onto his body, wrapping her arms around his neck and her legs around his waist.

"We did it! We did it!" Lauren yelled.

"Great job, Loe!" Dave said.

Beyond the outfield fence, Tualatin City's rooting section clapped and yelled its approval as well. The parents knew what it meant, too. The long summer softball ride was still alive, bound for one final destination. Their girls were qualified to play for the world championship of 11- and 12-year-old softball.

One player's father, suddenly overwhelmed, tilted his head back and bellowed toward sunset: "Whoooo Let The Dogs Out?"

It had become the team's battle cry.

"Whuuh . . . Whuu-Whuu . . . Whuuu!" came the reply from behind him.

The group of families that composed the team had its sweetest moment of a long summer. And for the Grill family, victory never felt so good. It felt like redemption.

Tualatin City Little League parents were cresting on the same wave as their daughter-players. The players had pointed to the World Series as nine-year-olds, and worked three years to get there. In the summer of 2000, the dream had drawn closer, finally becoming a reality. It came one pitch, one out, one inning at a time, on a string of successive weekends.

The group of families that were central to the effort had made the commitment to see it through. Softball was the focus of nearly every weekend that summer, for the players, parents and siblings.

They knew that they had a chance of making it all the way to the World Series, which incidentally wasn't very far from home. The World Series of Little League baseball, the most famous youth sports event in the world, brings an annual spotlight to Williamsport, Pa. The national counterpart for girls is the stately little league park located in the West Hills of Portland, on the grounds of Alpenrose Dairy.

Four families were at the heart of the tightly bound team. Mark Wiese was the manager, amiable and organized. He was detail oriented and had a light hand with the kids. It was his duty to make sure that substitution rotations were followed and that everyone played. His wife, Danelle, was the head of Tualatin City Little League. And their daughter, Leticia, tall and thin and bespectacled, played right field.

Tom Re was the pitching coach who made no attempt to conceal his energy or excitable personality. He was big and lovable, and dispensing bear hugs was not the least of his duties. He organized practice schedules and scripted practice drills so that every player knew what she was doing and when she was doing it. His daughter, Carlyn, tall and strong, alternated between first base and pitcher.

Doug Johnson was the father of Amanda Johnson, an athletically gifted shortstop with quick reflexes, fast feet and a strong arm. He was dubbed "the human pitching machine" for the countless pitches he threw to simulate live game situations for batting practice. Although he was not an official coach, he was an integral part of the staff.

The final coach was Dave Grill, an employee of a scrap metal company who oozed confidence and brought the team a sense of serene calm. His own athletic history was unspoken but evident in the way he carried himself and communicated with the girls. He was a former all-state high school football player in Utah. A small college star running back in the early 1980s at Portland's Lewis & Clark College. A scratch golfer whose scorching drives off the tee were the stuff of family legend. As a kid, he had been the best youth goalie in Portland's burgeoning ice hockey scene. And when he played a season of American Legion baseball in high school, on a lark, he posted a batting average of .618.

Lauren, his middle child, played catcher. Chatty, friendly and energetic to the point of hyper, she was one of several players with braces on their teeth. She was a natural leader, like her dad. She was a cornerstone behind the plate, preventing the passed balls and wild pitches that torment other teams of 12-year-olds. Her older sister, Nicole, 14, was along for the ride. Two years removed from her own little league experience, she gravitated toward a cheerleading role with a group of proud sisters. They waved pom-poms and painted each other's faces. Johnny, at 9, was the youngest of the Grills. He respected his sister's playing prowess, but was quick to remind any of them that when he got to 12, he'd do it even better. He cheered a bit too, when he wasn't feeling self-conscious about rooting for a team of girls.

Teresa Grill was at the front and center. She was unofficial team mom, driver, hair-braider, face-painter, cooler-stocker, hug-giver and one of the loudest parents in the stands. Dark brown curls framed her round face and she was quick to engage a conversation, though her eyes would sometimes stray back to the field. And when Lauren came up to bat, she would politely take a break. "Hold on just a sec . . . C'mon Lau-REN!" Her bright green eyes and easy smile held up through the nerves and worry that came during the crucial moments of dramatic games. And her irrepressible personality inspired the mothers and daughters that knew her best. They were also the ones who knew her as a cancer survivor.

When the best of the players merged for the "all-stars" portion of the summer—that's when little league organizations choose the best players to represent them in the biggest tournaments—Tualatin City fielded a roster that was rock solid. Dave, the onfield game-time coach, imparted a philosophy that stressed aggressive base running that pressured less skilled defensive teams. He dared other teams to prevent stolen bases. Runners at third base tagged up and charged for home on every popup to reach the outfield, no matter how shallow.

The Tualatin City Little League All-Stars gave their collective group of parents, relatives and friends a stirring month of weekends beginning in July. At the Oregon District 4 tournament, held at Alpenrose, Tualatin City began to flex its collective muscle. Pitcher Alicia Mesa pitched a perfect game in the 15-0 championship win over Murrayhill, a perennially strong club based in Beaverton, Oregon.

From there, Tualatin City advanced to the state tournament, and swept it in four games. Victories over Grants Pass, Hermiston and Corvallis set the stage for the championship game against Sunrise Little League, from Southeast Portland. Tualatin City was dominant again, winning 10-0.

Then came the divisional tournament, held at SeaTac, Washington. It was there that Tualatin City faced some rare adversity, losing an early game to Woodinville, Washington and falling into the loser's bracket.

The coaches gathered the girls in the outfield and tried to offer words of encouragement. Mark Weise began by saying that although the team had made some mistakes, it was still alive. If they played smarter and better, they could come back and win it.

Dave could see the seeds of doubt on the players' faces. He chose his words carefully and he delivered them sternly. He wanted their attention. He wasn't about to let the feeling of a loss fester, and he knew he must nip it in the bud.

He stepped up close to them and spoke with measured intensity. "We . . . will . . . win . . . this . . . tournament," he said, pausing between each word for effect. He looked directly into each player's eyes, making sure his point was clear. "You get that in your heads right now."

Dave's message was heard. It was a turning point in the team's attitude. Over the next couple of days, Tualatin City beat Montana in a loser-out game and earned a rematch with Woodinville. This time, Tualatin City was tighter and more focused, and beat Woodinville not once, but twice, winning the tournament and taking another step toward the ultimate goal: The World Series. The back-to-back wins over a quality team gave the girls a surge of momentum.

The West Regional—involving an even broader scope of teams, the 8 best from 13 western states, including softball-rich California and Arizona—was merely a formality. Tualatin City's closest game was 8-2.

The spectators sat on risers beyond the outfield fence, squinting westward into the sun, wondering if their cheers of encouragement could even be heard. But in Tualatin City's case, all that was necessary was a field, a ball, an umpire and an opponent. The team took care of the rest.

The week following the regional championship was a blur of dizzying excitement.

It began with a celebration at a Lynnwood, Washington pizza parlor. The coaches all rose to speak, each of them acknowledging the hard work and commitment of the players and parents. When the words "World" and "Series" were uttered together, it elicited a spontaneous cheer from the giddy players.

The Grills returned home to Tualatin by midnight and they all went to bed satisfied with their accomplishment, curious about what was to come next.

Dave woke on Thursday morning and went to work. Yes, he had to remind himself, he did have a job. Fortunately, his boss didn't seem to mind as long as the team kept winning. Dave worked the phone, calling customers to apologize for his recent absences. One by one, when they heard his reason, they all understood. They all wished him, and the team, good luck.

Teresa began a new list of to-dos, answering the dozen or so messages on the answering machine, most of them friends and family offering congratulations or looking for details on upcoming games. She tackled a mountain of dirty laundry and turned her focus to what needed to be done next to keep the speeding train on its tracks.

By Saturday morning, Dave had borrowed a flatbed truck from work so that Lauren and her teammates could ride in Tualatin's annual Crawfish Festival. From the end of the parade, parents hustled the kids to a nearby park where they reassembled and were met by two stretch limousines, one black and one white.

The players and the three coaches piled into them, enjoying the attention and luxury afforded to World Series qualifiers.

Similar limos were used to shuttle arriving out-of-town teams from the Portland airport to Alpenrose, a 52-acre dairy complex in the southwest corner of the city. The little league field has been in use since 1956, and as a kids' diamond it is truly a gem. Flowers bloom out of large brick planters behind the backstop. The field is dressed in patriotic bunting and manicured for events like the softball World Series, and every chalk line and grass edge is sharp as any field in the major leagues. There is bleacher seating for about 3,000 spectators.

Tualatin City wasn't the first local team to make it to the World Series, but it wasn't an annual occurrence either. A team from Gresham, Oregon won the world title in 1981. As recently as the early 1990s, a team from east Portland had made an appearance.

But everyone involved with the tournament knew that Midway Little League from Waco, Texas was the team to beat. Waco had won the world championship seven of the past eight years.

As the girls from Texas pulled up in their limos, Tualatin City was already several steps ahead in the arrival procedure and was fully dressed in its fresh new purple "West" uniforms. The team was in centerfield, preparing to pose for its official picture. When the girls from Waco stepped out of the cars, the Tualatin girls took notice. Dave heard the murmuring. "There's Waco."

Tualatin City's momentum carried into the World Series, and to victories over the team representing the "Central" United States, Tallmadge, Ohio, and the team from Canada. Both were easy wins that set the stage for the showdown that was the talk of the tournament: Tualatin City vs. Waco.

That game, on a warm Wednesday night, began at 8 P.M. in front of one of the biggest crowds to watch a softball game in

Alpenrose's history. Local television cameras from four different stations were present to gather highlights for the 11 o'clock news. For one night at least, little league softball had become the biggest game in town. And it felt every bit like a championship night, regardless of the tournament's double-elimination set up.

The winner, most figured, would go all the way.

Wednesday, August 16, 2000

Rachel Fahlenkamp's austere expression seldom changed. From beneath her ball cap, she exuded supreme confidence. Her icy glare toward home plate was serious and concentrated.

At 5-foot-10, Fahlenkamp was a giant among 12-year-old girls. She had arrived from Waco, Texas with her teammates from Midway Little League with one mission: Win. There was very little of the singing and dancing that gave other dugouts the giddiness of a slumber party. The girls from Waco, Texas were here to take care of business.

With the short sleeve of her bright orange "South" jersey hiked up onto her lean shoulder, Fahlenkamp gripped the yellow softball in her right hand. With a powerful windmill motion, her fist punched through a long arc. The ball shot from her hand and smacked her catcher's mitt with a hard "thud."

Another strike. Another out. Fahlenkamp never smiled. Her attention never strayed from the business at hand, despite the large crowd and electrically charged atmosphere. Most in the crowd were hoping for her to fail, and she knew it. It made her concentrate even more.

In the second inning, Eryn Lerum stepped into the batter's box for Tualatin City. Already down 3-0, the girls from the nearby

Portland suburb were facing their stiffest challenge of the summer and searching for a way out.

Fahlenkamp's fastball came in belt-high and Lerum caught up to it, redirecting the ball deep into the outfield, nearly to the wall. That sent the crowd, numbering nearly four thousand, to its feet with eager anticipation. Lerum tore around first and headed into second base with the first promising moments of the game for Tualatin City.

Slightly rattled, Fahlenkamp tried to settle back into control. But she threw a pitch high and wide and the catcher missed it. Lerum scurried to third base on the wild pitch, and the throng of Tualatin City supporters roared its approval.

Dave Grill, from the third base coaching box, gave Rachel Bywater the signal to bunt. He turned to Lerum and said, "We're going on contact. Be ready." Lerum nodded back.

Fahlenkamp delivered the pitch and Bywater deftly reached out with her bat and tapped the ball downward just a few feet in front of home plate.

With her pigtails flying, Fahlenkamp lunged forward, picked up the rolling ball, and froze for an instant. She looked down the first base line, where Bywater was approaching first. A throw there and the runner on third would surely score. So Fahlenkamp turned and fired a rushed, errant throw that skipped past third base. Lerum scored and the sea of purple rose to its feet again.

It was not, however, a long-lived celebration. Fahlenkamp and her teammates were not only good, they were better in nearly all the ways that Tualatin City had gained its deserved status as a championship contender. They made tough defensive plays crisper. They swung their bats with more confidence.

After giving up a run, Fahlenkamp regained her focus and shut down the momentary Tualatin City uprising. She retired all three batters she faced in the third and fourth innings. She pitched to just four in the fifth and sixth innings.

When it was over, the seven-time champions from Texas were 5-1 winners.

The players from both teams lined up in opposite directions and filed past one another, slapping high fives.

Tualatin City's magical run had hit a brick wall. The team gathered into the outfield and Dave tried to recycle some of the lines he had used to such inspiring effect after the loss to Woodinville.

"We are coming back and we are going to take two games from Waco," Dave said, studying the players' faces as he spoke. "We will win this tournament."

The reaction wasn't the same this time. Dave, despite his own undiminished confidence in the girls, knew that the response to his words had changed. In their eyes was something different. They would try, but their belief and hope had been damaged. Their expression told him: "We did it once. It's not going to happen again."

The girls of the Tualatin City Little League team gathered their gear, slipped silently into the back seats of their parents' vehicles, and went home to watch themselves on the local news before going to bed.

Waco's 5-1 victory over Tualatin City was one of its closest of the entire summer. It was a four-run win for a team that seldom won by fewer than 10.

As Waco's players and parents reset their sights on the championship, Tualatin City fell into a loser-out game against the team from Far East—Bacolod City, Philippines.

Tualatin City played one of its most memorable games of the entire summer. After falling behind by four runs, the girls rallied to win 7-6 in extra innings. The win kept alive Tualatin City's championship hopes, but the task ahead was daunting.

To win, they would have to beat Waco twice.

The rematch lacked much of the electricity of the first game. It had become obvious that Waco was simply too strong. The team from Texas won again, this time 6-1, and clinched championship No. 8.

As the final out came, ending Tualatin City's lingering hopes and completing its No. 2 in the world placing, the sky darkened. The temperature dropped. Light rain quickly became a steady downpour. The shower lasted all of about 10 minutes before letting up and allowing Waco to resume its celebration outside of its dugout.

The sudden rain punctuated the end of the line for Tualatin City, serving to wash the slate clean. The glorious summer was over. It was time for something new. The players, coaches, and families, knew it by the time they left the Alpenrose parking lot.

Sunday, August 20, 2000

No rest for the weary, Dave thought to himself.

With softball season finally completed, he allowed himself to look ahead. He was also Johnny's fourth grade football coach, and had already missed the first two weeks of practice. "I'll be there tomorrow," he told his assistant coach over the phone.

With the kids in bed, Dave sat down next to Teresa in the family room. They looked at each other and sighed. It felt like the first time either of them had paused in more than a month.

The adrenaline rush provided by Lauren's softball team had crested like a wave, gracefully crashed on Saturday, and finally began to recede on Sunday.

Monday would start a new week. Dave didn't want to think about the mountain of paperwork that he knew was stacked on his desk at work. Teresa would fall back into a routine of preparing lesson plans and getting her seventh-grade classroom ready for the start of a new school year.

"I'll let you give me a foot rub," Teresa said, giving Dave her saddest puppy-dog face.

"Alright," Dave replied.

She swung her legs up and plopped her bare feet into Dave's lap.

"Hold it," he said. "I'd better get some lotion."

When he returned with the bottle, Teresa was stretched out on the couch with her right hand extended.

"How's it feeling?" Dave asked.

"Pretty swollen," she said.

"Let me see," Dave said, taking a closer look at her puffy fingers. "I'll work on that when I'm done with your feet."

In 18 years together, 16 of them married, Dave had mastered the art of relieving his wife's tension through her feet. A foot rub had long been one of the ways they had connected with one another. It melted away the stress and rejuvenated both of them, mind and spirit. Many of their important conversations had happened this way, with Teresa lying down, one of her feet cradled in Dave's strong hands.

As Dave applied the warmed lotion to Teresa's foot, he could feel her begin to relax.

"So how are you feeling?" Dave asked, becoming aware that it had been too long since they had discussed it.

"I think I could sleep for days," Teresa said, resting her head on the side of the couch and closing her eyes, pretending to fall asleep.

"Yeah. But how are you *feeling*?" Dave asked again.

"Kind of got a knot in my stomach, but I think I just need to get back to a normal schedule," Teresa said.

"Do you think you should get it checked out?"

"I'll be fine. Put some more lotion on my foot."

As he did, Dave couldn't help but let his mind wander back to September 9, 1998. Memories of that day, he knew, would stay with him forever, and it was coming up on two full years since then. He had returned from a business trip and Teresa had confided in him that she had felt a lump in her right breast.

After she showed Dave what clearly felt like an abnormal growth, he had urged her to have it checked out.

He remembered her words. "I think I will, even though I'm sure it's nothing. Mom, Tamara and me, we all have lumpy boobs. It's probably just a fibrous tumor or something."

Dave knew it wasn't normal. He asked her to call her doctor.

"Yeah, I'm going to make an appointment," she said.

Dave heard the same tone in Teresa's voice now. She was optimistic, even when they both knew that there was very little reason to be. They had been through enough to know better.

"I'll be fine," she said, the slightest hint of uncertainty in her voice.

"I know you will," Dave said. "But you might mention the knot in your stomach to him on your next appointment."

"I will."

Dave's hands kept working over Teresa's foot throughout the conversation, but he finally reached the point where he felt the first foot was done.

"OK," he said. "Let me see your other foot."

All the years of practice had made Dave a pro at the application of lotion and pressure. Dave squirted more lotion in his hands and rubbed them together to warm it up before touching her foot.

From time to time, though, Dave liked to tease her. And to lighten the mood, he chose this to be one of those times. Dave deliberately shot some of the goopy lotion directly onto the top of her foot, which made her squirm and recoil.

"Brrrrrr! That's cold!" Teresa blurted.

"Oh, quit complaining," Dave snickered, as he began to spread the lotion over her foot.

"That's mean," Teresa protested.

"Do you want me to stop?" Dave asked, knowing that it would take nothing short of a sudden earthquake to get him out of finishing the job.

"No. Go ahead," she said as she sighed.

Dave rubbed the foot vigorously, pressing against the underside and kneading the arch with the palm of his hand. He carefully pinched each toe slightly, gently pulling on it, before moving on to something else.

"What a summer," Dave said, staring straight ahead and shaking his head as if he had a hard time comprehending all of it.

"I know," Teresa said. "I can't believe how fast it went. Now it's back to the same old grind. It's something we'll never forget."

She paused to consider the rush of the recent weeks.

"You know," Teresa said. "I think this was the best summer of my life."

"Yeah, mine too," Dave said.

Much like the summer, though, the same old grind would continue to keep the family going at a hectic pace. But it was nothing like the ride the family had just completed. Even Johnny and Nikki had been caught up in the excitement of watching their sister play ball.

The summer had been a much needed distraction.

For much of the previous two years, Teresa's struggle with breast cancer had cast a pall over the family, turning routine life into something entirely different.

The family had endured its share of trauma—sadness, worry, fear, fatigue—as Teresa endured her diagnosis and all that came after, which included two surgeries, chemotherapy, radiation treatment and the side effects: nausea, fatigue and hair loss.

One of the side effects was lymph edema in her right arm. The lymph nodes under Teresa's right arm pit had to be removed because the cancer had spread to them. Without lymph nodes to filter normal fluids, the body becomes susceptible to lymph edema, an ailment that produces severe swelling to the tissues of the arm and hand.

One of the therapeutic treatments for lymph edema is very simple, Dave and Teresa learned, and it was nothing more than a gentle finger-tip stroking of the affected tissue.

"How was that?" Dave asked as he finished massaging Teresa's left foot.

"Heavenly," Teresa said lazily.

"Let me see your arm now," Dave said.

Teresa sat up to let Dave take a closer look at the arm. "Ooh, it's a bit swollen," he said.

"I know, I haven't been keeping up with it like I should," Teresa agreed.

Dave scowled at her, then said, "Let me rub it a while." He knew Teresa wouldn't resist his offer.

After repositioning on the couch, Dave began gently stroking Teresa's arm the way he had been trained many months before by the physical therapist when the condition first appeared.

To Dave, it had seemed like an exercise in futility. The competitor in him wanted to attack the swelling by starting at the fingers and pressing the fluid upward and away. But the doctor had assured them that he should take the opposite approach. So soft, delicate touch was the pattern Dave followed.

After a few minutes, Dave could feel her relax by the dead weight of her arm in his hand.

Then, out of the blue, Teresa asked the question that Dave had asked himself a thousand times in the past year and a half: "What if it comes back?"

They had both thought about it, even discussed it in round-about ways. The summer had allowed them to put cancer on the back burner and focus on the positive objectives that were tangible with the softball team.

Teresa had been feeling relatively well, although the treatments had taken a toll, both physically and emotionally. But lately, she had been showing her old, usual spark.

"Well, I don't think it's going to happen," Dave said, as matter-of-factly as possible. There was no response.

Uh oh, Dave thought. Is she not telling me something? Is she concerned? Afraid? Wanting to discuss the what-ifs? Maybe she wanted me to say "Don't be ridiculous! There's not a chance in hell of it coming back!"

But then Teresa broke her silence.

"What if it does?" she said. "I don't think I could go through that again."

Dave did his best to reassure her.

"We have to trust the doctors," he said. "They seem pretty confident that they got it."

From the outset, Dave and Teresa had made a pact to be honest, truthful and candid with their feelings. They had agreed not to tippy-toe around the disease. Dave could feel that some of those "moments of truth" were about to come, if not this night, then soon.

"We'll cross that bridge when we come to it," Dave continued. He wanted to wince as he spoke the words, catching himself in a cliché.

"And we'll kick, scratch, claw and do whatever it takes to beat it," he said. His pep talks at least made him feel better, and he knew they cheered Teresa up too.

Teresa, by now, was resigned to the fact that Dave was trying his best to find comforting words, even if they did sound like they had come from a football coach in a locker room.

"OK," she muttered, laying her head against the back of the couch and turning her eyes up to the ceiling.

Several minutes of quiet went by. Dave continued to stroke his wife's arm with the tips of his fingers, wishing that his touch had the power to heal her.

"I think I'd better stop," Dave said, remembering the physical therapist's warning about overstimulation. "It's late anyway. We'd better get to bed."

Teresa was nearly asleep already and Monday would bring the start of a busy week.

She opened her eyes and smiled at Dave. "Thanks. That felt really good."

They walked up the stairs together and peeked into the rooms of the three kids. All were sound asleep.

As they climbed into their bed together, Dave could feel the tiredness in his bones. He knew that for Teresa the feeling was probably amplified. He lay in bed on his back, wide awake in the dark, and his mind involuntarily turned to one nagging question.

"What if it *does* come back?"

Teresa was thinking the same thing. But she had been thinking it much longer than Dave. She had even written a poem about the feeling, something she often did to express the emotions that welled inside her.

She called the poem "My New Best Friend":

I have a new best friend
We are together constantly
Never apart
My new best friend and me
My new best friend's name is
What if
What if they missed some
What if it comes back
What if I have to go through chemo again
What if I can't do it?
What if . . . ?

CHAPTER TWO

Dealing With Bad News

September, 1998

The Lump hung over their heads. It seemed lodged in their throats also, as the waiting dragged on from one day to the next.

Finally, Teresa went to get a definitive answer about what exactly the hard tissue in her right breast was, what it was doing there, and how to get rid of it.

Teresa's condition was noted in her medical file after a thorough physical examination: "There is in the lateral portion of the right breast a palpable area of thickening with a smaller dominant lesion laterally in the mid portion of the breast. This is mildly tender to direct palpation. There is no adenopathy in the axila, supraclavicular or cervical areas."

In other words, Teresa had a lump, of unknown origin and substance. So far, it was nothing more than what she already knew.

The doctor recommended that she have the area removed by biopsy. He scheduled a mammogram.

On September 23—Dave's 38th birthday —Teresa went in for the mammogram.

After the results came back, Teresa and Dave met with the surgeon, Dr. Mathis, to discuss the results and decide what to do next. Dr. Mathis was in his early 40s. Teresa and Dave were impressed with his easy demeanor and apparent expertise. He showed them the mammogram pictures and explained that in order to be sure what was going on, Teresa must undergo a surgical lumpectomy or a needle biopsy to get tissue for analysis.

The doctor examined Teresa's breast and recommended a lumpectomy.

"Look doctor, this is all new to us," Dave said, while Teresa put her shirt back on. "We're totally relying on you."

"Well, because of the size of the mass, I really feel that we need to go in and remove it and get a good look at what's going on," the doctor said. "Teresa, because you're, well . . . you're . . ."

Dave interrupted, thinking it was a good time to set a new tone with the doctor.

"Doc, we all know she's got big tits! What are you trying to say?" Dave said.

Dr. Mathis chuckled before replying: "You have enough tissue to allow me to remove the mass and any surrounding tissue without your having to look out of proportion."

Proportion was the last thing on Teresa's mind.

"I just want it out of there," she said quietly, restraining her emotions.

Dave was still trying to gain rapport and trust with someone that he suddenly knew he needed to depend on.

"Can I ask you a question?" Dave asked.

"Sure, anything," Dr. Mathis replied.

"Are you the best?"

The doctor responded without hesitation, gaining a bit more of Dave's respect in the process. "I'm not sure I'm the best, but I'm damn good."

That was enough for Teresa. "Then let's get it scheduled," she said.

At home, Teresa and Dave were talking quietly in their bedroom when they heard Lauren and Johnny walk in the door downstairs. They still didn't know about the lump, but they had a suspicion something was amiss with their mom.

They came upstairs and found both of their parents home.

"What's up? Why are you home?" Lauren asked, puzzled. "Is everything OK?"

"Yeah, things are fine," Teresa said, knowing that her attempt at a lie sounded feeble.

Nikki arrived minutes later, and joined the rest of the family in the bedroom.

"OK you guys, we do have something to talk about," Teresa said. "There is a little lump or something in my breast, and I'm going to have to have a surgery to have it removed."

The words silenced the room.

"It's just a precaution," Dave said. "We don't really think anything is wrong, but they just have to get it out of there so we know your mom is healthy and we can move on."

"Yes," Teresa said, picking up where Dave left off. She could see the worry beginning to mount on all three of her kids' faces. "It's probably nothing. Auntie Tami and Gigi have had lumps that didn't turn out to be anything to worry about. The doctor says I have to have mine removed. I'll only be in the hospital for a couple hours, and then I'll be home resting for a few days."

"Are you sure it's OK? Are you scared?" Lauren asked, suddenly beginning to feel overcome with emotion.

"There's nothing to be afraid of," Teresa answered in a soothing tone. "We just need to get it out of there. There's no explanation for it, but it's best to just get rid of it and make sure that it doesn't come back."

"When are you going to do this?" Johnny asked.

"Early next week, honey," Teresa said.

Six days later Teresa underwent the excisional biopsy that her doctor had recommended.

She tolerated the surgery well and was transferred back to the recovery area in stable condition.

Dr. Mathis came out to the waiting room to let Dave and his mom, Wilma, know that the procedure was over. As soon as he saw the doctor round the corner, Dave knew that the conversation was not going to be good.

"What did you find?" Dave asked.

"Teresa came through the surgery just fine but we have reason to be concerned," the doctor said. He described the tumor and said that it would be analyzed.

Dave was full of questions, but the look on the doctor's face answered most of them. He knew that the doctor wouldn't speculate until he had a copy of the pathology report in his hands.

"We have reason to be concerned" was a phrase that echoed in Dave's ear, yet it also contained a bit of hope.

The doctor left and Dave and Wilma continued to wait to see Teresa. Wilma had been a nurse for 30 years and she had read the doctor's face as well.

"He didn't like what he saw, did he?" Dave asked his mother.

"No, but we'll just have to wait and see what the pathology report says," Wilma said.

"I've got to go call Tamara," Dave said, excusing himself.

As he dialed Teresa's sister on his cell phone, Dave walked through a pair of automatic doors and out to the sidewalk.

"Tam," Dave said, hearing an answer on the phone.

"Yes, Dave. How is she?"

"We have reason to be concerned," Dave said, his voice beginning to crack in mid-sentence.

"What?" Tamara shot back, startled.

Dave took a deep breath to compose himself before continuing. "This is not good, Tamara."

"What did the doctor say?"

"He said we have reason to be concerned, but we won't know anything until he gets the word back from pathology," Dave said, pausing before going further. "Tam, I saw the look on the doctor's face . . . This is not good."

"Oh dear God," Tamara said, shuddering.

"Is there any way for you to get word to Ron and Jean?" Dave asked, referring to Teresa's parents, who were on vacation in Switzerland.

"Well, let's hold on and not alarm them until we know what's going on for sure. OK?" Tamara said.

"Fine," Dave agreed. "I'm going to get back to her now. I'll talk to you again when I know more."

"Thank you," Tamara said. "Tell her I love her."

The removed tissue was examined and the diagnosis made: "Infiltrating duct carcinoma with residual foci of intraductal carcinoma. Tumor extends 2.2 centimeters in greatest diameter and extends to the surgical lines of excision."

It was cancer, clear as day.

Back at home, it felt to Dave and Teresa as though random chance had come to pay an unwelcome visit.

Dave had held out hope that the lump could be removed and they could go on with their lives. But when the dark specter of cancer raised its wings above his wife, it felt like a punch in the stomach.

Dave hadn't considered himself very spiritual, but privately, he was praying now.

"God, please help her stay with me to get the girls through high school," he said inwardly. He desperately hoped that Teresa could make it that far, at least.

Adversity was something that the Grill family knew how to handle because it was an essential element in sports, something that Dave had excelled in all his life. Growing up in Portland's southwest suburbs, the son of a sporting goods salesman, Dave had been surrounded by all types of athletics.

But his favorite sport of all was football. The game was, for him, a perfect microcosm for life. He had woven the lessons it taught him into his life, marriage and parenting: Success comes by way of teamwork. Pick yourself up when you are thrown for a loss. Keep your head in the game. Be tough.

Like his father before him, Dave's football career reached its peak in a small college. Gary Grill had been a star halfback for Portland's Lewis & Clark College in the late 1950s. Dave, after a brief stint at Montana State, eventually followed in his dad's footsteps.

It was at Lewis & Clark College that Dave met Teresa. His first encounter with her was a memory that never faded.

He had walked into Leslie Baxter's class, "Introduction to Inter-personal Communication," and sat at a desk that faced hers. He was immediately riveted by Teresa. He watched her intently, even staring at times. She was the most beautiful girl he had ever seen.

After the first week of class, Teresa made the first move, approaching him and introducing herself. The first conversation sparked an instant friendship. But there was also an undeniable magnetism between the two of them.

"I'm going to marry her," Dave thought to himself.

Dave was familiar with the concept of love at first sight. The story of how his parents had met was often-told Grill family lore. His dad, Gary, had seen his mom, Wilma, at a barn dance in the late 1950s in the bucolic Willamette Valley farm town of Lebanon, Oregon.

Gary turned to a friend and said, "See that girl over there? I'm going to marry her."

Dave's courtship of Teresa had its own sublime moments. On a trip through the Rockies to visit friends in Montana, the inseparable couple made a daytrip south through Yellowstone and Teton national parks and stopped in touristy Jackson, Wyoming to have lunch and shop for souvenirs.

As they walked and window-shopped, Dave stepped up to the glass and began to inspect a tan pair of cowboy boots with snakeskin trim. Teresa watched Dave study the boots.

"That's a damn fine lookin' pair of boots," Dave said, wary of the price tag.

"I'll tell you what," Teresa said, wrapping her arms around his waist. "If you buy that pair of boots, I'll let you marry me in them."

Dave bought the boots. And he married Teresa on August 4, 1984.

Fourteen years seemed to go by in a heartbeat. Careers started, three kids came, and they always seemed happy. There was never a moment's doubt that Dave made the right choice buying that pair of snakeskin boots.

Then came the onset of the awful disease.

Dave, Teresa and their three kids were full of resolve, hope, and determination to stamp out the cancer before it spread, and then get on with their lives.

Teresa's doctor prescribed an aggressive treatment regime, and she began taking Tamoxifen, a drug that blocks estrogen receptors to prevent the hormone from contributing to tumor growth. And she took Pitocin to help alleviate the painful side effects of the Tamoxifen.

Getting adjusted to life with cancer took some time, and the challenges extended to even the most ordinary aspects of family life.

Not long after Teresa's lump was deemed to be cancerous, Dave had been to the neighborhood video store to pick up a couple of movies for the family to watch together on a Saturday evening.

When he walked in the front door, he carried with him *Sleepless in Seattle*. It seemed harmless enough. Tom Hanks and Meg Ryan, right? How could he go wrong?

With a fresh batch of popcorn in a large bowl set on the coffee table in the family room, Dave fed the tape into the VCR as Teresa and the kids found comfortable positions amid large pillows and couch cushions.

As the opening scene unfolded, Dave was overwhelmed with embarrassment. He cringed, then hung his head, hoping he could bury his face in the couch pillows.

Tom Hanks' character and his son begin the movie mourning the loss of his wife, presumably to cancer.

As the story began to unfold, Dave felt mortified by his own stupidity.

Teresa looked over at him and said in her most sarcastic tone, "Thank you. Nice choice."

Dave, disgusted, finally spoke as apologetically as he could. "I can't believe I rented this. Let's turn it off."

Teresa assured him she was OK.

"No . . . it's alright," she said.

"I am so sorry," Dave said. "I didn't remember what it was about."

Teresa tried to comfort him again. "It's OK."

It was the kind of mistake that Dave didn't make again. It was one of the many small but important lessons that those living around Teresa learned as time went on and she coped with a disease that threatened her life. Teresa's emotional response was to fight, not only against the disease in her body, but to maintain her sense of self. Her independence made it difficult for her to feel like a patient, much less a victim. "Victim" was a word that she despised.

The sudden changes in Teresa's life provoked strong emotions: fear, or anger, or frustration and finally, peace. When the feelings were strongest, she poured them out onto notebook paper. She called one of her earliest jottings, "With All Good Intentions":

> *With all good intentions*
> *They smile*
> *Kinda sad*
> *Light touch of fingers*
> *On my arm*
> *"How are you doing?"*
>
> *With all good intentions*
> *I smile*
> *"I am OK. Taking it one day at a time."*
>
> *Inside my head I am screaming*
> *How the Hell do you think I feel?*
> *With all good intentions*
> *Like shit!*
>
> *With all good intentions*
> *They offer*
> *"Let us take your kids for the weekend*
> *Give you and Dave a break."*
>
> *With all good intentions*
> *I smile*
> *"Thank you, we will keep that in mind."*

Reality check, inside I hear
"Yeah right, my kids don't even know you and
can't stand your kids. Send my family away in times
of crisis. Are you fucking stupid?"

With all good intentions
The doe-eyed looks
"Is your family holding up?"
No, they are on heavy sedation now.

"How is Dave handling all of this?"
Don't know, left me for a hooker right after we found out

"Are your kids OK with everything?"
Yes, they are thrilled that their Mom has cancer, can't wait
Until I lose my hair
I know the intentions are good
But sometimes people are so stupid

Just give me a hug
Tell me I am too ornery to stay sick for long

With all good intentions
I keep smiling

Thanksgiving Day, 1998

Dave sat on the edge of the bed, pulling his pant leg down over
his boot, when he heard Teresa call for him in the bathroom.

"Oh my God!" Teresa said. "Dave come look at this! Shit!"

By the time he reached the door to the bathroom, Teresa had
turned to him holding a brush that was so full of hair he could

barely see the bristles. In her other hand was yet another handful of hair. Teresa's chestnut-colored locks had begun to thin, but this was something else.

"Dave! Can you believe this?" she asked. She was near tears. They were getting ready to drive to her parents' house in Salem for Thanksgiving dinner. And suddenly she couldn't even brush her hair for fear that it was coming out in handfuls.

"Whoa!" Dave said. "Looks like you're due for a new 'do."

Dave tried to keep the mood light. He knew it must be an incredibly emotional moment to be faced with the reality of one of chemotherapy's most notorious side effects.

"Mom, what is it?" Nikki said, poking her head in. Lauren and Johnny were right behind her.

"Mommy! Your hair!" Lauren said.

"I know, sweetie," Teresa said. "It's coming out in clumps."

"What are you going to do?" Nikki asked.

"There's only one thing to do," Dave said. "We might as well give her a buzz cut."

"Dave!" Teresa exclaimed. "I don't want to cut it all off! I like my hair!"

"Well, are you going to go down to your mother's with bald spots on the side of your head? Are you going to have hair fall into your mom's mashed potatoes and gravy?" Dave asked. "Why don't we just buzz your head, and we'll buzz mine too."

Teresa smiled. She appreciated Dave's quick thinking in front of the kids. He was right. They might as well make a family event out of it. Cancer wasn't going to get them down, and it wasn't going to spoil Thanksgiving.

Dave produced the clippers and plugged them into an outlet near the sink. Teresa wrapped a towel around her shoulders and sat on the lid of the toilet.

"Mom, you're going to be bald!" Lauren blurted, stating the obvious. But the words were important. Everyone in the family let them sink in. Mom was going to be bald, and just to prove that it was OK, dad was too.

Dave started from the back of her neck and brought the clippers forward. Then he did it again, and again, until all of Teresa's naturally curly dark brown locks lay in a pile around her feet.

Teresa put her hand on top of her head and rubbed it, learning the odd feeling of being shorn so close. The kids reached out their hands and rubbed her head too, as if she were suddenly a family good luck charm.

"It's only hair," Dave said, trying to reassure his wife.

Teresa was quiet. She stood up and looked in the mirror for the first time without a hairdo. Her feelings were mixed. It doesn't look too bad, she thought. But also: I look like a cancer patient.

Dave took his seat on the toilet and Teresa inflicted the same hairstyle on him.

"You guys look so funny," Johnny said.

"Yeah, I hope you both wear hats so your heads don't get cold," Nikki said.

"Well I must say, this hairstyle looks better on you than it does me," Teresa told Dave.

Dave shrugged. "It's just hair. You're still beautiful."

In the weeks that followed, Teresa's overwhelming feelings of fear and pride and resolve continued to work themselves out in poetry.

One poem she wrote after learning of her cancer diagnosis came a couple of weeks after Thanksgiving. She titled it "Daily Prayer."

> *Please give me the strength to do today what I must do.*
> *Help me to be patient and understanding with my children.*

I know this is hard for them.
Make me gracious and accepting of all who want to help,
Understanding the importance of being able to accept as well
   as to give.
Do not allow me to become full of self pity and doubt.
Help me to keep believing in the future.
Give me the courage to tie a scarf around my head and face
   my job,
My community and peers with dignity and pride.
Grant me humor in dealing with that which makes me cry.
Make me forever grateful for a loving caring husband
   and family.
Give me the strength to do what I must do tomorrow.

Thursday, December 8, 1998

Teresa sat in the passenger seat of the red Chrysler, wishing that the drive to the clinic hadn't gone so quickly. She was never eager to arrive for chemotherapy treatment.

A block away, the sign came into view: Health First Medical Center.

"They should call it the Health First Poison Clinic," Teresa said dryly.

By now, trips to the clinic to receive chemotherapy were starting to become routine, but they were never welcome.

On this particular morning, Teresa would receive the last of four treatments using the drug Adriamycin. The first three treatments—which came every fourth week—had provoked the same nasty side effects.

Adriamycin is one of the most common drugs used in the treatment of breast cancer. It is a toxic compound that strips any weak cells from the body. In seeking out and destroying cancer cells, it also plays havoc with healthy systems.

Dave winced as Teresa opened the car door to step out.

"I wish I could take this one for you," he said.

"Thanks, I'll wait for you in the car," Teresa said, smirking.

Together they walked into the clinic. After checking in, Teresa was led back to the treatment area. A nurse weighed her, took her blood pressure and pricked her finger to take a blood sample. She was given a pre-emptive dose of anti-nausea medication.

Dave walked over to a self-serve beverage cart and made a cup of coffee for himself, and a cup of hot tea for Teresa.

The treatment area was a long room with six industrial reclining chairs. They were typically all filled with patients receiving chemotherapy.

Teresa forfeited her left arm to a nurse, who poked around for a fresh vein and stuck a needle into her arm. Once the needle was in place, the nurse attached a line that connected to the potent concoction that held the best chance she had for defeating cancer.

Dave pulled Teresa's headphones out of her bag and handed them to her. She set the headphones over her ears, hit the play button, and let Melissa Etheridge rock in her head while she closed her eyes. She kept her left arm still. If the drug were to leak out of the tube, it could burn her arm.

Eighty minutes later, the full measure of the drug was coursing through her veins, and Teresa was released to go home.

Dave had learned that he had a 40-minute window before the first wave of nausea hit. It was enough time to get her home and settled into bed.

He had set up everything she needed before they left. Her prescription anti-nausea medication sat on the nightstand next to her. Fruit sorbet chilled in the freezer. Gatorade and 7-Up were in the refrigerator. Extra pillows and blankets lay on the bed for Teresa to situate any way she wanted.

And a blue mop bucket sat on the floor next to the bed. The first few times Teresa needed to throw up, she could usually make it into the bathroom. But the bucket became a much-used companion by Friday, and certainly on Saturday and Sunday. The remainder of the weekend would take an agonizing toll. In addition to an upset stomach, there were head aches, joint and body pain, hot flashes and chills.

Teresa knew she had to endure just one more weekend of the Adriamycin aftermath. The next time she visited the poison clinic, she would begin another four-session cycle of Taxol, which had less severe side effects.

Hannah, Teresa's faithful black lab, lay on the bed next to her, staying close and keeping a watchful eye on her sick friend. Teresa appreciated Hannah's dedication, and wrote a poem about the dog, called "To Hannah":

> I have a guardian angel
> she watches over me
> with quiet patience
> and love.
>
> In the worst of times
> she's there for me
> always by my side
> never far from touch.
>
> When I sleep in sickness
> she lies beside me

her body giving me warmth
and comfort.

At night I know she is close
I can reach out my hand
and feel her touch.

My angel has four legs
and graying hairs on her chin
soft eyes clouded with age
look at me with devotion
gentle kisses on my chin
hairy shoulders absorb my tears.

My angel speaks
but never utters a word
her thoughts are shared with mine.

She asks little
but gives so much.

I have a source
of unconditional love
I am never alone
My guardian angel.

January 2, 1999

Not one of my better days, Teresa concluded.

It began with a weak, light-headed feeling when she woke up after another fitful night's sleep. But she felt compelled to get things done. There was so much to do.

Teresa joined Johnny in his room and began to help him organize his Christmas presents and prepare a list so that he could begin writing his thank-you notes. She discovered all of his pants rolled up into a ball on top of his dresser and then realized he didn't have hangers for them all. And before she could begin to solve the problem, dizziness and nausea welled up to the extent that she thought she was going to fall over.

She managed to cross the hall and go back into her bedroom, where Dave was still asleep. She pulled at his arm.

"Dave . . . you must call the doctor," she said. "Something is really wrong."

He sat up and snapped at her.

"You should just stay in bed!" he said.

Teresa fell onto the bed and buried her head into her pillow, starting to cry. Dave stepped out of bed and began to pace, rubbing his face with his hand and trying to wake up. He took another look at Teresa and could tell that she was in pain. As she continued to sob, he left the room in his underwear and went searching for the doctor's phone number.

Dave called the number, but since it was a weekend he was prompted to leave a message and then wait for a call back. When the call came, it wasn't Teresa's doctor, but an associate. His advice: "Get fluids in her."

As the chemotherapy treatments progressively become stronger, the recovery period gets longer, the doctor warned.

"Get fluids going now or bring her into the hospital for an IV," he said.

Dave finished dressing and walked out the door with a short list of must-haves: Gatorade for Teresa, doughnuts for the kids, and a strong coffee for himself.

While Dave was gone, Teresa called her mom. Could she help finish Johnny's room? Could she take back the bathrobe to the store that was two sizes too small?

Two hours later, as Teresa remained in bed, Dave and Teresa's mother and father, Jean and Ron, talked quietly in the kitchen.

Jean patiently and dutifully fed Teresa mango sorbet with a spoon. They decided to call the doctor again and he admitted her to the hospital. Ron and Dave took her there.

Nikki prepared a hot water bottle and wrapped it in a blanket, and gave it to her mom as she gingerly walked out of the house and toward the car, dressed in baggy sweat pants with a bright red bandanna tied over her bald head and a pair of new designer sunglasses meant to cut down the glare for her sensitive eyes. She felt like a poster child for cancer. She crawled into the front seat, clutching the hot water bottle and a pillow.

Ron took the wheel and Dave sat in the back seat, where he made two phone calls before they had reached the freeway: One to his parents, Wilma and Gary; another to Teresa's sister, Tamara. Dave was frequently left with the role of "updates" for the closest family members.

At the hospital, the pain was even worse. Teresa's communication was reduced to tearful blubbering and shaking her head. So much for her self-image of a strong and brave woman, she thought. Her head was pounding so hard she could hardly see. She was checked into a room and got into a bed, while Dave filled out paperwork. Two hours went by, and Ron did his best to occupy Teresa's mind by conversing about anything he could think of—including favorite restaurants that had gone out of business.

Finally, the IV came. It was a four-hour drip, complete with anti-nausea medication and Benadryl. Teresa sent Ron and Dave home and fell comfortably asleep.

When she awoke, Dave was asleep in the chair next to her bed. A grocery store bag sat on the table. She could see what was inside of it—a package of string cheese. Teresa hadn't eaten much in the past week, and the cheese sounded good. But she couldn't reach it. And she didn't want to wake her sleeping husband.

She knew this wasn't easy on Dave. If the roles had been reversed, she knew it would be eating her up inside to see Dave lying in a hospital bed. She took comfort in his presence, rolled over and fell back asleep.

An hour later, Teresa woke again and the bag of cheese was within arm's reach. Dave was gone. She wondered where he went as she quietly ate the cheese. She began to doze off again.

By the time the process was done, Teresa felt much better. The nurse, and Dave, both agreed that she looked well again. Teresa ate a bowl of chicken noodle soup and then topped it off with two Dixie cups of lime sherbet. A doctor offered to let her stay the night if she wanted to. Teresa wanted to go home.

They were home again at 9 P.M. Jean had put away all of the Christmas decorations, cleaned, organized Johnny's presents and entertained all three kids.

Teresa couldn't believe how tired she felt even after all her napping. Still, she wanted to end this frightening day by feeling the warmth of Dave in bed next to her, where she felt safest. It was a day she prayed never to repeat—although she was growing more and more certain that she would. It was a bad day, for sure, but nothing too out of the ordinary for a cancer patient on chemotherapy.

I must be careful, she thought. I won't be so scared of what to do the next time.

Early the next morning, she began to write again, penning another poem named for the feeling of anxiety that she hated most: "Scared."

Shit
Double shit
I have to face the fact
I am scared
Scared shitless in fact.
I have been doing the strong, brave
I can handle anything routine.

The fact is, I am scared.
Knowing me, you know how hard this is to admit
I hate being out of control of my body
My decisions
My fate.

I laid awake Christmas Eve terrified
What if it were my last?
Who would do all the things I do every year.

My daughter turns 13 tomorrow
A real teenager
She needs me and I don't want to miss this.

I look at the kids and panic
Like I need to shove so much in them today so
I can enjoy it
What if I am not around later?

I know what the doctors tell me
Prognosis is good
But this was never supposed to happen
In the first place.

Keep positive
Keep fighting
Attitude is everything
Who makes up this shit?

I am scared as hell
Yes I'll keep fighting
Not because of some quote in a
Sappy daily meditations book.
Because I have too much to lose.

January 3, 1999

Nikki couldn't help but mope in the days before her thirteenth birthday. Clearly, it seemed, her mom's health was going to prevent her from keeping alive the family tradition of special birthdays.

In the Grill home, birthdays 1, 5, 10 and 13 held extra significance because they marked the passing of a milestone. And as Nikki moved closer to the day that would officially make her a teenager, she began to worry that her birthday might be forgotten altogether. She complained to anyone who would listen.

Nikki could tell just by looking at her mom that there was no way she would have the energy and patience for a party.

"Here is my most important birthday and I can't have a party," she bemoaned in a conversation with her grandma Wilma.

"Why not?" Wilma, Dave's mom, asked.

"Because my mom is so sick," Nikki replied.

"Well, yes you can," Wilma said. "We'll have it at my house!"

Nikki's eyes lit up in a way that they hadn't in months. "Really?"

Teresa, also, knew it was going to be difficult. There was nothing that she wanted more than to conduct her family like normal, but these clearly weren't normal times. She quietly thanked Wilma for her offer, and added that she would help as much as possible.

And so when the big day arrived, Wilma, or "Grammi" to her grandkids, came to the rescue.

Nikki arrived early at Wilma's door the night of the party to see palm trees, nets holding seashells, glass floats, and a basket holding paper leis. Hawaiian decorations covered the porch, the windows and the front door to the condo.

A large "Happy Birthday" banner hung over the entry way to the living room.

"Oh, Grammi!" Nikki said, gleefully, jumping with excitement. "It's just perfect! Thank you so much!"

Soon, Nikki's friends began to show up, dressed in Hawaiian shirts, shorts, halters, flip-flops, sarongs and grass skirts. It was a slice of summer in the middle of a damp, cold Oregon winter.

The girls quickly got into party mode, as Teresa and Wilma made preparations for the cake-decorating contest. There was karaoke, dancing and splashing in the hot tub.

Contest time brought two girls to each cake, where they slathered thick layers of frosting and candy sprinkles on their plain white cakes. Teresa and Wilma then judged each one, making up prizes as they saw fit: Prettiest, Most Frosting, Biggest Disaster, Most Original, Most Unusual.

Frosting was everywhere. It covered not only the cakes, but the girls, the table, the carpet and the kitchen counter.

But the laughter and joy provided by the party was a welcome release for Teresa and Nikki.

The girls spent the night, and the living room was filled from wall to wall with sleeping bags. The giggling continued into the early morning.

The partygoers awoke to strawberry waffles with ice cream before their parents came to retrieve them in the morning.

The success of the event brought an important realization to the family. Cancer had become a fearsome foe for Teresa, yet the family managed to move on and make the best of the situation. With a little help and some imagination, the Grills still knew how to enjoy a good party.

CHAPTER THREE

The Black Hole

Wednesday, October 25, 2000

Nikki was getting nervous. Her first date was just two days away and she felt woefully unprepared.

She had danced many times in front of her bedroom mirror to the tune of her favorite songs. But she hadn't danced with a boy.

"Can you guys show me how to dance?" She presented the question to her parents at the dinner table.

Teresa smiled. It was the kind of moment she lived for as a mom.

"Sure honey," she said. Teresa had presided over her share of middle school dances over the years, serving as a chaperone at dozens of them. She was keenly aware of the social importance of events like these, and how they magnified in the minds of 13-and 14-year-olds. Teresa had once bought a pair of new pants for a boy at her school so that he would have something nice to wear at a school dance because she knew the child couldn't afford them.

But at dances like these, looking good was only half the battle. All sense of cool could be undone if the rhythm was off and the moves weren't right.

When dinner was through and the dishes removed from the table, Lauren and Johnny went upstairs to work on their homework.

Nikki was eager to get started.

"So what do I do?" she asked Dave. They moved to the living room and kicked off their shoes. Nikki sat on the couch with her legs curled under her, and Teresa moved next to Dave.

"It's easy," he said. "You just flow with the music." He began to move his hips and shoulders loosely.

Teresa felt a gnawing uneasiness in her stomach but she forgot about it and smiled her approval of Dave's moves.

"But how do you flow? I mean, what about slow dances?" Nikki asked.

The conversation downstairs was too much for Lauren and Johnny to ignore. They came down the stairs and sat down with Nikki to watch.

"Dave, why don't you put on some music?" Teresa suggested.

Dave turned on the radio and a pop song filled the room. He moved back to the center of the living room and took Teresa's hand in his.

"If it's a fast song like this, you just move with the rhythm," Dave instructed. "You don't have to be spazzy. You just flow with it."

"It won't be difficult for a fast song," Teresa said. "You'll just bounce along like everyone else."

Nikki readily understood that. She had been to dances before. She was more concerned with interacting with her date.

"But what about a *slow* song?"

Dave pulled his wife close, placing his right hand on her lower back and taking her right hand in his left.

"This is how you dance," Dave said, leading his wife in a circle on the carpet. "But what's going to happen is he'll probably put his arms around you like this."

Dave let go of Teresa's hand and locked his fingers behind her back. Together, they swayed, like any awkward ninth graders would at their first important high school dance.

"It's not hard. You just move back and forth. And try not to step on his feet," Teresa said.

Nikki and Lauren giggled.

Dave slid his hands further down his wife's back and playfully grabbed her rear end.

"Now if his hands slide down like this, slap him upside the head," Dave said, deadpanning.

"Eww, that's gross daddy!" Lauren chimed in.

Teresa smiled and kissed Dave on the cheek.

"OK, now you come dance with me," Dave said to Nikki.

Teresa and Nikki switched places. Nikki bounced up to stand in front of her dad and Teresa found a comfortable spot on the couch between Lauren and Johnny.

Dave put his arms around Nikki and led her around the living room for the next three songs. He gently guided her. Nikki reacted accordingly, stepping lightly but naturally and confidently. He could tell she was getting the hang of it.

Teresa sat contentedly on the couch offering her critique of their performance.

"I think you've got it, honey," Teresa said. "See, it's really not too hard. It's easy, isn't it?"

Nikki agreed. "Yeah, I guess it is."

Teresa reached out her hands and tapped Lauren and Johnny on their legs.

"OK guys, show's over," she said. "Back upstairs to your homework."

Dave surprised Nikki at the end of their final song by dipping her backwards before raising her back up and letting her go.

"Thanks, daddy," she said, smiling. She reached up on her tippy-toes and put her lips together. Dave bent forward and turned his chin, offering his cheek for a quick kiss.

Friday, October 27, 2000

Teresa tried to smile. It was an important night for Nikki, and she was trying her best to enjoy the cool, crisp night at Tualatin High School with her daughter. It was homecoming. Nikki, a freshman and member of the student council, was among a handful of ninth graders charged with the task of constructing the class float, and she had worked on it all afternoon.

Teresa had volunteered to hitch the float to the Suburban and pull it around the track at halftime of the football game, which coincided with the announcement of the Homecoming king and queen from each class. Dave had left the day before for Eastern Oregon, for his annual elk hunting trip.

For the most part, the Grill family had fallen back into their usual busy routine. Dave was back to working at Metro Metals and coaching Johnny's football team. The kids were all back in school and into a variety of activities.

Teresa, in addition to teaching at Athey Creek Middle School, was taking graduate courses in education administration two nights a week at George Fox College in Newberg so that she could resume her attempt to earn a Master's degree. It was her goal to become a principal. She also spent the early part of the fall coaching Lauren's soccer team with Tom Re.

Teresa thought of herself as a cancer "survivor" and was determined to leave it in the past, God willing. She tried not to think negatively, but it was also impossible not to have an occasional what-if? moment. Teresa kept her mind focused on her many tasks. She always had somewhere to go or something to do, or someone to pick up.

On this night, the discomfort was almost more than she could bear. She winced with pain as she hopped up into the driver's seat, put the gear shift lever into low and pulled the makeshift wagon covered in streamers past the politely applauding crowd in the stands. They made one circuit of the track, and Teresa could see the kids on the float smiling and waving all the way around in her rearview mirror. She clenched her jaw tight and thought about how it would be over soon enough. "Just get through it," she thought.

She wasted no time getting home at the first opportunity. In the past month, the ache in her stomach had become more than a frequent nuisance. And liberal swigs of Pepto-Bismol and Maalox weren't doing the trick. At times, the pain flared to excruciating levels, and this was becoming the worst yet. Next to childbirth, she thought, this was as much pain as she could ever remember.

By the time she finally got home, she was scared. After a short rest on the couch, she dialed Dave's cell phone. She knew he wouldn't pick up, but she wanted to leave him a message.

Dave was far out of cell range, but he had the phone on. His day had been filled with a long, fruitless hike through the sage and juniper over a familiar piece of dry, rocky terrain near the tiny town of Fossil. He hadn't spotted a single elk all day. It was the end of Day 2 of a planned four-day trip with Teresa's dad, Ron, and his friend, Doug Jacobson.

He was getting his sleeping bag ready by lamplight in the tent when he told Ron and Doug that he needed to check in with Teresa at home.

He walked to the pickup, got in and drove onto the gravel road, toward the high point on the ridge where he knew his phone would find a signal. He knew the road well, and in about 10 minutes came upon the hill that rose above everything else for 20 miles. He tried his phone and it worked.

"Teresa? It's Dave," he said as he heard the other side pick up. "Is everything OK?"

"I'm just . . . wiped," Teresa said. Dave could hear the fatigue in her voice through the weak connection. In the back of his mind, Dave kicked himself for even making this trip. He knew it was too far away for him to be. He had been thinking the same thought all day long.

"I'm not feeling well. It really hurts tonight," Teresa said. "Maybe I'm coming down with the flu or something."

"I think I better come home, then," Dave said.

"Could you? I think you better," she said.

That was unlike Teresa. Dave knew that unless it was urgent, Teresa would have encouraged him to stay another day and keep hunting.

He felt a sudden chill. "She knows something," he thought.

Dave hustled back to camp and told Ron and Doug that Teresa wasn't feeling well and that he needed to get home.

By Saturday night, Dave was home and Teresa had scheduled a doctor's appointment for Monday. Her oncologist was out of town so she made an appointment with the surgeon who had performed her biopsies, Dr. Mathis. The doctor told her that he would order an ultrasound test to look into Teresa's body, scan her tissues, organs and bones and look for whatever was causing her so much pain.

But the way Teresa felt that weekend, neither one of them was very optimistic. Something was definitely wrong. Dave began to brace for a new round of unpleasant news.

Teresa, meanwhile, could feel the gathering storm clouds and was uncertain whether she would have the energy to stop them. She put her feelings down in a new poem she called "The Black Hole":

I'm heading for a black hole.
It has been coming for about two months
Slowly it is creeping around me.

Life was good
On the top
Quite a fall

I have no choice
I must go through with it
My very life depends on it.

The hole is dark and filled with
Fear, pain and uncertainty
My body must travel alone
My soul will not be.

I know there is a light at the end
I can see it
The light of my friends and family
I feel the presence of those who love me
As I pass through the darkness
Supplying me energy and hope
I hear your voices
Courageously calling my name
Towards your outstretched hands
I will grasp
Into your arms I will fall
You are my lifeline.

I thank you for being my light
This journey could not be made alone.
The blackness of the hole is not without end
I will embrace you on the other side.

Friday, November 3

After Teresa's Monday appointment to draw blood for testing, and undergoing an ultrasound exam to determine what was causing the flaring pains in her abdomen, it was another long week of nervous waiting.

Friday came, and Dave was returning from a day trip to Bend, where he'd had a meeting. Teresa called his cell phone in the mid afternoon from Danelle Wiese's house. She had been resting on Danelle's couch with a heating pad wrapped around her waist, sipping hot tea.

"Did you get the results?" Dave asked, nervously.

"Yes," Teresa said, taking a deep breath to pause. She wanted to avoid more of the tears she had shed earlier in front of Danelle. "They said I've got lumps on my liver."

The words hit hard. Dave thought about pulling over, but pressed on through the mountains toward home.

In a flash, Dave's mind reverted back to all that he had learned through Teresa's breast cancer treatment. His sister, Lisa, an M.D., had instructed Dave on the basics of cancer and how the disease worked.

Lisa had been a valuable resource from the beginning and could answer almost any of Dave's questions. He had also taken it upon himself to read everything he could on the subject and gathered information on the internet. Without realizing it, Dave had mastered Cancer 101.

And he knew now that the usual places for cancer to metastize were the brain, the lungs, the liver and the bones.

"Lumps on your liver," he repeated, hesitantly.

Dave had sensed the fear in her voice and wanted to soothe her. He hoped she couldn't sense his fear as well.

"Yes," Teresa said, softly.

Both of them were 99 percent sure that "lumps on your liver" was going to produce the same diagnosis as the lump in her breast had: Malignant cancer.

"The doctor has ordered a biopsy on Monday so they can figure out what they are and what to do next," Teresa said.

"Are you doing OK?" Dave asked.

"Yeah, I'm with Danelle and Kathy. I'm doing OK," Teresa answered. "Are you going to the football game?"

Dave had planned to meet their husbands, Tom and Mark, at the Tualatin High School game in Dallas, about 15 miles west of Salem.

"Well, I was going to, but do you need me to come home?" Dave asked.

"No, I'll be OK here. Go watch the game and try not to think about it," Teresa said. "I'll be fine. There's nothing we can do about it until Monday."

"You're sure?" he said.

"Yes, we're going to make dinner here and I've got the girls and Johnny," she said. "I think the game is on the radio, so we might tune it in."

"OK, then I'll head over to the game for a while," Dave said. "I'll see you later. I love you."

"I love you too," she said.

They hung up. Dave put the phone down and put both hands on the steering wheel. He bit his bottom lip and cringed.

"Fuck," he said aloud.

Tualatin High's football game at Dallas was one of the biggest in the state that week, which also marked the end of the regular season. Both teams were undefeated and the conference championship was on the line. Dave decided he could use the distraction, and drove across Salem's rush hour traffic, and then westward toward Dallas.

Dave wondered if he could even concentrate on the football game, but he knew he needed time to clear his head. Teresa was upset. He was scared. And from that point on he felt certain that this was the beginning of the end. Teresa was going to die soon. He tried not to think of it, and he hoped the football game could offer a few moments' relief.

Dave met up with Tom and Mark and some other friends from Tualatin, and joined the overflow crowd standing near the Timberwolves' cheering section. They could tell something was up.

"What's happening, buddy?" Tom asked, discretely.

"We got the test results today. Not good," Dave said.

Tom looked at his friend and his heart sank. He reached to put his hand on Dave's shoulder.

"If Kathy or I can do anything, you let us know," Tom said. "We've been thinking about you all week."

Dave stayed at the game until the second half, but he had trouble paying attention to it. He needed to get home and he was still 50 miles away. He prepared himself for whatever happened next, knowing that things were about to get difficult again.

Monday, November 6

Dave was in a hospital corridor when he spotted a friend of theirs, a radiologist. Teresa had already checked in and was in an exam room preparing for her needle biopsy procedure.

"Hi. How are you doing," Dave said as the doctor approached.

"Dave Grill? What are you doing here? Is anything wrong?" he said, with a puzzled look on his face.

"Teresa is in today for a liver biopsy," Dave said. "She has some lumps that need to be checked out."

The look on the doctor's face changed from pleasantly surprised to suddenly uncomfortable.

"I'm sorry to hear that," he said. "Look, I'm running late. I'm in a bit of a hurry to get to a meeting."

They exchanged good-byes. The doctor retreated in the opposite direction—not wanting to tell Dave that he was getting ready for Teresa's procedure.

There was another short delay before another radiologist arrived.

Teresa laid face down on a table, sedated. The radiologist took a long needle and pressed it into her back, to her liver. He drew out a tissue sample from one of the areas that came up as a "lump" on the ultrasound.

From there, a histology technician prepared the specimen so that a pathologist could review it and determine what it was.

In his heart, Dave knew what it was. And Teresa knew what it was too.

The procedure itself was painful, and after the sedative wore off, soreness began to throb. Dave brought Teresa home for a few hours, but she couldn't find any way to be comfortable. The pain continued to grow worse. So Dave took her back to the hospital.

Then they waited. Time dragged slowly as Dave and Teresa waited, nervously, for the pathology report to come back and for Teresa's oncologist to get back into town.

Dave could sense the clock was ticking. It was fourth down and a mile to go.

Wednesday, November 8

Two days of waiting left Dave's emotions frayed. The answers that he and Teresa were seeking seemed delayed and he couldn't figure out why. And with every passing minute that he stayed by Teresa's bedside, he knew that time was slowly slipping away.

Dave stepped out of Teresa's room and into the hallway to find a drinking fountain, and saw her oncologist approaching in his direction, a stern look upon his face.

"Dave, how are you doing?" he asked. "Is she OK?"

"Come in and take a look," Dave said, holding the door open for the doctor to enter.

Teresa was in her bed, but it was propped up at an angle to support her back. She was alert and casually watching the television news coverage of the virtual tie in the presidential election.

The doctor came to the foot of her bed, grabbed one of her feet through the covers, and asked "How are you doing, Teresa?"

"I've been better," Teresa said, dryly.

The doctor wasn't in the mood to continue with small talk, and the ground rules he had long ago established with Dave and Teresa dictated that he cut to the chase. He leaned in on the wheeled service table that was next to Teresa and rested his elbows on it.

"Teresa, you've got a liver full of cancer," he said.

Those words seemed to suck all of the air out of the room. The spoken affirmation was the sum of their worst fears. And yet it was no surprise. They had known it.

Dave felt devastated. Teresa's eyes told him that she was too. They began to well with tears, and she put her hands up to her face.

Dave broke the dreadful silence.

"So . . . what do we do?" Dave asked.

"It is a chronic condition," he said. "We have to treat it with chemotherapy, and you'll have to be on it for the rest of your life."

The words fell like a death sentence. Teresa wept, with one hand now clutching Dave's. They both knew, from past experience, that "chemotherapy for life" was an unacceptable solution. And what did "for life" mean, anyway? How much longer could she endure the struggle? A couple years? Six months?

Dave knew at that moment that his wife's death was imminent. And Teresa was realizing that, for certain, cancer was going to kill her.

"My God," Dave thought. "She has to go through this for the rest of her life?"

The doctor continued to explain, calmly and seriously, the next steps: when the chemotherapy would start, which medicines might be used, and how the treatment regime worked.

None of it was definite yet. The oncologist was still waiting on more information to come back from pathology. Dave tried to pay attention, but the words blurred as his mind drifted to the inescapable truth that his wife was dying.

"Chronic condition" was the key. No matter how well the chemotherapy drugs fought the cancer, it was never going to defeat it.

"David, I can't do this any more," she said, considering the prospect of starting over with chemotherapy. "I . . . cannot . . . do it."

She lowered her head into her hands and began to cry.

Dave moved to her side and put an arm around her shoulders.

"I wouldn't ask you to," he said.

Friday, November 10

Two more days passed with no news. No word from the oncologist about what to do next. No idea when the first chemotherapy treatments were to begin. No idea who was doing what, if anything, to come up with a new game plan to save Teresa's life, or at least give her a fighting chance to prolong it.

Dave wanted action of some kind, be it wrong, right or indifferent. He could see that inaction was giving the cancer time to entrench itself further in Teresa's body, to grow unchecked.

Dave made repeated phone calls to the doctor, but never heard back. He asked for updates on the pathology findings. He inquired about the new plan of attack. But the response didn't come.

Dave could sense the strength of Teresa's spirit beginning to wane, and his own frustration began to mount.

He decided to go to the doctor's office, since he couldn't reach him by phone.

"Can I help you, sir?" the receptionist asked.

"I'm here to see the doctor. My wife is a patient of his and he isn't returning my phone calls. If I have to wait, I'll wait," Dave said sternly.

"He's with patients and won't be available today," the receptionist said.

At that, Dave's temper began to boil.

"I will wait if I have to, but I am going to see him today. I demand to see him," Dave said. "Would you tell him I'm waiting in his lobby?"

The receptionist tried to reaffirm her stand, but could see that it wasn't going to work.

Twenty minutes passed.

The door to the waiting room opened and the doctor popped out.

"What's going on Dave?" the doctor asked.

"We need to talk," Dave replied.

The two went back to an examination room and quickly sat down. Dave didn't mince words.

"Doc, we have lost our window of opportunity to start treating this thing because Teresa has lost her will," Dave said. "She's done. She's not going to go through this."

The doctor offered only a puzzled look.

"There is no reason for her to give up on this," he said. "I am still working on a treatment plan for her. I got the pathology results for her back earlier today but I need to confer with another doctor to figure out the best route to go."

The doctor's words didn't offer enough comfort.

"Well, whatever you do, I think she's done at this point," Dave said.

The doctor still seemed amazed to hear the finality in Dave's words.

"I will come over to the hospital when I'm done with my patients here and we can sit down and talk and I will have a plan of action that we can talk about then," he said.

Dave had calmed some, but was still rattled. "I highly suggest you do that."

He turned and left.

A few hours later, the oncologist walked into Teresa's room. Dave could tell by the look on his face that the doctor was somewhat surprised to see how quickly she was slipping, even if he didn't admit to it.

He patiently explained to Dave the nature of the pathologist's findings, and what he thought they should do next.

"We need to start the chemotherapy, and we can start it tonight if you want to," said the doctor.

The doctor's words had a ring of hope in them, but Dave felt they were a couple of days too late. Teresa's spirits had ebbed severely over the 48 hours, and they weren't coming back.

Teresa took the first chemotherapy treatment, but it was different than what she had gone through when she was fighting breast cancer. This time the drugs were not as harsh, and focused more precisely on a specific target: the liver. The treatments she had been through in the past made her nauseated and sick for several days.

After it was over, Dave took her home. Her parents, Ron and Jean, and the kids—Nikki, Lauren and Johnny—met them there.

Saturday, November 11

Kathy Hart entered the Grill house clutching a bouquet of purple flowers.

Her son, Taylor, had been passing along the heartbreaking news about Johnny Grill's mom. Taylor had been begging his mom to go over and visit.

"I am so sorry to hear about what you're going through," Kathy said, offering condolences to Dave. "Taylor has been informing us all after he talks with Johnny."

"Well, she's actually home from the hospital, but she's upstairs getting some rest," Dave said, looking tired.

"That's OK," Kathy said. "I just wanted to leave these with you."

In the living room, Taylor and Johnny had wasted little time starting their usual roughhousing.

Jean O'Brien put a quick stop to it.

"Boys!" she said. "Please keep it down. Your mother needs some peace and quiet so she can sleep."

Kathy suddenly felt slightly embarrassed for interrupting. She could tell that the entire family, and not just Teresa, could use some rest. Everyone she saw seemed to wear the burden of their worries on their faces.

"Taylor, come on, let's go," Kathy said, impatiently. "We need to get going."

Just then, she could hear movement at the top of the stairs. It was Teresa, up from her bed.

"Hello," Teresa said, trying to force some cheer into her weak voice.

"Oh, hi," Kathy said, nervously.

Teresa noticed the flowers in Dave's hand and moved to come down the stairs, slowly. She clutched the rail and carefully, painfully put one foot in front of the other.

Kathy watched her, shocked at how much Teresa had deteriorated since the last time she saw her. She forced a smile to mask her surprise.

Teresa continued to labor on the stairs, straining to make each step down.

Kathy moved up to greet her so that she didn't have to come all the way.

"I just wanted to drop these flowers by. Taylor wanted to see Johnny for a couple of minutes," Kathy said.

Teresa reached out and touched Kathy's shoulder.

"Thank you," Teresa said. She mouthed the words with almost no sound coming out.

After a brief hug, Kathy stepped back and made eye contact with Teresa. She felt frozen, and suddenly experienced a tingling sensation that gave her immediate goosebumps. It was a peculiar feeling that Kathy had never before felt.

Teresa leaned close once again in the stairwell that hid them from view.

"Take care of my boy for me."

The words were unspoken. They seemed to emanate from Teresa's soul. The message was delivered from her pleading eyes and it was unmistakable. It was a moment between mothers.

Kathy backed away, in tears, and offered her good-byes. "I will."

Within an hour after Kathy's departure, Teresa asked Dave to take her back to the hospital once again.

Tuesday, November 14

"Daddy, will you come dance with me?"

Ron O'Brien, by now, was ready for duty. Over the past three days, since Teresa had come back into the hospital, a member of the family had been with her 24 hours a day. From Teresa's parents, Ron and Jean, to Dave, to Tamara, to Wilma and Gary, and an assortment of other relatives and close friends, there was always someone to keep her company and be there if she needed anything.

But Ron was the one who never wanted to leave.

And the job he had carved out for himself was important. He helped her to the bathroom.

The cancer kept Teresa in a constant state of pain, and moving was difficult. Ron had volunteered for the task of bathroom escort. He approached her bed and reached under her arms to pull her up into a sitting position. From there, he picked up Teresa's feet and rotated them off the side of the bed.

Then Ron reached his arms around his daughter again, embracing her closely in a bear hug, and stood her up. He carried most of Teresa's weight as, together, they waltzed six feet to the bathroom door. Once inside, Ron carefully lowered her so she could sit on the toilet.

When she was through, Ron reversed the procedure, and led his dancing partner back to the bed.

On the rare occasion that Ron was out of the room, a nurse handled the duty.

But Teresa's father brought a delicate, heartfelt touch that turned a struggle into a dance.

Friday, November 17

Dave walked into Teresa's hospital room and found her sitting up straight, more alert than he had seen her in several days. Some of the color had returned to her cheeks and she looked contentedly peaceful.

"Good morning," Dave said, walking in and smiling. "What's going on?"

"Hello!" she beamed back.

"Grandma Clara and some pink angels came to see me last night," Teresa said, matter-of-factly.

"Oh?" Dave said, bemused. "What did they have to say?"

"They just told me that they're here for me and that everything's going to be fine," she said.

Dave smiled and nodded but was slightly puzzled. It wasn't like Teresa to talk like this, and he knew that her medication dose hadn't been increased. She was still on just enough narcotic to ward off severe discomfort. But it wasn't a high enough dosage to provoke hallucinations. Regardless, her obviously improved mood was a welcome change.

"Well . . . what did you think about that?" Dave asked her.

"It made me feel good," Teresa said. "I know that they'll look after me. They're waiting for me."

Dave wasn't exactly sure what Teresa had experienced, but the serene sound in her voice was significant. He could tell that Teresa was at peace. She had come to accept what was going on and was prepared for whatever came next. She seemed confident and assured that her grandmother and her angels were going to greet her soon.

When Dave returned to the house after school, the kids greeted him at the door to ask, "How's mommy doing?"

Dave, for once, had an encouraging story to tell them from Teresa's hospital room. He gathered them in the living room.

"She smiled this morning," Dave began. "She told me she was visited by Grandma Clara and a pink angel."

"Really? Grandma Clara?" Nikki asked. All three kids knew their great grandmother before she had died a few years earlier. They all knew that she had been one of Teresa's favorite people. "That's funny. Is that because of all the drugs she is taking?"

Dave was inclined to agree that the pain medication probably had a little something to do with it.

"I don't know," Dave said. "But I know Aunt Tammy saw a pink light in her room too. I don't really know what it is, or what it means. But it was the first time in several days that your mom smiled and seemed happy."

The news brightened the children's faces. They could all picture their mom, smiling. It was a mental image to replace the last one they had of her at the hospital.

"I like that," Lauren said, letting the new information soak in. "Mom's got Grandma Clara and pink angels watching over her."

"I think there really could be some truth to that," Dave said. "I just want you all to know that your mom loves you. I think you should all keep praying that those pink angels protect her and keep her smiling."

Sunday, November 19

Dave scooted the chair as close to Teresa's bed as he could so that he could touch her hand as they talked.

Teresa's stay at home had been short. She had asked to come back to the hospital, where she felt safer and where the medical staff could ease her suffering more ably than her family could. But with each passing day, the pain medication took its toll on Teresa's appearance.

As the cancer raged on in her liver, Teresa's skin became sensitive, particularly on her torso and sides, close to where the tumors bunched together. Her face became puffy and her eyes occasionally had a glazed faraway look to them, particularly after a new dose of medication.

It had been six days since Dave brought the girls up to visit their mother and it had made him uncomfortable how they had nervously giggled in the hallway on the way out of the hospital to the car. "That didn't even look like mom," Nikki had said.

And Dave knew they were right. So he sat them down and asked them to remember their mom the way they had always known her, as the vivacious teacher, coach and mother that she had always been. He thought it best that they not return to the hospital and witness the drugs ravaging Teresa, distorting her.

Teresa had asked the doctor to give her the minimum dose of pain medication necessary to ease her comfort yet maintain coherence. There was much yet to discuss with Dave and other family members and friends. She wanted to be an active participant in those conversations, some of which she knew would be among her last.

With Johnny's blue baby blanket, a Scooby-Doo and a stuffed lion sharing the bed with her, Teresa gestured for Dave to sit down beside her and hold her hand.

"I've had a wonderful life, Dave," Teresa said. "I couldn't ask for anything more. I'm so happy that we had that summer together. The kids were so happy."

"I know," Dave said. "You were happy too. We'll never forget it."

"Are you worried about what's going to happen when I'm gone?" Teresa asked.

Before Dave could reply, she continued.

"Because I don't want you to be," she said. "I know you can do it. I know you will make all the right decisions. And you've got lots of help. Gigi and Papa, your parents, Tamara, Lisa. Don't forget you've got a great support group."

Dave had spent the last week of nights running over how to manage raising three kids on his own. He was exhausted from trying to wrap his mind around the enormity of it all. But Teresa's confidence in him was reassuring. He had always respected her intelligence and her empathy with the children. It comforted him to know that Teresa had faith in him as a parent about to embark upon an uncertain future.

"We'll be fine," Dave said. "Don't worry about us. You've raised three great kids. I think we can pull through it together."

A few moments of silence passed.

"Dave," Teresa said.

"Yes."

"I want you to promise me something," Teresa said. "I want you to promise me that you will go on and be happy. I don't want you to be miserable. I want you to move on. You and the kids go on and be happy. Promise me that you will."

"Yes, Teresa. I promise," Dave replied. He would have said anything at that point to set Teresa's mind at ease. It humbled him how her thoughts were focused on his well being, and on the kids, rather than herself.

"I believe in you, Dave," Teresa said. "Whatever you need to do, you do it. Always know that you have my support, 100 percent. These things are very important. I know you'll be strong for them. You've always been so strong for me."

Monday, November 20

"Guys, gather around," Dave said, standing in the middle of his living room. Johnny was on the couch watching TV and Nikki and Lauren were both standing in the kitchen.

"Time for another update," Dave said. Nikki and Lauren joined Johnny on the couch.

The kids sat in silence. They knew that their prayers weren't going to keep their mom from leaving them. They fixed their eyes on their father.

There were no more light-hearted messages now. This one was serious.

"She's on a lot of medication now and I'm not sure how much more I'm going to get to talk to her again," Dave said. "She's asleep most of the time now."

Lauren spoke up.

"Daddy?" she asked.

"Yes."

"Do you think she is hurting?"

"I don't think so, honey," Dave said, gently. "I don't think she can feel very much. But the medicine she is on now is only for her discomfort. It isn't making the cancer go away. We can only hope that the chemo will slow it down some."

Dave looked at each of their faces. He hated to tell them that there was no hope left for their mother, but he also felt an obligation to tell them exactly what he knew. He hoped being upfront and candid with them would serve to soften the blow when the terrible announcement came.

Lauren's red eyes began to tear up again. She reached forward and grabbed her dad by the neck, hugging him tightly and began to sob.

Tuesday, November 21

Teresa had a full room of visitors—Dave, his parents, and her parents and Tamara—but she was in so much pain she could barely focus her eyes on them.

She gripped the rails on the side of the bed, and couldn't suppress her agony.

The sight made her visitors recoil, and Dave went out to find a nurse to inquire about increasing the frequency of the medication drips that were relieving Teresa's discomfort at 15-minute intervals.

"She's struggling," Dave said to the nurse. "Is there anything you can do to boost the dosage or shorten the interval?"

"I'm going to have to call the oncologist and ask him to come up and talk to you about that," the nurse said.

Dave returned to the room. Jean and Ron stood on either sides of Teresa's bed and pleaded with her to give them a way to ease her suffering. But the situation was growing hopeless.

All eyes were focused on the electronic timer that measured the intervals between new doses of morphine. Each time the machine clicked on again, a fresh drip began to dispense the pain-relieving cocktail that surged through a tube and into the shunt that led straight into her chest. And each time the machine clicked on, the loved ones at her bedside felt a similar relief from their own anguish.

Minutes later, the doctor poked his head into the room. Dave moved toward the door and motioned for the doctor to join him in the hallway.

"How are things going here?" the doctor asked.

"She is in a lot of pain," Dave said. "I don't think she's getting enough morphine quickly enough. She says she wants more. She keeps saying 'I can't do this any more.'"

"Well, let's go in and let me see her," the doctor said.

The oncologist pushed open the door and all eyes turned toward him. He walked directly to Teresa's bed and studied her face and body language.

"Teresa? I hear that you are in a lot of discomfort," the doctor said. "Is that true?"

Teresa, with her hair stuck to the sides of her face with sweat, grimaced and nodded in the affirmative.

"You told me you wanted enough to ease the pain, but still be able to hold a conversation," the doctor said. "Is that still the case?"

Teresa looked at the doctor. She shook her head "No."

"Teresa. I can increase your medication to make you comfortable, but if I do that, you won't be able to talk with your family any more," the doctor said. "Do you understand what I mean?"

Teresa didn't hesitate.

"Yes," she said.

Dave, standing with his back to the far wall, closed his eyes. A surge of emotion hit him and he clenched his jaw to prevent tears. At that moment, everyone in the room knew that Teresa's last words were at hand.

"OK, Teresa," he said. "I'll take care of it for you." He turned and left the room.

Dave felt like he, and everyone else standing around Teresa's bed, was caught in a vise. No one could stand to watch her suffer. And no one could bear the thought of letting her go.

But the vise was squeezing Teresa the tightest.

Thursday, November 23, Thanksgiving Day

Tamara sat at her sister's bedside, alone. By now, Teresa was heavily medicated to the point where it was no longer possible to speak with her one on one. She lay there, as if sleeping.

Tamara refused to give in to the idea that she had communicated with Teresa for the last time. There was energy in the room that Tamara could feel, and it seemed to emanate from her sister. Had she been awake, Teresa might have scoffed at her about that, the way she had in the past when Tamara talked about her interest in New Age spirituality.

But in that room, Tamara felt a strong bond with Teresa. And recent sightings of a pink light in the room, and a visit from Grandma Clara were matters that she took seriously. Tamara scooted her chair close, holding a yellow notepad in one hand and a pen in the other.

Tamara reached her left hand out and grasped Teresa's warm fingers, hanging limp at her side.

"Teresa, I know you can hear me," Tamara said out loud in a soft voice. "I know you can communicate with me by thought even though you can't speak. I am going to make my mind go totally blank, and write down everything you communicate to me. Say good bye to your children."

Then, Tamara felt something move the pen. It was a voice that wasn't hers. She scribbled as quickly as she could to keep up. Over the next few minutes she had covered more than three pages of her legal pad. Her fingers ached from gripping the pen so tightly and writing so feverishly.

But then the words stopped.

Tamara held Teresa's hand a few seconds longer, then let go and opened her eyes. For the first time she looked at the pad and pages of scribbling.

Tamara folded the sheets of yellow paper and stuck them in her purse. She wasn't sure what to do with them. She certainly couldn't return to the house waving them over her head. And presenting them any time within the next week might compound already raw emotions.

She left Teresa's room.

At Tom and Kathy Re's house, Dave and the kids and the grandparents and an assortment of friends were gathered for an unhappy Thanksgiving. It was a day that few of them felt thankful for. Instead, there was an overriding feeling that they were all preparing themselves for bad news.

Tamara slipped into the house and joined the family for turkey dinner. She didn't say anything about her visit with Teresa.

Saturday, November 25

The morning left Dave feeling drained. He could see that Teresa was fading away, one breath at a time. He sat patiently at her bedside, stroking her forehead and sweeping his hand back into her hair. He ran the back of his forefinger over her cheek and felt its warmth. They were well past the point of no return now.

He sensed the final day had come.

As he stroked her face and hair, Dave spoke gently to his silent wife.

"It's OK to let go," he said. "Go ahead, Teresa. It's OK to go now."

The words pushed him to the brink of his emotions, but they felt like his final responsibility as a husband.

He was ready for it to be over, and he knew that she was ready as well.

Dave tried to prepare the kids that their mother's life was coming to an end, and that it would now be only a matter of hours and minutes. He drove the five short minutes to the house and delivered the final bulletin.

"Guys, I don't think she's going to make it much longer," he said.

Lauren's eyes were reddened from days of waiting and crying. Nikki was less emotional, preferring to spend time alone in her room. Johnny idly watched TV, broken hearted.

Shortly after 3:30, Dave decided to return to the hospital again. His gut was telling him that she might not make it through this day.

As he walked off the elevator to the third floor and began to walk toward Teresa's room, Dave caught the eyes of a nurse that had just emerged from her door. The nurse looked down, her face full of remorse.

Then she glanced up at Dave and made eye contact.

"I'm sorry, but she's gone," the nurse said.

Dave impulsively hugged her. "Thank you for taking such good care of her," he managed in a cracked whisper.

He proceeded into Teresa's room, located at the end of the corridor.

Jean, Ron and Tamara were all in the room, on the far side of Teresa's bed. They gathered around Dave and hugged him.

"Why don't you go on in and we'll wait outside?" Jean said.

Dave took a seat next to Teresa's lifeless body. He sighed, then bowed his head.

His final words felt like a prayer, since he knew she was no longer in the room with him.

"We're going to go on with our lives, just like you asked," Dave said. "You'll always be with us. I'm going to miss you, and love you, forever."

He bent over and kissed her on the forehead.

It was no more than five minutes. Then Dave stood up and walked out, where he met Teresa's parents and her sister. They stood together, stunned that Teresa's life had come to a conclusion.

All that was left was to tell the kids.

Dave pushed the front door to the house open. He looked at his boots as he slowly walked in the door and wiped his feet. He didn't want to make eye contact until he was ready.

Lauren sprang to her feet at the sight of her dad, with her grandparents and aunt behind him.

Nikki and Johnny sat on the sofa with his parents, Gary and Wilma.

Dave leaned back against the door leading to the garage, and tried to compose himself before he said the words. All three kids turned their attention to him.

"Guys, mom didn't make it," he said.

His eyes began to well, and he reached out to them. The three kids ran to him, squeezing his body in their arms.

They knew before he said it, but the words still felt crushing. The kids hugged their dad even tighter, and he could feel them begin to sob. He reached his arms around them, bowed his head and rested his cheek against the top of Johnny's head. And squeezed his eyes shut.

Dave could already feel Teresa's absence in their hug. The family hug used to have five bodies, 10 arms. It had suddenly been reduced. This ball of arms and heads and tears was his family now.

"Your mom was very strong but she couldn't take the cancer any more," Dave said. "You know your mom as well as I do. She wasn't the type of person that would want any of us to dwell on the fact that she just died. Mourning her is fine. But she expects us to go on."

The three kids released their dad and returned to the couch. More hugs and tears came from both sets of grandparents.

"We're not going to use this as a crutch and not do the things that we need to do," Dave said. "Mom expects us to go on and live and be happy."

Then he sat down too. Over the next hour, they all cried and they all laughed, retelling the stories of favorite memories about Teresa.

Johnny spoke up. "Sometimes when you love somebody you just have to let them go."

The sentiment summed up a sorrowful room that was determined to find resilience.

Tamara looked at the time and said, "I don't think anyone here has eaten for days. I'm hungry. Let's go some place and have dinner."

They chose a nearby Mexican place called El Sol. It was a favorite of Teresa's.

Before they left, Dave went into the bedroom and made several phone calls to the people he felt needed to know right away: Kathy and Tom Re, who had hosted them for Thanksgiving; Keely Jacobson, Teresa's best friend since college; Brett Poulsen, one of Dave's best friends, in Utah, and a few others. He asked the few he reached over the phone if they wouldn't mind spreading the news.

∞

Dave figured many of the families with the closest connections had migrated to Hillsboro, west of Portland, for the afternoon to watch the Tualatin High School football team's state playoff game. He thought, under a normal set of circumstances, that he probably would have gone to the game himself.

The restaurant was somewhat busy, but the wait staff was able to get the Grill family a table for nine fairly quickly up front near the door.

As they waited for their food to come, Dave spotted the unmistakable gray Suburban that belonged to Tom and Kathy Re. He felt a sudden twinge of panic. Little did he know the Res had spotted Dave's vehicle in the parking lot also.

Dave's cell phone rang. "Dave, this is Kathy. This might not be very good news, but everyone who was at the game is on the way over to El Sol. The Johnsons. The Wieses. Everybody. Do you want me to divert them away? Because I will. If you need privacy, we understand. We can go someplace else."

Dave paused for a second.

"No, that's fine," he said, wondering if he was really going to be OK with it and how the kids were going to hold up.

"I didn't tell anyone at the game, so know one knows yet," Kathy said.

"That's OK, Kathy," Dave said. "Have them come on in. She'd want us to all to be here together."

Not the best place to break the news, Dave thought. But it was the situation they were in.

Dave went to the door, calmly telling each family as they arrived in turn that Teresa has died earlier that day. The news was met with sorrow, and in some cases, shock. Many of their closest friends knew that Teresa had become drastically ill, but not that she had slipped so far so fast. Just a few weeks earlier she had seemed fine. They all expected to see her again.

Each time another family arrived, the uneasiness repeated itself. Johnny, seated between Dave and Wilma, leaned his head into his dad and fought to control his tears.

"Do you want to go home, John?" Wilma whispered to him. He turned and nodded to her.

Wilma waited briefly for the best opportunity to escape, and wrapped an arm around her grandson and led him out.

Dave instantly wished he had ordered the food to go and brought it back home. But as the scene wore on, and he explained for the fifth and sixth time what had happened earlier that day, Dave saw strength in his kids. Nikki and Lauren, especially, were holding up on the worst day of their young lives. Dave saw his kids persevere, he began to see a greater lesson at work: We have to eat. We have to go on. We have to face people. It was a reality check, and the first of many.

CHAPTER FOUR

Teresa's Memorial

Brett Poulsen got out of the way of the two redheads behind him, toting their suitcases into his Sandy, Utah home. All three of them had just arrived from Fillmore, Utah, 150 miles to the south, where they had spent Thanksgiving with their mom and stepdad.

For the 34-year-old twin sisters, this was the second leg of a trip from their home near Nashville, Tenn. They had spent a few days with their mom, Kay, for her 60th birthday. Once they got settled in at Brett's they could go and visit their dad. They were careful about trying to spend equal time with each parent.

Kaysie called her dad while Brett, a burly 280-pounder with a red goatee, a big smile and a chirping voice, went to the patio to greet his two excited Labrador retrievers.

After Kaysie made her plans, she went upstairs where Kellie was unpacking and changing clothes.

"Oh, I know, I've missed you too," Brett said to his dogs, walking back toward the phone. He had checked his messages in the car on the ride up from Fillmore, and the one that interested him most was from Dave Grill, whom he simply called "Grill." His affection for his old high-school buddy ran a little deeper than for any of his other Brighton High School classmates. Even though they spoke only once or twice a year, Brett considered Dave his dearest friend.

The last he had seen of Dave and Teresa was in June of 1999, when they spent a long weekend with Brett and his girlfriend, Karen, and attended the guys' 20th high school reunion.

It was there that Brett had learned about Teresa's breast cancer, but by then the only visible sign was her nearly bald head. Brett had playfully teased Teresa that most women lost their breasts when they have breast cancer, but since "her boobs were so damn big, they just took the cancer out the side." One former classmate tapped Brett on the shoulder and whispered, "What's with Grill's wife? Is she a punker?"

Punker?

"No, you asshole! She's a cancer survivor!" Brett replied emphatically. But after the fun weekend with them, he rarely thought of it. Teresa seemed healthy.

When Dave and Teresa left Salt Lake City, Brett gave them both heartfelt hugs. As he leaned closer to Teresa, he remembered whispering into her ear: "You stay healthy, you hear me? And please let me know if there's anything I can do."

Teresa had merely smiled.

Then a year and a half passed.

The message on the answering machine had been short and lacked specifics: "Please call." Brett got a sudden cold chill and thought, "Something's wrong with Teresa." But then, as quickly as the thought occurred, Brett suppressed it. How could something be wrong with her? She had a clean bill of health. There was no reason to suspect that had changed. So he began to assume that Dave wanted to bring the family out for a ski trip over the winter break. He smiled at the thought of it. He loved the whole family.

As he dialed Dave's number, Brett felt an involuntarily smile. It had been too long since he had spoken with his friend. He was excited to hear his voice again and find out the latest news on the kids. He considered Nikki and Lauren nieces, and Johnny his nephew.

But there was no small talk.

"Brett, we lost Teresa," Dave said.

The words, so quick out of Dave's mouth, didn't compute at first. There was a moment of silence on the line while Brett processed it.

"What do you mean? I thought she was fine," Brett protested.

"Yeah," Dave said. "It came back fast."

The rest of the conversation was short. Brett promised to be there as soon as he could.

Upstairs, Kellie and Kaysie were busily getting ready to visit their father. They chatted as they primped, combing hair and touching up makeup. The stressful part of the vacation—the time spent at their mother's for Thanksgiving and the birthday party— had come to an end. They looked forward to the rest.

"Girls!" Brett cried out. "GIRLS! Kaysie and Kellie!"

They ran to the top of the stairs and looked down.

"What is it?" Kellie yelled back.

Brett, their hulking brother, was in tears. Kaysie and Kellie looked at each other, puzzled, and rushed downstairs to see what the problem was.

Brett slouched at the bottom of the stairs, tears streaming down his round cheeks. He looked up, and his sisters were instantly shocked by his visible pain and torment. The phone, still in his limp right hand, threatened to fall on the floor.

"Teresa has died," he said.

"Oh my God," Kellie said. "How? When? Why?"

Kellie and Kaysie hugged their brother, trying to console him and find out what happened.

"Cancer," Brett said. "She had breast cancer, and I knew that. But she was better, and cured, and came to the reunion last year, and . . ."

Kellie shook her head, and her own tears started to come. She had never seen her big, strong football-loving brother so emotional. She knew that Dave Grill had always been more than merely a dear old high-school friend, but someone he idolized. She also vaguely recalled that his wife had been ill.

"I'm still waiting to find out more," Brett said, briefly composing himself. "Dave's still on the line. He had another call come in, so I'm waiting."

He removed his wet glasses, rubbed the moisture out of his reddened eyes with his thick fingers and heard Dave's voice again.

Kellie and Kaysie stood next to Brett, rubbing his back as he clutched the phone and listened, with his chin quivering and his free hand wiping the moisture off his eyes. At intervals he would lose control and bawl with his whole being.

Dave and Teresa had been more than just longtime friends. Brett had held them on a pedestal: The perfect couple. Parents of the perfect kids. They were the standard that Brett hoped to achieve some day. He had never known love quite like that before. Watching Dave and Teresa together had given him something to shoot for.

Some of his tears were squeezed out in anger. "How can that be screwed up? Why does that have to end?" The questions raged in his head as he waited for Dave to come back on the phone.

"Talk to us, Brett," Kellie said. "What's going on?"

"She died on Saturday. The cancer came back into her liver about a month ago and it just took her like that," Brett said, snapping his fingers.

Brett's mind reeled back to the first time he met Teresa. Almost eighteen years earlier, while visiting Dave in Portland, they had gone to a local watering hole, The Rusty Pelican, where

Teresa waited tables, to see if Brett "approved" of Grill's new girlfriend.

The stamp of approval had come instantly. How could he not approve the curly-haired beauty with such quick wit and intelligence? His buddy, usually Mr. Hard-To-Get, was clearly smitten. "Oh yeah," Brett had said, nodding. "She's pretty damn cool."

Brett was stopped cold by the appalling news.

Teresa gone?

A new feeling began to overwhelm him. It was like a cold shiver running up and down his spine. It grasped his mind as well his body.

And then, in a flash, he felt a moment of clarity and a new sense of purpose.

His buddy was going to need help. Dave would now have three kids by himself. And Kellie . . . simply must come with him. His mind raced to all of the ways they were compatible.

With more than 20 animals that needed tending back on the twins' farm in Tennessee, it seemed unlikely that Kaysie would be able to go. He was fine with that.

But Kellie was another story. Brett felt a twinge of guilt because Teresa had just died, but something was telling him that he simply must try to put Kellie into Dave's orbit, just to test the gravitational pull that might start between them.

Brett felt compelled to help try and keep the family perfect. He had been unable to protect his buddy from his recent suffering, but looking ahead now, he saw an opportunity to repair things.

"You're going up there with me," Brett told his sister.

"I don't know if I could, Brett," Kellie said. "You know how I've always had a torch for him since I was 12. How could I just show up at a time like this?"

"Go with me because I need you there with me. Go because we're representing our family together. Just help out and take a look around," Brett said.

∞

Kellie descended the stairs in her red-and-black flannel pajamas and fuzzy footie slippers. She was exhausted from a long, emotional day and was getting ready for bed.

She walked into Brett's kitchen to find him hovering over the sink. He held his hands under the faucet, collecting cold water and then splashing it over his face. His tears were gone, and now so too was the reddened puffiness around his eyes.

As Brett turned to her, Kellie could see something else on his face: Focus and renewed determination.

"Well . . . I don't . . . know much, but I do know one thing," Kellie said, stammering slightly. She tried to pre-empt the strike that she saw coming. "I'm not going with you to the funeral."

"Now Kell, hear me out," Brett said, wiping his face with a towel for the final time and beginning to dig in for a battle. Brett, a real estate broker, knew his negotiation skills were about to come in handy. This was an argument he couldn't afford to lose. The cold chill seemed to tell him that he wouldn't.

"No, Brett, don't even go there," Kellie said, turning to watch as Kaysie joined them in the kitchen.

"Kell, now just listen," Brett said, bluntly. "You are going with me to Portland. You have to go with me. You don't have a choice. Now is your chance. And cold and calloused as it sounds, now is your opportunity to pursue Dave Grill. You've always wanted him and now this is your chance."

"No Brett! I can't!" Kellie said, raising a voice wrought with emotion. "I can't see him again! I can't do this!" She begged him to stop this "nonsense."

"You can and you are," Brett said. "The casserole women are going to attack Dave once things start to settle back down."

The casserole women, as Brett called them, were the single mothers, divorced mostly, that he knew populated Dave's neighborhood. They would surely show up on his doorstep with casseroles and condolences, and some might try to pry their way into his life.

He cringed just thinking about them.

No, he thought. The solution was becoming more and more clear. It was Kellie.

Kaysie chimed in, taking the side of her brother, which was a rare event. Kaysie almost always sided with her twin.

"Kellie, listen to Brett. It's true," Kaysie said. "You can go and at least find out if you still feel the same way about him."

"I can't go," Kellie pleaded. "I have to get back to Tennessee and go back to work, and help with the animals and stuff."

"No you don't," Brett said, backing her weak argument into a corner. "Kaysie can do it."

"That's right," Kaysie said. "I can do it. I've got to get back and see Mark and relieve him from all the chores and help everyone who needs cleaning work done, but you can stay. I wish I could go and give my condolences to Dave and Wilma and Gary, but somebody's got to get back to Nashville."

Kellie knew she was grasping and could begin to feel the force of their prodding push her in a direction she wasn't yet ready to go.

"I'm not going to go! And you two aren't going to make me!" Kellie said, turning to leave the kitchen.

Brett wasn't having it. "You're going with me," he said, as if swearing a promise. "And yes, I can make you go because I'm bigger than you. If I have to I'll literally set you on that plane. I'm gonna call the airline right now and order two tickets."

Brett reached for the phone.

Kellie was dumbfounded. "You two are incredible! I can't believe you're going to make me go. I'm scared. Don't you know how nervous I am about seeing him again? Especially now!"

Kaysie approached and put her arm over her sister's shoulder, and led her back into Brett's kitchen. They sat down at the table.

"You'll be fine," she said. "You may see him after 20 years and think, 'What was I thinking?' But then again, you may not. He may still be the most gorgeous thing to you. And you might find that you love him like you used to."

Kellie knew that the two of them had her best interests at heart, even if it did feel like they were ganging up on her and shoving her out onto a stage where there was a blinding hot spotlight and a critical audience awaiting.

"I don't know," Kellie whined, beginning to back down a degree. She turned around at the sound of Brett on the phone with Delta Airlines. He ordered two roundtrip tickets, set to depart Salt Lake City on Thursday.

Brett finished his call, hung up, and proceeded immediately to dial a new number while his sisters watched and wondered what he was up to.

Kellie had a sinking feeling in her stomach.

"Hey, it's me," Brett said. "Just wanted you to know I've booked the airfare. The girls are here for Thanksgiving, and Kellie is going to come with me up there for the service and to see you guys. Kaysie needs to get back to Nashville and her boyfriend and work and stuff, but Kellie and I will be there on Thursday."

Kellie closed her eyes and swallowed. He was talking to Dave.

"I know we're coming kind of early," Brett continued. "But we'll be there to help out wherever needed, OK? Great, we'll see you then. Take care buddy. Bye."

Brett hung up and Kellie could now feel herself completely trapped. She couldn't back out now. Deep down, she knew that her protests were more a formality, a show. The truth was, her heart and mind were both in agreement with Brett and Kaysie.

Kellie hated the origin of this opportunity: Teresa's death. She hated herself for even using the word "opportunity."

But it was a fact. And Dave Grill and Portland, Oregon were her new destination, if only for a scouting mission.

She stood up from the table and could already feel her legs begin to tremble. Her decision had been made for her. She left the room wondering if she was going to throw up.

Thursday, November 30

Kellie's stomach churned as she gazed out the window, downward into a layer of white clouds. Brett, almost too big for a standard airline seat, was next to her, quietly thumbing through a magazine.

"The weather in Portland is 44 degrees and overcast," said the pilot over the intercom. "We are making our descent into Portland and should be there in about 12 minutes. Please fasten your seatbelts, and attendants please prepare the cabin for landing. Thank you for flying with Delta today and enjoy your stay in Portland or wherever your final destination will be today."

Kellie continued to stare out the window, watching the wisps of white slide over the top of the wing. But she had heard the pilot's announcement.

"Fasten your seatbelts," he said.

Ha. If he only knew.

Brett had been surprisingly upbeat all morning. His mind wandered to past encounters with Dave, Teresa and the kids and he happily told all of his stories to Kellie. He told her how he had sincerely loved Teresa and admired her since the day he had been introduced. He explained to Kellie nearly all he knew about their three kids. Nicole was the oldest, with a quiet, confident personality and a brilliant smile. She excelled in music and acting. Next was Lauren. More sensitive, but also more determined. A star athlete with a gregarious personality that Brett was sure Kellie would get along with. And then there was Johnny, the little man of the family who would carry on the Grill name. Destined to be a football star, Brett said confidently.

All of the Grill kids were bright and charming. It was just one more reason that Brett idolized Dave and Teresa. Not only had they been his ideal couple, they had turned into ideal parents.

"This is going to be fun, Kell," Brett said. "I'm telling you, we will be partying this week."

Kellie looked at her brother with a puzzled look that bordered on disgust.

"Fun?" she asked. "Brett! We're going to a memorial service. This is not a happy time for Dave or anyone in his family."

Brett disagreed. He knew this was not going to be a typical funeral.

"Yes, it is going to be fun," Brett said. "Wilma said it's going to be a celebration of Teresa's life. It will be fun. Trust me."

Kellie knew Wilma and Gary, Dave's parents, from their long association with her family. In fact, she had seen them within the past year, when they had come to visit Nashville. She knew that at the very least, she could talk with them.

Seeing Dave again was another matter. She hadn't seen him in the flesh in 17 years.

"How are you doing? Are you going to be alright?" Brett said, noticing Kellie's nerves. Not only that, she had been fighting a sinus infection all week. The altitude of the plane played havoc with her runny nose.

"I don't know," Kellie said softly. "I think so."

Kellie and Brett arrived at their gate and walked together to the baggage claim. Kellie waited for the carousel to start dispensing bags while Brett went over to pick up the keys to a rental car.

They drove south on I-205, through east Portland and the suburbs before arriving in Wilsonville.

Brett led Kellie into the Wankers Corner Saloon and they took a seat for lunch. It was a restaurant Brett knew well. He had been there with Dave several times before. He ordered a Crown Royal and 7-Up. And then another.

"Ahh . . ." Brett sighed. "We're in Oregon, where they put real booze in their drinks. Not like Salt Lake where everything is watered down."

Kellie wasn't impressed. She didn't drink alcohol. She ordered a hot tea to go with lunch.

After lunch, Brett and Kellie found their way two blocks to the Comfort Inn and checked into their room. Then, without hesitation, Brett dialed up Dave on his cell phone.

"Hey buddy, Kellie and I just rolled in," Brett said. "What can we do to help? That's what we're here for."

"Well . . . OK. You got it. We'll be over," Brett said. Then he hung up, and turned to Kellie, smiling.

"What did he say?" she asked.

"He said the way to help is to come over to the house and have a beer with me," Brett said.

∞

Kellie took a deep breath. She couldn't control the overwhelming jitters she felt in her stomach. The sensation made her remember her awkward teenage years. She thought she might have an anxiety attack.

Kellie hadn't felt this way in a very long time, particularly over a man. And certainly not as an adult.

Brett kept a sharp eye on his sister. He was concerned, but he also knew she was tough enough to handle it.

"Are you going to be OK?" he asked.

"Yeah, I'll be fine," Kellie responded. But it felt like a lie.

The arrival of a giant moment seemed to be around the next corner. As a 12-year-old, Kellie had peaked over the window sill from an upstairs vantage point just to get a glimpse of Brett's friend Dave drive up in his blue Camaro.

Once in the house, she had tip-toed up to doorways to get a closer look. Even then, Dave Grill had taken her breath away.

And now, as a 34-year-old woman, the mere thought of seeing him again was stealing her breath once more. Long years of deeply hidden desire and love for a man who was off limits were about to yield to a new reality. Dave was now single, even though it was unwillingly and unintentionally. And it was a status that Dave himself hadn't even paused to consider.

Brett drove onto 70th Street, then down a short hill to Dave's house. Kellie held her breath, looked straight ahead, and saw him.

Dave was crouched with his back to them, washing the back end of the white Suburban in his driveway. He wore a baseball cap, navy blue sweatshirt and jeans. The sun shone down on his broad shoulders. He stood straight up when he turned to see Brett's rental car pull up alongside the curb. He smiled.

There was a white-haired man standing with Dave. It was John O'Brien, Teresa's father.

Brett put the car into park and practically jumped out of the car. He excitedly walked around the back end, grasped Dave's hand and pulled him into a bear hug.

Kellie, meanwhile, watched from the passenger seat. She took another deep breath, removed her seat belt and opened the door, slowly, deliberately. She went to stand up and struggled to move her legs. They felt paralyzed. She was momentarily frozen, literally, by her fear.

"Oh my God," Kellie said silently, in prayer. "Give me the strength to do this."

She gathered herself and got up out of the car. She approached Brett who was already with Dave and John, and could sense that her knees were shaking. Her eyes focused on Dave, now just a few feet away.

Her eyes sized up Dave Grill, and the reaction was beyond her long-held childhood fantasies. She had considered, while on the plane, that time and age may have weakened her attraction to him. That maybe her feelings would seem silly once she saw him.

But she instantly realized that was all wrong. From his strong jaw, to his dark handsome green eyes, and his welcoming smile, all the pieces came together. She was mesmerized. Dave's blue sweatshirt covered a torso that was strong and lean. She sensed the power of his arms and could see the muscles of his legs fill out the denim of his jeans.

She felt lovestruck, immediately followed by a wave of embarrassment and guilt.

"Hey buddy, how are ya?" Dave said, embracing Brett. The words sounded to Kellie's ears like a long-lost but ever-familiar tune.

"I'm good," Brett responded. "Are you OK?"

Brett's first impression was far different than Kellie's. He could see the wear and tear on Dave's face, from the bags under his eyes, to the unshaven face, to a pallid gray color in his cheeks.

"Yeah, we're going to be fine," Dave said, bravely.

Dave turned his eyes to Kellie for the first time. He put down a rag he had been using to wipe up some gas that had spilled on the back of the Suburban earlier in the day at the gas station.

"Oh my God, Kellie, how long has it been?" Dave was amiable and welcoming. His warm smile calmed his guest's jangling nerves, though he was completely unaware of it.

Kellie swallowed hard, knowing his attention was on her.

"Too long," Kellie smiled. Before the words were completed, Dave engulfed her with an embrace.

Kellie was desperately thankful for the tight hug, because at that very instant she thought she might fall down.

"Brett and I figured out that I haven't seen you since we all came to Oregon when I was a junior in high school 17 years ago," Kellie said. She finished the sentence as she stepped out of the hug.

Brett was focused on John O'Brien, whom everyone called "Ron."

"Hey Ron, how are you doing?" Brett said, reaching to hug him. Ron started to cry just a bit. Brett knew both of Teresa's parents, Ron and Jean, very well. Brett had even gone on Dave and Teresa's honeymoon with them, up at Detroit Lake in Oregon, where they all stayed together in Ron and Jean's cabin.

"I'll make it," Ron said, wiping his eyes. "It's just so hard."

"I know," Brett said, his eyes beginning to mist as well. "We are so sorry about your loss."

Kellie nodded her head as a lump began to well in her own throat. "Yeah, we're so sorry."

"Thanks," Dave said.

"Kellie, this is Ron O'Brien, Teresa's dad," he continued.

"It's nice to meet you," Kellie said softly. "I'm just so sorry it's under these circumstances."

She shook Ron's hand and felt it trembling. She felt his grief instantly and in a matter of seconds was drawn in to his sadness. He had just lost his daughter, his baby.

Kellie had taken the time to consider Dave and his loss, and the loss of his kids. But at shaking Ron's hand, Kellie began to think about Teresa's family, and their pain, for the first time.

She felt heartbroken for all of them.

∞

The four of them began to walk up the short path to Dave's front door.

Stepping up into the house, Kellie entered yet another ring of the protective circle that had rallied around Dave and his kids.

Teresa's mother, Jean, greeted them first. At 5-foot-10 inches, Jean cut an imposing figure. She welcomed Brett with a hug and then stuck out a hand to shake with Kellie after a brief introduction. Even in her despair, Jean was poised.

Further into the house, there were more introductions. Tamara, Teresa's sister, was sitting in the family room typing at the computer. Brett did most of the talking and Kellie followed, right behind his shoulder.

Dave briefly left the room and returned moments later with beer. He offered one to Brett, who gladly accepted. And another he offered to Kellie, who declined and politely said that she did not drink.

By this time, Brett could feel some of the vibe in the house. They were happy to see him, and yet he could tell they were wondering why *she* was here. Brett didn't care. He knew whatever static they might run into, it wasn't likely to come out into the open. And besides, he knew his sister. She was tough.

They moved to sit on the couch when Kellie was startled by sudden crashing and banging from upstairs. Then came the thunder of feet down the stairs.

Lauren and her cousin Makenna, Tamara's daughter, rushed into the room. Dave introduced Brett and Kellie to them, and Brett stood up to accept their hugs. Brett backed away and suddenly became emotional after releasing Lauren.

Johnny and his cousin Al were next. Brett grabbed Johnny and gave him a bear hug as well.

Dave introduced Kellie to Lauren and Johnny, and added a kicker: "If you're nice to Kellie she just may let us come and visit her and her twin sister Kaysie in Nashville sometime. They live there, and they have horses and dogs and cats and they know tons of people in the country music business because they write songs."

Dave winked at Kellie as he said it, as if to assure her that he was half-teasing.

"Cool," Johnny said.

"How many horses do you have?" Lauren asked.

"We now have eight," Kellie said, beginning to relax for the first time. "We keep having babies."

"Wow," chimed in Makenna, instantly impressed because of her own love of horses.

Kellie smiled at them, but turned her attention to the black Labrador lying on the floor by the television set. She stood up and walked over to Kellie, nuzzling her grayed muzzle into her lap.

"This is Hannah," Dave said. "She's Teresa's dog and she's an old girl."

Kellie looked into the dog's cloudy blue eyes and could tell that Hannah was old and beginning to go blind. She stroked the top of Hannah's head and scratched her under the chin. The dog sat down and rested her chin on Kellie's leg for the next hour.

"She misses Teresa a lot," Dave said to Kellie. "They were pretty good buddies. I think she knows that Teresa is gone. We're beginning to wonder if she's going to survive her broken heart. She hasn't eaten much since Teresa died."

"She seems to like you though."

Kellie was glad he noticed.

"Oh, she's so cute but her eyes are sad. I feel bad for her. She's such a sweetheart."

Time rolled by as the conversation turned to Brett to Dave to Tamara to the O'Briens and even to Kellie.

Nikki walked in the door. She had spent the afternoon at her school, where she was auditioning for a play.

Brett stood up for another hug. Dave made yet another introduction. "Nicole, this is Kellie Poulsen, Brett's sister."

"Hi, nice to meet you," Nikki said.

"Oh, hon, nice to meet you too. I'm so sorry," Kellie said sympathetically.

"Thanks," Nikki said, smiling. She, too, wore a brave face, Kellie thought.

Nikki sat down and joined the adults' conversation. Kellie could hardly take her eyes off of her. She was amazed by all of them for the way they handled themselves in what surely was a horrific time. They had just lost a wife, mother, daughter, sister, aunt. And yet to sit with them, they all played good hosts.

They seemed to be comforting Brett and Kellie more than the other way around.

The front door opened again, and in walked Wilma and Gary, Dave's mom and dad. The sight of them excited Kellie. They were a familiar sight and no introductions were needed. Here were two friends and allies that she knew wouldn't look at her with suspicion.

The gathering moved over to the kitchen table, and more friends joined them. Exhausted, Jean, Ron and Tamara left to go back to their motel. The men drank beer and someone asked Dave to go grab his Brighton High School senior yearbook. They reminisced as they turned through pages. Nikki and Lauren teased their father about notes various girls had written to him.

Later, Dave went into his bedroom, looking for a few extra photos. He opened the door to a small cabinet in the nightstand on Teresa's side of the bed. There, instead of the pictures he was looking for, was her wallet.

He picked it up and sat on the bed, unsnapping it and holding it open. There were a variety of credit cards, some of which he knew he should probably move to his own wallet. There were coins that he emptied out into his hand. And there was Teresa's license, which he slid out of a clear plastic protector and held in his hand. She looked jovial in the picture and he studied it for a few seconds, running his thumb across her face as if he could feel her brown hair.

He flipped through the small photos that she kept in her wallet. Johnny. Lauren. Nikki. And in the back, there was a picture of a shaggy-haired football player, down on one knee, posing on a field: Brett Poulsen.

Brett Poulsen?

Dave couldn't help but smile and shake his head.

He took the wallet and the pictures downstairs and called out to his buddy in the kitchen.

"Well, I can see how you rate!" Dave said, feigning as though he were perturbed. "Teresa had pictures of each of the kids, and you, in her wallet. But do you think she carried one of her husband?"

Brett set his beer down. The revelation brought a swirl of emotion to him. There was pride, flattery, and something else: confirmation. In a heartbeat, Brett felt better about his role in trying to match Dave with his sister. He knew there was an aspect of imposition in it. But that picture in Teresa's wallet was an indication for Brett that there was an unspoken connection all these years between them. He knew that she trusted him.

Although the news swelled him with a sense of honor, Brett kept the deeper meaning to himself.

"Well she could see your ugly mug anytime," Brett retorted.

Brett, Dave, Gary and Tom Re went through Hamms one can at a time until an entire half-rack was gone. Dave went off in search of Pabst Blue Ribbon. For Dave, the cheapest beer always seemed to taste best.

With his inhibitions lowered, Brett could feel his ideas about Dave and Kellie creep up to the tip of his tongue, like a competitor on a diving board. Looking across the kitchen counter at Tom Re, it began to spill out of him. He felt the beer had forged a bond between them. Brett could tell that Tom was torn up over the loss of Teresa, and he wanted to explain his solution to the Grill family's crisis.

"Tom, what if . . ." Brett said, then paused. He considered going further before good sense stopped him. He played off the beginning of his sentence and went another direction.

It was Dave to whom he really wanted to bare his soul.

The conversations and storytelling continued into the evening, then late into the night.

The girls, Nikki, Lauren and Makenna cornered Kellie near the kitchen sink. They were full of questions and Kellie's bubbly, enthusiastic personality began to emerge. They talked about the most random things: Self-defense; her wolf back home, Timber; Kellie's old boyfriends; who she knew in country music; and about her experiences as a model.

Kellie began to grow hungry, and out of the blue, asked the girls if they were interested in going out for ice cream.

She received a quick, unanimous "Yes!"

"Is there a Baskin Robbins nearby?" she asked them.

It was closing in on midnight.

"There's a Haggen's Grocery Store," Nikki said. "It's open 24 hours a day."

"Perfect! Let's go!" Kellie said.

She asked Brett for the rental car keys, and the three girls followed her outside to the car.

Lauren was almost bursting out of her skin with joy. "Hey, I have an idea," she said, beaming. "Let's call all of each other by our favorite names. Like if your favorite name is Suzie, then that's who you are for the rest of the night! Alright?"

"OK," Makenna said. "I'm Tiffany, but you can call me Tiff."

"I'm Tegan," Nikki said.

"Well, I'm Claire," Lauren said. "Who are you Kellie?"

Kellie felt suddenly drawn into their teenage world again and was happy to go with it. After brief consideration, she giggled and said, "Well, I'd have to be Randi."

It was settled. The two younger girls got into the backseat while Nikki went for the passenger seat so that she could give Kellie directions to the store.

Kellie was still trying to keep all of their real names straight, yet now faced the challenge of remembering their pretend names as well. She was able to get through it without messing up once.

The chatter filled the car all the way to the store.

Makenna, aka Tiff, spoke up in a serious tone that got Kellie's attention. "Kellie... uh, I mean Randi?" she said, giggling at her mistake. "I have to tell you something."

"What is it, Tiff?" Kellie said.

"I think my Aunt Cheese sent you to us," Makenna said. Aunt Cheese was a nickname that she had for Teresa.

Kellie felt a sudden surge of emotion well up in her throat, but fought to suppress it.

Makenna continued her thought: "I think that she knew how sad we all were and that she had Brett bring you here to help us through this time."

Kellie turned her head to see the other girls, Dave's daughters, nod in agreement.

"Oh . . ." Kellie said. "You girls are so sweet. It is so weird that you would say that because I feel the same way. I feel like I was meant to meet you guys and be here with you through all of this. I know we've only known each other for a few hours, but I feel like I've known you all of my life."

"Same here!" the girls said in unison.

"That is so cute that you called your Aunt Teresa, 'Aunt Cheese,'" Kellie said. "I can tell you have a special bond with your aunt."

It seemed to Kellie as if the loss was as hard on Makenna as it was on Nikki and Lauren.

The serious moment left again as soon as it had come. Soon, they were all back to laughter and pretend names and talking about their favorite flavors of ice cream.

They each found the Haagen Dasz of their choice, and followed Kellie up to the register.

It was a short drive back to the Grills' neighborhood. Once they had reached the side streets, Kellie pulled over. She turned to Nikki and asked if she wanted to drive.

The 14-year-old didn't have to be asked twice. She flung the door open and raced around to the driver's side, where Kellie turned over the wheel to her. Nikki drove up and down the streets of their neighborhood, grinning and concentrating.

They came upon an ambulance coming down the road in the opposite direction with its lights flashing. Nikki calmly pulled the car over to the side to allow it more room to go by.

"Let's go see where it's going!" Lauren shouted from the backseat.

Nikki looked over to Kellie, and they nodded in agreement. Nikki turned the car around and "chased" after the ambulance, following the flashing lights and sirens without exceeding the speed limit.

They followed it to a house several blocks down the street from the Grills, and pulled into a driveway where they could watch and eat their ice cream and giggle.

A man walked out of the house, toward the ambulance. He didn't seem to be in any urgent need of help, or to be in any pain.

"What a faker!" Lauren yelled, breaking up everyone in the car.

The man did eventually get into the ambulance, and it calmly took him away without the spectacle of lights or sirens.

They decided to leave too. It was getting late. Nikki drove the few blocks back to the house and parked behind another car on the curb.

As they got out, Nikki walked around the back of the car and wrote "Tegan" with her finger on the dewy back windshield. Lauren did the same, writing "Claire." Makenna then wrote "Randi" and "Tiffany."

Kellie never felt so right being so silly. How is one supposed to act around children of a mother who has just died, or the niece of a dearly departed aunt?

Kellie knew of no rulebook or guidelines. She decided to act the way that she felt, and these girls made her feel good.

Friday, December 1

As agreed upon the night before, Kellie returned to pick up the girls. The plan called for her taking them back to her motel so that they could swim in the pool. It would give her some more time to spend with her new friends. And it would help Dave to have a few less people to worry about entertaining. More relatives were flying in for Teresa's memorial.

Kellie pulled up to the Grill residence in the rental car, still feeling the ill effects of a cold that she had been fighting for a week. Without her makeup on, and her unwashed hair pulled back into a ponytail, Kellie felt sheepish about getting out of the car for fear that Dave would see her.

Silly, she thought. Dave could care less.

When the door opened, there was Dave, smiling at her and holding a hot cup of coffee in his right hand.

"Good morning," he said, greeting her. He then turned to shout up the stairs.

"Kellie's here! Hurry up and get your stuff together!" Dave said, looking back to offer Kellie a wink.

"How are you doing? Did you get enough sleep last night?" Dave asked her.

"Ugh . . . I can't seem to shake this cold!" Kellie said, aware that he was looking at her raw, red nose. "I just hope I don't go and give it to anyone while I'm here."

Kellie could tell that Dave didn't look his best, either. A week's worth of scruff was becoming a beard, evidence that he had ceased paying very close attention to it.

Hannah, Teresa's old black Lab, came to the door to greet Kellie with her tail excitedly wagging. Or at least as excited as old Hannah could get. Kellie reached down to smile into Hannah's cloudy eyes, and then turned up and was momentarily caught in Dave's green eyes.

Lauren bounded down the stairs, loud and energetic, and playfully bumped into her dad when she reached the bottom.

"Hi!" Lauren said to them both, grinning.

"Well hi yourself, kiddo," Kellie said. "Are you guys ready to go?"

"Yeah, we just need to get our suits on," Lauren said. "Just a couple more minutes."

Lauren grabbed Kellie's hand.

"C'mon!" Lauren said, practically pulling her new friend back up the stairs.

Nikki and Makenna greeted Kellie in unison with a loud "Hi!" as she got within a few steps of them.

Kellie turned to watch Dave vanish from view. As she followed the girls down the hall, the cluttered messes she saw in the bedrooms took Kellie aback. Clearly, the absence of a mother was already evident in the housekeeping. Kellie was alert to such things. She and Kaysie operated a housecleaning business in Tennessee. Songwriting, which was their love and their "profession," seldom paid the bills.

Kellie followed Lauren into her room and watched the girl as she went rifling through her dresser, adding to the piles of clothes on the floor.

"I can't find a suit for Makenna," Lauren said. "Maybe I can find one in Nikki's room." They walked into that room and Kellie noticed a similar mess.

Dave walked up the stairs to join them. He noticed Kellie stepping over the clutter, but it didn't occur to him to be embarrassed by it.

Kellie commented on a picture hanging on the wall, a water-color painting of a skier coming down a mountain.

"This is so neat," Kellie said.

"Yeah," Dave said. "Ron, Teresa's dad, painted it. He's quite an artist."

"Really?" Kellie said. "He's good."

"Oh, hold on a second, I know something you would love," Dave said, moving away into his bedroom. He returned with a painting of an old wagon wheel propped up against a barn door.

"Ron painted this one too," he said.

"Wow, I do like that one!" Kellie said. "It reminds me of grandpa's farm in Cedar Valley, in Utah, remember it?"

"Yeah, I went there a couple of times with Brett," Dave said.

Kellie became suddenly aware of her closeness to Dave in the narrow hallway and it nearly overwhelmed her. She turned back to the girls, "Did you find that swimsuit yet?"

"I don't know how they find anything in those filthy rooms," Dave said, finally noticing them enough to apologize for them. "You girls are coming back here after swimming and cleaning these rooms! Company is arriving and these rooms will not be like this. Right?"

"Right!" Nikki and Lauren said in unison.

The girls each grabbed a towel, and all of them filed down the stairs.

At the pool, the three girls splashed, screamed, pushed each other under the water and giggled. Kellie was glad to see them all enjoying themselves when she knew that deep down they were all still crushed by their loss.

Kellie steered clear of them in the pool, trying to keep her head and ears dry so as to not worsen her cold. During a break in the girls' horseplay, Lauren suddenly got serious.

"Sometimes I still can't believe mom is dead," the 12-year-old said.

The words stopped the other girls, and Kellie.

"I know," Kellie said empathetically. "I didn't even know her except for that one time I met her at the Lewis & Clark football game. And it's hard for even me to believe she's gone."

Kellie's memory still held snapshots of that fall day 17 years earlier. She was a high school junior when she and her parents made the trip to Oregon to watch Brett play in one of his games for Southern Oregon. But when he got hurt that week and couldn't play, the Poulsens decided to drive north and watch Dave's game instead.

Dave Grill was still Kellie's secret crush. But how was she going to compete for his attention against college girls? At the game, she was introduced to Teresa O'Brien, Dave's new girlfriend.

It was a polite encounter that left Kellie with mixed emotions. She was stung, but she was also impressed with Teresa. Dave was taken.

That was the only time she ever saw Teresa in person. And until two days ago, it was the last time she had seen Dave.

"Why did she have to die, Kell?" Lauren said, mournfully. "It's just so unfair."

"I don't know, sweetie," Kellie said, struggling to find something comforting to say.

Nikki and Makenna drew nearer to them, joining the conversation.

"Why couldn't a bad awful prisoner die?" Nikki asked. "Someone who murdered or raped people? Why mom? She was so good."

"I don't know," Kellie said, shaking her head. "Life can be so unfair sometimes."

Lauren was clearly taking it the hardest, Kellie thought. Her tender age, combined with her raw, open personality, made it all the more difficult for her to contain her overwhelming emotions.

After a final round of splashing and laughing, they got out of the pool and went up to the motel room and changed into dry clothes. Kellie let Lauren tie her hair into French braids.

Kellie took the girls back to the house so they could clean their rooms, but before she dropped them off they made plans to meet again in the afternoon.

∞

Kellie arrived at the doorstep yet again to pick up the girls, and they happily greeted her. Nikki held a bag of carrots, which they had bought at the store to prepare for their next excursion together: feeding and petting horses.

The three girls were impressed with Kellie's knowledge of horses, and were thrilled at the idea of going and finding some to feed carrots to.

Nikki gave Kellie directions and they drove five or six miles south of Tualatin, into the Stafford area of large estates with rolling green pastures separated by white fences.

"There's some horses!" Kellie said gleefully, pulling the car over as she surveyed about 10 animals all in individual paddocks about a quarter acre each. Kellie quickly surmised it to be a boarding facility and judged that the large barn up at the top of the hill contained an arena for showing.

The girls ran to the first fence and began holding carrots out, and Kellie reached down to pull up some long green grass. A couple of the horses walked over to them and began nibbling on the handouts. Kellie pet one and urged the girls to follow her lead.

"Just like this," she said, stroking the gelding's neck and muzzle. "Yeah, he likes that."

They began naming the ones that were the friendliest. "Snowflake" was the gelding, a white Arabian. "Prince" was a sorrel quarter horse gelding, and "Sassy" was a black thoroughbred mare.

Makenna asked which horse would be the most suitable to ride out of the three. Without hesitation, Kellie determined that "Prince" would probably work out the best.

A tall blond woman approached them and Kellie stopped feeding the horse, hoping she wasn't about to get reprimanded by a protective owner.

"I hope you don't mind that we've been petting and feeding your horses," Kellie said, trying to gauge the woman's reaction.

The woman walked up to "Prince" and put a lead rope and halter on him.

"No problem," the woman said, smiling. "He probably loves all the attention."

"What's his name?" Kellie asked. "We've been calling him Prince."

"Oh, wow, I bet he loves that," the woman said. "His name is actually Drake. And mine is Diane. Diane Riefert."

"Well, hi, nice to meet you," Kellie said, extending her hand. "I'm Kellie and these girls are Makenna, Lauren and Nikki." The girls all smiled.

"Do you want to come to the barn with me and help me get him ready?" Diane asked. "I'm going to ride him tonight."

The girls gleefully answered "Yes!" and they followed along, with Kellie.

"That would be so nice," Kellie said. "I have eight horses in Tennessee so I forget how much people who aren't used to them get such a kick out of being around them."

"Tennessee?" Diane asked. "Do you live there?"

"Yes, I'm a country music songwriter," Kellie said proudly. She always was eager to identify herself that way. It sounded so much better than "I clean houses for a living."

"Cool," Diane said. She handed each of the girls a brush and instructed them on the basics of how to groom Drake. "Would you like to ride him when you're done brushing him?"

The girls couldn't believe their luck. Of course they wanted to ride him. Kellie and Nikki walked with Diane to a phone so that they could call Dave and get his permission first. He said OK.

"So why are you here, Kellie?" Diane asked, making conversation as they returned to the girls.

"Well . . ." Kellie said, awkwardly unsure how to answer. "I'm here with my brother Brett ..."

She looked up and saw the faces of the girls gazing on her. She could tell Lauren's eyes were beginning to fill with tears, bracing for what she knew Kellie was about to say.

"We're actually here for a . . ." Kellie tried to continue, but stammered. ". . . for a memorial service for Lauren and Nikki's mom."

Diane's disbelieving eyes widened.

Kellie continued. "She died a week ago today from cancer."

"Oh . . . " Diane said, momentarily regretting that she'd asked the question. "I'm so sorry to hear that."

She set the saddle she was carrying down and gave each girl a hug.

Makenna and Lauren tried to fight back their tears, wiping them away with the palms of their hands. The sight almost caused Kellie to lose it too, but Diane offered her a hug as well.

"My brother is their dad's best friend of 22 years," Kellie said, trying to fill in the blanks. "I came to be with him during this tough time. Actually, I just met these precious girls yesterday."

Diane looked stunned once more.

"You're kidding me," she said. "You guys act like you've known each other forever."

"I know," Kellie said. "I feel the same way."

"We think my aunt sent her to us to help us through it," Makenna said. Nikki and Lauren nodded.

After taking a few turns on Drake, Kellie and the girls thanked Diane for her hospitality. Kellie exchanged phone numbers with her and said her good-byes before walking with the girls back to the car.

∽

After shuttling the girls off to a birthday party, Dave picked up Brett and Kellie at their motel and headed a few miles down the freeway toward their next function: dinner at his parents' condo south of Wilsonville, across the Willamette River.

Brett's emotions had rocked back and forth for the past day and a half, and he started to get teary once more as he stepped out of the Suburban at Gary and Wilma's. He hugged Dave as the two walked together toward the door.

"I'm sorry Bud, I'll quit huggin' ya," Brett said. "I don't know why I keep doin' that. Probably all of that ass touchin' from when I was your center back at Brighton High. I'll quit, or soon I'll be grabbin' your ass!"

Dave laughed.

"Yeah," Kellie said, trying to gracefully interject into the joke. "If there's any ass grabbin' going on, it better be mine. And I don't mean by Brett!"

Kellie would like to have caught her words and shoved them back in her mouth. But after she cringed, she felt the slightest bit of relief that her bottled up attraction had leaked just a bit. Dave had not responded to it, and she wondered if maybe he hadn't even heard. He stepped into the condo and momentarily out of sight. It was just long enough for Kellie to take a deep breath.

The inside of the condo was crammed with Dave's extended family, including his sister and her family, and Ron and Jean and members of their family. It was noisy from conversation, punctuated by the noise of children. Johnny and his cousins were on the back patio in the hot tub.

As Dave greeted all the newcomers to the week's gathering, Kellie sought out the few familiar faces that she felt comfortable with. She told Wilma about her afternoon with the girls and the horses, and caught up briefly with Dave's sister, Lisa, whom she had barely known back in Utah.

Kellie was also aware of curious glances from across the room, mostly from women that she didn't know. She suspected they were Teresa's relatives, but felt it wise not to approach them.

"Hey Kellie, tell everyone the incredible story about the girls getting to ride the horses today and how that all came about!" Wilma said over all of the other voices in the living room.

Kellie stopped in mid-chew, then swallowed. All 25 faces turned toward her, and she could feel the scrutiny coming from most of them. It said, "Who the hell are you, and what are you doing here?"

Kellie felt trapped in the spotlight, forced to tell her story to a group that included more strangers than friendly faces.

She proceeded to explain it all, piece by piece, detail by detail, using her hands and her enthusiasm to try and win over the crowd. But she could tell in the faces of Teresa's parents, sister, aunt and cousins that there were puzzling questions brewing.

"Why are we listening to this woman? Who invited her? Why, exactly, is she here?"

It hadn't taken long for Kellie to notice the tension in the room from people who were protective of Teresa and unaware why a stranger was in their midst. She had felt it from the first time she stepped into Dave's house.

But the confusion they felt seemed to be intensifying with every passing hour. She felt shunned by some, openly disliked by others.

Kellie didn't take any of it personally. She knew she was filling a role by supporting and comforting her brother and her family's longtime friends, the Grills.

But why was she *really* here? It seemed like a perfectly valid question, even to Kellie. She was here because she had no choice in the matter. Brett had forced her. Or maybe it was even more than that. The girls' said they felt Teresa had brought Kellie to them, to help distract them through a tough stretch of days. And the more she thought about it, the more Kellie was inclined to agree with them.

But was she also here to test the waters with Dave? And if she was, then weren't the glaring eyes justified?

Deep down, Kellie felt pangs of guilt. She knew that part of the reason she had come, perhaps the only reason that Brett had forced to come, was for the entry point into Dave's life.

To that end, Kellie felt as confused as any of them.

Late in the evening, after many of the guests had left, Brett, Kellie, Dave and his parents were all that were left. They reminisced about the time spent as friends and neighbors in Salt Lake City.

Naturally, the conversation moved to music. The Grills shared the Poulsens' fondness for country music. All of their car radios were tuned to it. Kellie mentioned a benefit concert that she was planning to attend when she returned to Nashville, at the famous Wildhorse Saloon.

"Who are you going with?" Dave asked, forgetting for a moment that it was a loaded question.

"I'm taking my best friend, Joni. There's no man in my life currently," she said.

"Oh," Dave said playfully. "I'll go with ya, that sounds fun."

The words, and the way Dave said them, with a smile and wink in her direction, affected Kellie all over again. She knew he was only teasing. But those green eyes, she thought, are going to be the end of me. She longed for those words to be serious. She fantasized about how wonderful it would be to actually take Dave to the concert.

"I wish you could," Kellie said, catching his glance for a moment and then shying away. "It would be fun."

Wilma chimed in. She knew how much Dave enjoyed country music, both listening to it and occasionally dabbling with composing it.

"You'll have to go to Nashville sometime, Dave," his mother said. "It's so much fun."

It had been little more than a year since Gary and Wilma had come to Nashville and visited Kellie and Kaysie and been to some shows with them.

Midnight came quickly, and broke up the gathering.

Dave dropped Kellie and Brett off at their motel and continued on toward home.

Brett was asleep by the time his head touched the pillow. But Kellie tossed and turned for what seemed like hours. She kept reviewing Dave, all of his mannerisms, the sound of his voice and the athletic grace in his movement. She could also see the kids:

Johnny in his swim trunks in the hot tub, the girls with the horses. Everything and everyone she had met since arriving in Portland.

This was too much information for her brain to process. It shut down for the night.

Saturday, December 2

"Brett," Kellie said, whining nasally. The sun was beginning to peak in through the drapes on the windows of the motel room.

Brett was rummaging through his suitcase, looking for something.

"Yeah? Good morning Kell," he said with his back to her in the dim light.

"Brett, I just had an awful night. I couldn't get to sleep until about 5," she said. "I absolutely could not stop thinking about Dave. I feel like I'm obsessed, and we're here for his wife's memorial service. I can't help feeling so guilty about it!"

"No, Kellie, really, don't be," Brett said. "Seriously, I am so glad you agreed to come. It's really working out great having you here."

Kellie thought for a moment about the word "agreed," but then let it pass without comment.

Brett turned on the television and flipped the channels until he found CMT, Country Music Television. He laid back down on his bed, propping himself up against his pillows and watched the Billy Ray Cyrus video for "Some Gave All."

As the sad video played, it broke up both Brett and Kellie. Thoughts of Teresa and Dave and the kids had become first and foremost in their minds. It didn't take much to trigger the emotions.

"I'm taking a shower and then going over to see Wilma," Kellie announced. "I need to tell her how I'm feeling."

"OK, Kellie," Brett replied. "I think that's a good idea. She's a great lady and a good ally to have. She'll understand."

Kellie went into the bathroom, slipped out of her pajamas and turned on the hot water. She stepped into the shower and hoped the water would recharge her and wash away the guilt that she felt conflicting with her other emotions.

She let the water beat down on her face and she began to pray silently for guidance. Was she doing the right thing by going to Wilma? Was there any way that something good was going to come out of all of this? The stresses of the long night worked themselves out in her tears. She felt tired and scared.

As she prayed, she reached up and grabbed the shower head, holding onto it to help support herself so she wouldn't fall. In her mind, she begged Teresa for forgiveness for the swell of feelings she could no longer contain for her husband. The water poured onto her face and washed the tears that squeezed out of the corners of her eyes. Something felt so right about this, and yet it felt so wrong at the same time.

The last couple of days had felt like a test as much as it had a visit. But who was testing her? Teresa?

Kellie wrung the last of her thoughts out in the shower. Then she stepped out of it to dry off and begin a new round of challenges.

Brett went into the bathroom after Kellie came out. She wrapped her hair in a towel and set it up on her head. She sat on the edge of her bed and reached for the phone, dialing Wilma.

"Good morning! How are you doing?" Kellie said, cheerfully as ever. "I've got something to bring you and I was wondering if you would let me bring it over."

Wilma said her morning was free and that she could come on by any time.

The something was a sympathy card. It was little more than an excuse to come over and reveal the real purpose of the visit.

Kellie finished getting dressed and ready.

"I'm taking off, Brett!" Kellie yelled toward the bathroom door.

"OK!" she heard. "Good luck! You're the strongest person I know! Proud of you! Love you!"

Brett's words refilled her with confidence as she pulled the motel door shut behind her.

The drive to Wilma's was less than 10 minutes, far too short to rehearse all the things she knew she needed to say.

As she knocked on Dave's mom's door, she could feel her heart in her throat. It was the same uneasy feeling that she was beginning to feel accustomed to over the past couple of days.

"Dear God, please guide me," Kellie whispered to herself, waiting for the door to open.

∞

Wilma opened the door and greeted Kellie with a warm hug.

"Come in, come in!" Wilma said, delightful as always.

Kellie exchanged greetings and stepped in and followed Wilma to the kitchen. In the room next to it, Gary sat in an easy chair and held the TV clicker in his hand. He had settled on a program about golf. He stood up and offered Kellie a hug, too, and then sat back down.

"Can I make you some tea?" Wilma asked. "I'm making myself a cup."

"Oh that would be wonderful," Kellie said. "I'm still trying to take care of this scratchy throat of mine."

Wilma shooed Gary into the spare bedroom to watch his golf so that, "Us girls can talk."

Kellie took the sympathy card from her purse and handed it to Wilma. She had picked it out before leaving Salt Lake City.

"Oh, you didn't have to do that," Wilma said, taking the card and opening it.

Kellie protested by shaking her head. "You know me, I send cards to everybody."

Wilma held it up and began to read it:

Dear Wilma and Gary,

I'm at a loss for words yet I want to express how sorry I am at the death of your precious daughter-in-law Teresa.

The unfairness and injustices of this life are sometimes so overwhelming and so confusing.

It is so hard but you all will pull through this.

How do I know? Because you are so very special and wonderful. And you are the Grills!

I love you dearly,

Kellie

Wilma began to feel a tear coming on and set the card down. She hugged Kellie again and thanked her for the kind gesture.

They fell into some small talk about Kellie's trip, and her impressions of the Portland area. They talked about Wilma's childhood and the Willamette Valley town of Lebanon, where she grew up, and how her father had been a state senator. Talking about him got Wilma emotional once again. It had only been a few years since her parents had died.

As they talked, Wilma mentioned Dave and how rough Teresa's illness and death had been on him and the kids. Even though he didn't show it outwardly, he was devastated, Wilma said.

"He's got some deep scars but he doesn't let anybody see them. I'm worried about him," Wilma said. "Dave and Teresa had such a hectic schedule with those kids. I'm not sure how he's going to manage it all by himself. Between lessons and practices and games and you name it . . . these kids are into it."

"I can't even imagine," Kellie said, shaking her head.

"I mean I will help some, with things like cooking and cleaning and laundry when I have time, and he has many friends around that will help him, but it's going to be a big adjustment," Wilma continued.

Wilma changed the subject and began to ask Kellie about the men in her life. The first night in town, it had come up in conversation that she had never married but that she had been proposed to once. She had gotten serious about the guy for a time, but it was months into the relationship before he owned up to an ex-wife and 10-year-old son. Kellie was disgusted by his lying and broke it off. There had been a string of failed attempts to make relationships work, but she couldn't seem to get it right, or meet the right guy.

"Wilma, I don't know what it is, or if it's me, or what," Kellie said. "But I am a jerk-magnet! There's no other way to put it."

"Well, I can't believe that," Wilma said. "You're so good with kids. Dave and Tamara's kids think you hung the moon. It's been so nice to have you here to help out watching them with all of this craziness going on this week."

"Oh, thanks," Kellie said. "It's been fun to get to know them and see Dave again . . ."

Kellie's thought trailed off. She knew where she needed to go next but was afraid of what Wilma's reaction might be. Her hands began to shake and she put her cup of tea down on the counter.

"Actually, that's one of the reasons I came here to you this morning," Kellie said, stammering. "I . . . I wanted to . . . umm, talk to you about . . ."

Wilma picked up on Kellie's changed tone and could see how nervous she had suddenly become.

"What is it, dear?"

Kellie's lighthearted cheerful chatter had been replaced by a serious, pensive tone that was wrought with fear.

And just then, Gary walked into the kitchen.

"I'm starving!" he said boisterously, as he opened the refrigerator. "I'm going to make a BLT. Anyone else want one?"

Kellie said no thanks and inquired about his golf show.

"It's good, but I think after I have my sandwich I'm going to clean the hot tub out on the back patio," he said.

Wilma was annoyed by the interruption, because she knew Kellie had something pressing on her mind. But the two women turned their conversation to idle chatter for a couple of more minutes while Gary meticulously constructed his sandwich.

Kellie's jangling nerves continued to cause a rumbling in her stomach. Each excruciating minute that passed brought her closer to tears.

Gary, oblivious, took the first bite of his sandwich and sauntered out the door.

Wilma was growing anxious too.

"Well, now we can talk again. Where were we?" she asked. "You were saying you needed to talk about Dave?"

"Yeah," Kellie started again, pausing on each word. "I . . . well, I . . . I don't know how to say this exactly."

She took her eyes off of Wilma and directed them at the floor.

"I'm just going to go ahead and say it," Kellie said.

"OK," Wilma said, patiently.

"I feel so foolish and weird to say what I'm about to say, but I have to say it," Kellie said. She was shaking again and wasn't sure if she could get through it.

"I have to say some things that might seem horrible for me to say, especially right now because of everything that's going on. Please forgive me for saying it now, but I have to because if I don't it won't get said . . . and . . . at least not in person I mean," Kellie continued, a rambling mess. She knew that with every apology and attempt to cushion the blow she was getting closer.

"It's OK, Kellie," Wilma said, sympathetically. She had scooted closer to Kellie, who by now was seated on a couch. Wilma's soft brown eyes coaxed Kellie and made her feel that whatever she had to say, it was OK. She was safe.

"Anyway . . . I don't know if you know this or not, but I have always, and I mean always, had a huge crush on your son," Kellie said, finally getting to the point. "Ever since I met him when I was 12."

Wilma looked a little stunned.

Kellie kept her newfound momentum going:

"I know this is so odd to tell you this now, but it's just that I am having such a hard time trying to mask my feelings and keep it hidden. When I came here with Brett to see you guys and attend the memorial, I had no idea that all of these feelings would come back again and be so strong."

She stopped to take a deep breath.

"Wilma, I feel so guilty to feel this way about Dave, especially now and with Teresa's death so recent, but I can't help myself. I am so confused."

Wilma put her hand on Kellie's and held it.

"It's OK, Kellie," Wilma said. "You can't help what you feel."

"When I met the kids it was the clincher," Kellie said. "I was sunk! Hook, line and sinker. Dave is gorgeous and he has the most awesome personality. Wilma, I think that I am hopelessly in love with your son and his kids and I don't know what to do about it!"

There, Kellie thought. It was out on the table. She could feel some of the weight had slid off her shoulders, but she was still shaking, and crying. Her chin quivered, not yet knowing how her admission was going to be accepted. Her secret was out.

"Oh, Kellie," Wilma said, sliding next to her to offer a hug. She offered Kellie a tissue. "You sweetheart."

"I'm so sorry," Kellie said. "I know it sounds sick and twisted with Teresa only gone such a short time. It's just so real and so powerful and I know how close you are to Dave, and I was thinking that maybe sometime, whenever—even if it's five years from now—you could tell him about me and then maybe we could date or whatever."

Kellie's rambling had started all over again. Her thoughts were spilling out faster than she could edit them.

"I know we live thousands of miles apart, it's just that I have to try. I've loved him so long and I have to try," Kellie continued, mashing a wad of tissue in her nervous hands. She stopped momentarily to sniff and wipe her eyes again.

"Well, let me tell you this," Wilma said. "Dave is like me. He is a realist. He knows that Teresa is gone and she isn't coming back. He is a father of three children and has to go on. I don't know when and who, but he will date and probably marry again. My God, he's only 40 years old. I would love it if it could be you!"

With those final words, Kellie's cloud was lifted. Not only did she have an accomplice to her secret, she had an ally.

"You are very brave to tell me all of this," Wilma said. "And I will tell him sometime."

"Thank you," Kellie said. She felt relief and triumph. Her mission, difficult as it had been, was accomplished. She knew that she could fly away without any regrets. The shaking was beginning to subside, and she picked up her cup and took a sip of cold tea.

The phone rang and Wilma moved to answer it.

"Here," Wilma said. "She's right here. Let me let you tell her."

Kellie's expression moved from puzzled to shocked. It was Dave!

Wilma handed the receiver to Kellie, smiling a knowing smile. Dave had instructions for Kellie to meet him, Brett and Dave Kitches, another former high school buddy who had just flown into town, at a bowling alley in Wilsonville. The kids were going to be there too.

Kellie's hand shook violently as she scribbled directions down onto a notepad and she tried to compose herself.

"Uh huh," she said. "Ok. Yep. See you there. Bye."

After hanging up the phone, Kellie stood up and hugged Wilma. Gary came into the room and got a hug too.

Kellie told them the plan and said her good-byes. As she went out the doorway, she saw a sparkle in Wilma's eyes. She took it to be a sign of hope that somehow and some way, things were going to work themselves out in everyone's favor. The timing clearly wasn't appropriate, but one day it would be. And maybe the Grill family would be whole once again.

Sunday, December 3

Kellie stood in front of the mirror in the motel bathroom and inserted the last of the bobby pins to hold her long red hair in place on top of her head.

She touched up her eyeliner and checked one last time for something to fix. She was careful not to do too much makeup, because she was sure that her tears would make a mess of it if she did.

In the other room, Brett concentrated on a needle and thread, trying to reattach a button to his shirt. Dave Kitches had stayed in the same motel the previous night, and he was getting ready too. Brett paused from his button project long enough to show Kitches how to tie a perfect double Windsor knot in his tie.

The morning of Teresa's memorial service was quiet and solemn for them, and it marked a change from the past few days, which had been remarkably upbeat and lighthearted.

Kellie wore a black dress that came down to her knees. She slipped her black nylon-covered foot into her shoe and went in to check on the guys.

"Are we ready?" she asked.

"Yeah, Kell," Brett said, annoyed at his wardrobe. Not only did the button need reattached, he felt like his pants were too tight. "Let me grab my coat and I'll be ready."

They stopped for late breakfast at Shari's, idly waiting for the time to melt away, and discussed the memorial, what they would see and how they would deal with it. And more importantly, they were curious to see how Dave and the kids would cope with it.

The car ride to the chapel on the campus of Lewis & Clark College was subdued. Kellie held Dave's instructions in her hand while Brett drove through a cold, gray drizzle as he headed north on I-5 and into Southwest Portland.

They arrived an hour early to find a swarm of people, mostly clad in black, already there. Dave Kitches, Brett and Kellie sat together, near the front, about three rows behind Dave and his family. But for the next half hour, their necks craned to the rear of the chapel as they watched people come in.

The chapel had seating for 700 people and Dave had printed no more than 250 programs, thinking that would be plenty.

But it wasn't.

Thirty minutes before the 2 P.M. service was to begin, the chapel was packed. Rev. Larry Bingham, a pastor that Dave and Teresa had known in Tualatin, was preparing to preside over the service. He approached the microphone and asked those already seated to scoot closer together.

"It looks like we're going to have quite a crowd today," the pastor said. "Please try and sit as closely as you can so we can accommodate as many people as possible. Thank you."

Dave, Brett and a few others brought up folding chairs from the basement, and put them at the ends of the pews. By 2 P.M., nearly 900 people were squeezed into the chapel, or standing in the back where they could hear.

The weight of Teresa's impact on so many lives was palpable before the first act of the service began.

In addition to family and friends, there were teachers and colleagues and former students.

At the altar was an oversized color portrait of Teresa, a photo that Dave had blown up. It was surrounded by large bouquets of flowers.

Rev. Bingham welcomed his audience and thanked them for coming.

"We are here today to remember the life of Teresa," he began. "And I think it is clear to all of us by looking around this chapel today that she touched so many lives."

The pastor continued with a bible reading and a prayer.

Then he introduced Nikki, and she wriggled out of her pew, straightened her skirt and calmly walked to the microphone.

Hundreds of people clutched their programs tighter, squeezed the hand of the person next to them, or simply let the first tears fall.

Nikki had spoken up early when Dave began planning the service. She wanted to sing.

Many of the family members advised her against it. It would be too emotional, they said.

"If I don't get to sing I will be so upset," she protested.

Dave, however, made no attempt to talk her out of it. He knew it was important to her and that the song would provide a release valve for her stored up emotions.

The 14-year-old took the microphone, turned to face 900 sympathetic faces—and the DVD karaoke system that held the music to her song promptly cut out.

Kellie quickly shoved a Kleenex in the direction of Brett, who took it. She offered another one to Dave Kitches, who whispered, "I'm fine."

A tense, awkward silence filled the room as Nikki waited for the music to start, and the crowd of people bore her anxiety for her.

A minute went by, then two. Nikki held up the microphone to apologize for the delay, then kept smiling. Brett felt his own tension mount, to the point he was nearly ready to stand up and scream at the operator of the sound equipment.

Nikki remained placid and decided to read a speech she had written for the occasion, though she had intended for it to come after the song.

"I think I'll start with something I wrote for my mom," Nikki began, holding a sheet of paper steadily with her left hand.

She swallowed and took a deep breath before calmly beginning.

"As I lay in bed Wednesday night trying to think about what I was going to say, I thought about my mom's life and all the things she accomplished. I realized that night that today we would be celebrating the life of an angel. In Webster's Dictionary I found two very good definitions of an angel. The first one was 'a very kind and lovable person.' The second was 'a helping or guiding spirit.' All who knew my mother would have to say she met both of those descriptions.

"She was very kind and loving to all her students, friends and family, and she definitely helped and guided each of us in our own special way. She helped, loved, lead and cared for people all of her life. My sister said, 'She never pushed too hard, but instead guided us and made us set goals and helped us achieve them. She was sometimes a little bossy, but she never let us be bossy because she wanted us to be respected. She was a wonderful mother.'

"I believe her reason for leaving us was because she had done so many things here on Earth that she needed to go on to a new place where she could expand her skills in teaching and guiding. Her whole life she worked and taught. And when you work at anything, you keep getting better and better at it. She was so good at what she did, Heaven was the next place up on her ladder of achievement. There she can watch over all of us and many others.

"She was taken away in the arms of an angel so she could become our angel. She was born an angel and will live on as an angel forever in Heaven. We are in her hands now and I have to thank her for stepping up onto that last rung to watch over us all."

Nikki folded the sheet of paper and looked up at the silent audience. Reading off the page had actually calmed the few nerves that she felt. She took a cue from the back of the room that the sound system was ready for her.

Meanwhile, the tension in the room had turned into admiration for such an eloquent speech. Yet many in the crowd all wondered the same thing: Is this girl really going to be able to sing at a time like this?

The music started, Nikki brought the microphone closer to her mouth once again, closed her eyes, and began to sing the first notes of Sarah McLachlan's song, "Angel."

Dave Kitches tapped Kellie's knee, motioning for a second chance for that Kleenex. She turned to him, saw his reddened eyes, stuffed a tissue into his hand and turned her own tear-filled eyes back to Nikki.

Dave, sitting next to Lauren and Johnny, was transfixed. He had never heard her sing with such power and soulful emotion. As he responded to every perfected note, he grew more and more impressed. He recognized a poise and grace that he knew could only be traced back to one person: Teresa.

On this most heartbreaking of days for his family, Dave knew he was witnessing a great moment. And it was the first of many to come that he knew Teresa was going to miss.

Nikki concluded her song and put the microphone back in its stand. For a moment, she surveyed the crowd's reaction and saw the proud eyes of her father. She felt proud too, because she knew she had nailed the song.

Dave quickly slid out of his seat and began clapping as he rushed up to his daughter, breaking up the silence and pulling her into his chest and squeezing her in a tight hug. The crowd began clapping as well, filling the sanctuary with a roaring cheer of approval, rare at such a solemn event.

"Thank you, honey," Dave said into Nikki's ear as he kissed her cheek. "You were incredible up there."

If the song hadn't gotten them all to weeping, Dave's gesture of love for his daughter did. Neither Dave nor Nikki was crying, but they both were caught up with their emotions. They felt comforted, like the song said, in the arms of their angel.

Nikki's song set the tone for the rest of the memorial service, and in a profound way, for the rest of their lives. The scar they all carried was fresh and it still ached. But the resolve in the girl's voice, and the tenderness in her father's heartfelt hug, told everyone in the room that the Grills would heal from their wound and carry on.

After Nikki and Dave were seated, Lisa and Wilma went to the microphone together, hand in hand.

Wilma had intended to let Lisa read the words she had prepared, but following Nikki's performance she felt compelled to show the same bravery she had just witnessed from her granddaughter.

Wilma began with an introduction to the poem she had written.

"I had the good fortune to spend a great deal of time with Teresa in her final days. We shared tears, laughter and the messages of love she had for Dave, her children, her family, and her love for them was expressed often. During the middle of one night, I wrote this in hopes that it would bring some comfort to them."

Wilma cleared her throat and began her poem:

> How do you say goodbye to someone you love?
> The answer is—you don't!
> They never leave you
> They have become such a part of you.
> You see them in every sunflower and blue iris
> You feel them when you need their presence most
> You hear them in their children's laughter.
> Tho the earthly person is gone,
> She waits for us in a new place

A place we know is beautiful
And full of peace.
How do we know?
She spoke of angels sitting with her in her room on several
occasions,
Of Grandma Clara on the end of her bed,
Watching as she got up,
And it made her happy!
So, I let you go now, my love,
Because you can never leave me—
You have become such a part of me!

Family friend Dan Jacobson came to the lectern next and read an obituary that he had written for Teresa.

Rev. Bingham followed him and read passages from the Bible, offering solace and reassurance to the room full of family and friends that Teresa was beginning her new, eternal life. Then he introduced another family friend, Doug Johnson, who came up front to sing an operatic rendition of the Lord's Prayer.

When he was through, the service took a more personal turn as Ron, and then Tamara, delivered words about the impact Teresa had made on their lives. More relatives and close friends followed. Their stories were thoughtful, poignant statements about love and loss, fun and humor.

When they were finished, the microphone was opened to anyone in the room who wanted to tell a story or express their feelings about Teresa.

Brett raised his hand and took the microphone to tell his story about going on the honeymoon with Dave and Teresa, to a cabin on Detroit Lake. Kellie could feel Brett's leg quivering, and wasn't sure if he was going to make it through to the end. But he did.

Another dozen people spoke, to offer their fondest remembrances of Teresa, or simply to say, "Thank you."

One of her former students, who had come across town on the city bus, took the microphone and wanted to publicly thank "Mrs. OBG" for the extra effort that she had spent on him. Several years back, Teresa had bought him a pair of shoes when his family couldn't afford them.

Dave had remembered Teresa telling him about the boy years ago, but had never seen him. He couldn't believe that he had made it here. And based on what Teresa had told him about the boy's shyness, was even more surprised that he stood up to speak.

Dave was the last to go. He went up to the front, where everyone could see him, and held up the microphone. He was still calm, still in control of his emotions. He was dumbfounded by the number of people that had come to his wife's memorial.

"I don't think I ordered enough food," Dave said, making a joke about the size of the crowd. "I am really surprised so *many* of you came, but it is wonderful to see you all and it is a testament to how many people Teresa touched.

"I met her here at Lewis & Clark, so I suppose that it's appropriate that we end it here," he said, beginning to fight back tears. "I truly loved Teresa. She was the love of my life, and I'm going to miss her."

Five rows back, Kellie was riveted. She couldn't take her eyes off Dave. This man was going through so much, had lost the most important person in his life, and was still able to face this crowd of people with courage. He would greet every one of these 900 people and continue to be a rock for his three kids to lean on. She was fascinated by him.

"I want to thank all of you for coming," he continued. "And I know that so many of you want to offer your help to us, or want to bring us something to eat. But let me assure you, we are doing fine. If there is something we need, we will not hesitate to call and ask. But if I don't call you, please don't be offended. It just means that we're doing fine."

Dave introduced the final piece of the ceremony, the video tribute, and thanked those that had quickly put it together. It was the same friend that had spliced together home videos the previous summer to make a highlight tape of the Little League World Series team.

Dave had pulled together about a hundred photos of Teresa, spanning her life. A friend had turned them into a slide show, and overlaid an audio track that included a couple of Teresa's favorite songs: "I Hope You Dance," by Lee Ann Womack, and "The Dance," by Garth Brooks.

Kellie and Brett had already previewed the video at Dave's house, and it had moved them to tears. Brett had blubbered watching it with Ron O'Brien and the mere sight of him set Brett off during the service.

The video cast a light on all that had been wonderful in Teresa's life: Her kids, her marriage, her robust personality and pursuit of knowledge and enjoyment. Serious, reflective photos were offset with humorous, candid shots that evoked laughter.

When it ended, Rev. Bingham returned to the lectern and offered a few final words, then brought the ceremony to a close, offering directions to the campus cafeteria.

The guests rose from their seats and filed out of the chapel.

So few people chose to eat—fearing that there would be nothing left for those that really wanted to—that Dave was left with trays full of leftovers.

Dave and the kids patiently greeted everyone that extended a handshake or hug. They thanked all the guests, many of them surprises, for coming. They shared stories back and forth about Teresa. And more tears were shed. But the general mood of the occasion was upbeat, just the way Dave had wanted it. He was convinced that his wife would have preferred a celebration to a sad, mournful funeral.

Members of the family and Dave's closest friends returned to the house. Brett and Kellie returned to the motel to change their clothes before returning to the house on 70th Street. There, the party continued for hours, with beer, leftover food, karaoke, and more tears. Dave knew the day had gone just the way Teresa would have wanted it to.

In the midst of it, and after the Hamm's had worn down Brett's inhibitions yet again, he spotted Keely Jacobson, one of Teresa's closest friends, sitting on a couch with her hands over her face, crying.

Brett approached her, sat down, and put his arm around her.

"I'm putting them together," Brett said quietly, with a nod toward Dave, who was standing near Kellie.

Keely looked back at him with a blank, puzzled gaze. "What?"

Brett got up to find a fresh beer. A few minutes went by and Keely came up to him, looking slightly more composed.

"That's OK," Keely said, tentatively nodding her approval. "Just not yet. It's too soon."

The next morning's 8:30 A.M. flight came early. As they walked out of Dave's house for the final time, Brett gave his buddy a farewell hug before shuffling off to the car. Dave thanked Kellie for coming and filling such a helpful role distracting the kids and driving Brett back to the motel each night.

Kellie, lucid as ever, gave Dave a hug as well.

"I want to be one that you call," she said.

CHAPTER FIVE

Starting Over

Monday, December 4, 2000

Ron and Jean were hours ahead already by the time Dave pulled the Suburban out of the driveway and made his way onto Borland Road.

The next piece of business for all of them was a small, private graveside service at a small cemetery in Dufur, a tiny town located about two hours away, on the dry rolling plains that sweep down the eastern flanks of Mt. Hood.

Behind Dave were a half dozen more cars, filled with more family members and friends.

Dave drove past Athey Creek Middle School, and turned his head to the left to look at it. Several of the teachers had come to yesterday's memorial and he thought of them as he drove by. But his attention suddenly turned to the radio. He turned up the volume.

Garth Brooks' song, "The Dance" started to play.

With the song still so fresh in their minds from the day before, Dave spoke up to the riders in his backseat. "Hey, do you hear that?"

He picked up his cell phone and called back to Dan Jacobson, who was driving the car with all of the kids. "Are you listening to KWJJ?" he asked.

Dave leaned back into his seat and let the words of the song sink in. Appropriate, he thought, that the song should set the tone for them all as they set out for Dufur.

The words to "The Dance" just about perfectly summed up the way Dave felt about his time with Teresa being cut too short.

Dave let the words fill the Suburban. They were no longer attached to the memorial video, and this was the first time Dave had heard this 10-year-old song on the radio in some time. But he was suddenly aware that whenever it came on, it would instantly remind him of all things Teresa.

The convoy headed north to meet I-84, and then east through the Columbia Gorge to The Dalles.

By the time Dave pulled the Suburban into the small parking lot outside the cemetery fence, he could see that Ron and Jean had prepared Teresa's marker. Teresa's remains had been placed in a small hole. Next to it were several tall flower arrangements. Dufur was the place where the O'Brien family had settled as pioneers. For that reason, it was decided that Teresa's remains should be put to rest there.

Dave and the three kids all covered the small box containing Teresa's ashes. He wore an old pair of cowboy boots, the same pair that he had bought when he and Teresa were dating at the outfitter store in Jackson, Wyoming so long ago. It was the same pair that he had gotten married in. As he knelt down beside the small hole in the ground, he felt the sole of his right boot tear away from its stitching, exposing his white sock.

Another fitting moment, Dave thought. The boots had spanned the relationship, and now they, like it, were done.

The drive home was somber. The memorial weekend was through and now Teresa was laid to rest.

Dave felt numbness that the rush of activity of the previous couple of weeks, with all of its lows mixed in with a scant few highs, was just about done. The next day would bring an entirely new chapter.

The end of the World Series had felt a little bit like this, a transition point between something that held all of their focus and energy and the unknowns of what came next. This time, it had come with extremes that felt a thousand times more important.

Dave steered the Suburban off of I-205 and drove past the school again. And as he did, another familiar song began on the radio: "I Hope You Dance."

It was almost too much for him. The timing was uncanny to the point of spooky.

Dave felt chills up his spine as the first notes began to register in his ears, and he instinctively reached for the volume knob to turn it up. Nobody in the vehicle said a word. He glanced into the rearview mirror and saw Keely Jacobson with tears rolling down her cheeks.

The lyrics of Lee Ann Womack's biggest hit of 2000 had become a mantra within the Grill family even while Teresa was still alive. The uplifting message about squeezing the most out of life reminded Dave of Teresa's outlook, and even some of her poems. Her take on life had been clearly expressed many times during the course of her marriage, her teaching, and her friendships:

"You can choose to be a victim, or you can choose to dig in and fight your way out of the problem and arrive at something better," she would say. "If you choose to fight, I'll be right there by your side."

As he pulled into the driveway, the song faded out.

"It's been a long day," Dave said, turning off the ignition and looking back into the red-eyed passengers in the back seat. They looked too numb to move. "I think it's time to go inside."

As he walked into the house, there was a dizzying sensation still buzzing around him. Had he really just been through that? The words of the song resonated in such a way that it almost felt like Teresa had spoken them.

It was certainly an eerily odd coincidence. And one that gave him cause to wonder. Was Teresa letting him know she had arrived safely in heaven?

∞

Kellie watched the Columbia River out of the small window as the jet pushed her higher into the sky. Small raindrops swept across the glass pane, and soon all she could see were white, cottony clouds.

She leaned back into her seat and closed her eyes. She was exhausted from four emotional days separated by fitful nights of sleep. The competing forces of elation and hope fought battles with the remorse and sorrow that she also felt.

Brett was tired too, not to mention hung over. His headache left him in a quiet mood. He put his head back against the small airplane pillow, shut his eyes and tried to sleep.

Kellie couldn't stop thinking about Dave Grill, or for that matter, Nikki, Lauren or Johnny. She wished she could have stayed with them. In a span of four short days they had come to mean the world to her.

She reran the entire trip—especially the interactions with Dave, his mother and the kids—over and over, searching for ways she might be able to offer solutions to their problems. Her mind went back to her last moments with Dave. "I want to be one you call," she had said. She wondered if he really would. Or, could it be another 20 years until she saw him again? And even if he did call, what then? How could anything worthwhile come of it with 2,500 miles between them?

Kellie's mind began racing again. She was beset by questions she couldn't answer and feelings she could hardly comprehend.

She looked over to Brett. He was sound asleep, snoring gently into the pillow.

She pulled two sheets of notebook paper out of her carry-on bag and set them on a magazine in her lap. She found a black pen and began to scribble on the first sheet.

12-4-00

Dave,

As I fly away from you, I already long for you—you and all that you ARE! And all that you have always been to me. How can one man be so much? You are a pillar of strength and a wishing well full of knowledge and love. A giver, a provider, a person truly unique and rare. You are a precious gem, rugged yet polished. Your life is so full of purpose and meaning, plans and ideas. I am so proud of you and how you remain solid and steady even in this time of devastating tragedies and harsh events.

Your composure, courage and bravery during the obstacles of Teresa's death have amazed me. The gift of control and power you possess truly keeps me in awe.

As I analyze your situation I must admit that I have begun fantasizing about you and your recent "availability." I must confess that I'm held in a silky tangled web, held spellbound and captured by you and your precious loving children. I'm confused and scared of my feelings, yet I feel I must act on them at this time. (Even if this time is so unstable and emotionally draining.)

What the future holds is anyone's guess. There are no guarantees ever—I know that, you know that. But that doesn't scare me as I write this letter.

I know God holds today and controls our future. I am truly amazed at the many coincidences and happenings that seem to be taking shape and forming around you and me. God knows the wishes and desires of my heart, although it may be "bad timing" for me to write these things to you. (Because in NO WAY ever would I want to show any disrespect to Teresa and her untimely death.) Maybe Teresa's death is too recent, and I pray that I'm not hurting you by saying all of this, but then again maybe I must say all of this now just so you'll know. Life does go on!

You are only 40 years old and although it is so hard to think of now at this difficult time, you will probably seek the comfort and love of another woman in your life. As your mom says, you are a realist, and I know you know what I'm trying to express and say to you. And, who knows? Maybe Teresa wants us to try this. Maybe SHE is once again working on doing "What's best for you and the kids." Maybe she's TAKING ACTION in bringing us together.

And as for the timing of me telling you this now—as you've said through all of "this," there are no rules or guidelines. So I have to follow my heart.

Dave, this will probably sound crazy to say now (especially at this awkward time), but the truth is I Love You. And deep down, I have always loved you ever since I was 12 years old. You still have a hold on me. Your friends and I LOVE TERESA! (And the beautiful, wonderful woman she was and always will be.)

I pray that God, Destiny and Fate will shape us and move us, that it will control our paths and if all goes as I am hoping maybe I will one day touch your heart the way that you have touched mine. As long as you have been a presence in my life I've never had a chance, an opening, with you, until now. You were married and I respected, admired and honored your choices and commitments.

You're "something else!"

Well, Mr. Grill. It's your move. I'm throwing the ball. It's up to you to catch it. If you feel it, please take this chance. There's no pressure or obligation. I'm just opening a door that I hope you will walk through, as I can't believe this rare opportunity has arrived.

Love, Kellie.

Kellie read her letter once through, and it made her feel better knowing that she had conveyed all her feelings.

Kellie folded the sheets of paper, put them back in her bag and looked out the window again. The plane was descending into Salt Lake.

She said her goodbyes to her sleepy-eyed brother and kissed his cheek. She walked down a long corridor to the gate for the next part of her trip, back her twin sister Kaysie in Nashville.

As she sat down and waited to board, a new wave of questions came to mind. What would Kaysie think of all this? Would she be supportive? Would she understand?

Aboard the plane her fatigue finally overtook her anxiety, and she slept almost all the way back to Tennessee.

∞

All of the guests and family members and friends were finally gone from Dave Grill's house in Tualatin. It was the first night alone for Dave and his three kids. He felt drained, beyond tired. Not so much physically, but mentally and emotionally he felt utterly drained.

Teresa was no longer with them. All of her mortal remains were inside a small box in a hole in the ground 100 miles away.

The grandparents were gone, back to their homes. The visiting kids were all gone, getting ready for school to resume. And their friends were back to their own homes and their own lives.

Occasionally, there was a phone call from someone. "How are you doing?" they would say. "I was just calling to make sure everything was OK."

He politely told everybody the same thing: "Yes, we're doing fine. We're going to be OK."

Dave had been wondering if he'd been too stern in a sit-down he'd had with the three kids.

"We are not going to use this as a crutch," he'd warned them. "We are going to go on and do the things that we need to do."

He held out his hand and counted those need-to-do things off on his fingers. They were a father's words, nonnegotiable.

"We are going to do our homework."

"We are going to keep the house clean."

"We are going to go to bed by 9 P.M."

"We are not going to mope around here and have a pity party."

All three kids looked at their dad and agreed. They knew they had to move on as well, painful as it may seem.

But they were also dazed, and so was their dad.

After a month of upheaval, Dave wanted his kids to get back into a regular routine, resume their activities at school, and interact with their friends.

He knew nothing else was going to move them all further away from the raw emotions they all still felt.

Teresa had made Dave promise to move on, and for the first time he began to consider what that meant. He was a single dad now. A widower. Things he never expected to call himself in his lifetime.

Dave determined that when the kids needed emotional support he would show compassion and support, but he did not want to coddle them. It was OK to grieve, he said, but he wasn't going to allow them to use their grief as an excuse to fail or curl up and do nothing. He knew that Teresa would have agreed with him.

He gave the kids, and himself, a few days rest. They were in survival mode.

On Wednesday, Dave went into the office for a half-day and returned a few of the messages that had piled up on his desk. It felt good to get out of the house and turn his attention to something other than sorrow that filled his home.

The evenings after the kids had gone to bed became quiet, then lonely. It was during those times in the late evening that Dave felt alone for the first time he could remember. Teresa wasn't coming back. He said the words out loud a couple of times, just to let them sink in.

He tried to put his mind to something useful, like laundry and sorting through bills. Mostly, he just shoved all of the bills aside. It was difficult to concentrate on them, because his mind kept wandering away and stopping on one simple question that he couldn't seem to get his mind around: What next?

The kids went to bed Wednesday night knowing that they had school to return to in the morning.

Downstairs it was still and quiet. Even Hannah was curled up and asleep in her usual spot next to the couch. He could hear the clock on the wall ticking, something he hadn't ever noticed.

Dave went into the laundry room to sort clothes into whites and darks, and then shoved the first load into the washer. As he closed the lid, he felt a sudden, overwhelming tension in his chest and throat. It was a sensation he had never felt before, but he knew it wasn't a heart attack.

Dave took a deep breath, closed his eyes and spoke out loud: "Teresa . . . how am I going to do this?"

As soon as the words were out, the pressure in his chest and throat began to subside.

Dave pulled the knob to start the water in the washer and his mind drifted back to the conversation that he had with Teresa at her bedside, when both of them were coming to acknowledge that the end was near. He remembered how she made him promise to go on, to be happy. He recalled her demand that he follow his heart and guide the kids without her. He realized that the pain of missing her was a feeling he was going to have to learn to live with.

His mind tried to process it all. She wasn't coming back.

Dave went upstairs and flopped down onto the bed while he waited for the load of laundry to complete its cycle.

Bored and lonely for one of the first times in his entire life, Dave spotted the videotape from Teresa's memorial service. He got up, slid it out of the box, and pushed it gently into the VCR. He turned on the television.

He sat back down on the bed and watched the first few seconds go by before his eyes welled with tears. He rolled over onto his side, curled his legs into a fetal position, and for the first time since Teresa's death, permitted his anguish to leak out. In the privacy of the bedroom he once shared with his wife, he sobbed into his pillow, crying like he never had before.

When he awoke, the room was silent. The VCR had shut itself off automatically. The TV was on but the screen was black. He was still dressed, lying on the top of the bed spread. The pillow was still damp from his tears. He could tell that it was still pre-dawn. There was no light coming in through the curtains.

He rolled to the side for a glimpse at the clock radio on the nightstand. It was 3:33 in the morning.

∞

Kellie grabbed her two suitcases off the baggage carousel and walked outside to the curb. Sure enough, around the far corner she came. Perfect timing, Kellie thought. Kaysie pulled the white GMC Jimmy 4x4 to the curb and hopped out to greet her sister.

"Hi," Kellie said, with a tired drawl, still scratchy from her cold.

"Hi yourself," Kaysie said. "You look and sound awful." Kaysie picked up Kellie's suitcases and shoved them into the rear hatch of the SUV.

"Thanks," Kellie said, sarcastically. "I feel awful, too. What a long flight. Ugh."

Kaysie steered them out of the airport and back onto the freeway before asking the first of her many questions.

"Well . . . ?" Kaysie said. Even though she had spoken on the phone with Kellie almost daily while she was gone, she was eager to have a face-to-face recounting. Kellie knew she wanted the nitty-gritty.

"What's the verdict? Is he really all you cracked him up to be?" Kaysie asked.

Kaysie and Kellie knew that their life together as twins could be altered forever by the answer to those questions.

"Oh my God, Kiz . . . he's more," Kellie said, trying to muster all the energy she could. "He and the kids are so incredible. They are going through so much right now and they're so strong and . . . they're just precious.

"I honestly don't know what to do because I'm so sad to leave them."

Kaysie was eager to know more.

"So what do you think is going to happen?" Kaysie asked.

Kellie knew her twin well enough to know that she was beginning to analyze the situation, and figure out its potential impact on them both.

"I don't know," Kellie said. "I asked Wilma to tell Dave what I told her whenever she felt the time was right."

The sisters continued to talk about when that might be as Kaysie took them east on Interstate 40, headed for their farm. Kellie was anxious to see all of her pets—dogs, cats and horses. She had been away from them for two weeks. The only thing she wanted to see more were her photos, so she made Kaysie stop at a Wal-Mart so she could get her pictures developed in an hour.

After dropping off the photos, they went to Taco Bell to grab a quick bite, and then sat down and kept talking. Kellie did most of the talking, taking her sister through each hour of her trip. She told Kaysie about all of the people she had met, the characters in the family that had suddenly mattered so much to her. Some liked her right away, and others had cast an evil eye her way throughout the trip.

Kellie had missed her sister tremendously. It was rare that they had spent as much as a week apart their entire lives. They had grown up, and into their 30s, together.

Then they had moved to Tennessee starting a house-cleaning business while never giving up on their dreams of making their way into the country music business as songwriters. They had done well in their life together, but neither of them had gotten married. For Kellie, it had been one failed attempt after another to find what she was looking for in a companion. She had started down the path several times only to find it blocked with lies and deceit and unfulfilled hopes. It had been an especially sore subject over the past six months, after yet another attempt at love had failed. There were numerous nights that she had cried herself to sleep, unsure about whether she was doomed to remain single.

She prayed to God nightly, asking for guidance and a purpose in life to which she could devote her heart and soul.

Kaysie, meanwhile, had a steady boyfriend. She and Mark seemed happy. Kellie suspected that her sister had found her man.

Kellie showed Kaysie the photos she had taken in Oregon, taking time to identify each person in every photograph.

Then she produced the letter she had written on the plane. She unfolded it and read it to her sister, becoming emotional at points but pressing on.

"Kellie!" Kaysie said. "You can't send that letter to him yet. It's way too soon. He'll think you're a psycho."

Kellie was having a similar feeling about it.

"I think you ought to give it some more time," Kaysie said. "Just play it cool and try to get to know him better."

Kellie knew it was sound advice. She just wasn't sure if she had the patience to go along with it.

Kaysie turned onto Tater Peeler Road, and then into the driveway of their house. Inside, Kellie set her bags down, went to see her animals and thumbed through the mail. Then she walked into her bedroom and prepared for bed.

First, though, she called Brett to thank him once again for dragging her to Oregon.

Saturday, December 9, 2000

In the evening, the phone rang.

"Hi Kellie this is Makenna," the girl said.

"Well hello! I thought it was Tiff?" Kellie said, trying to make a joke.

"Oh you're right! How are you doing, Randi?" Makenna said.

There was concern in Makenna's voice and Kellie picked up on it immediately.

"What's going on kiddo?"

"I was calling because of Lauren," Makenna said.

"What about her? Is everything OK?"

"Well, she's having trouble sleeping because she is so sad about her mom," Makenna said. She explained the ride up to the burial in Dufur and how they had stopped in Cascade Locks for lunch. Makenna had bought Kellie a silver horse belt buckle in the gift shop. She also explained that Lauren had been sullen for most of the trip, staring out the window and trying to keep her emotions in check.

"Would you mind calling her?" Makenna asked. "I think it might cheer her up a little bit if she could talk to you."

"Yes," Kellie said. "Oh, the poor thing. It's no wonder she can't sleep. I don't know how they can get through this. They're so brave!"

Makenna and Kellie exchanged good-byes and they hung up.

Kellie dialed the Grill household and talked with Lauren for about 15 minutes.

Sunday, December 10, 2000

Dave met his mother at the door and took the bags of groceries from her arms. Wilma had taken it upon herself to do some shopping and she intended to make Dave and the kids a home-cooked meal.

"How are you doing?" Wilma asked.

"Oh, hanging in there," Dave said.

Dave began putting things away into cupboards while Wilma assembled the things for dinner on the counter.

"Kellie Poulsen called the other night to talk to Lauren," Dave said.

"Oh. That's nice of her. Is Lauren still having a hard time sleeping?" Wilma asked.

"Yes, but I think talking with Kellie helped. All of the girls seemed to bond pretty well with Kellie when she was here," Dave said.

"I know. She was great with them," Wilma said. "But I want to caution you about something . . ."

Dave was puzzled.

"Be careful that you don't break that little girl's heart," Wilma said, aiming a wooden spoon at him.

Dave raised his eyebrows. He had no idea why she would say such a thing.

"Before the memorial, Kellie came over to see me and we had a long talk," Wilma said. "And the bottom line of it is: She has feelings for you. And she has had them for a very long time, since you both were kids. Well, she was 12, so that made you and Brett about 17. But she has had a crush on you ever since."

The revelation left Dave speechless, but as he processed the new information it did seem to make some sense. There had been little tell-tale signs in Kellie's behavior that he hadn't thought twice about. Why would he?

"She felt incredibly guilty that the feelings were there all over again, but she told me because she thought I was the only one she could tell. And it wasn't easy for her to do it," Wilma said.

"Who else knows about this?" Dave asked.

"Well I'm pretty sure Brett and Kaysie know," Wilma said. "But she asked me to keep it a secret and only to tell you when enough time had passed."

Dave was completely clueless about the infatuation. Kellie had definitely grown up from a skinny red-haired kid into a beautiful woman, he thought. He felt flattered that she had feelings for him, appropriate or not.

"Well I had no clue about that," Dave said. "Brett never said anything about it to me in all these years."

"I know," Wilma said. "But just be careful, will you? If you talk on the phone, please don't lead her on. This isn't something she takes lightly. She was very emotional when she was here."

"OK," Dave said, still a little stunned. "I'll be careful."

Dave determined not to use this piece of news to his advantage. For one thing, he didn't yet feel emotionally available. And for another, Kellie was more than two thousand miles away.

A couple of days later, Dave stumbled upon a small wooden jewelry box of Teresa's that was in the top drawer of her dresser. It was a small light-colored cedar box, eight inches long by five inches wide. The inside was trimmed in leather. He had made it for her early in their marriage.

Most of the things he found in Teresa's little keepsake box didn't surprise him. There were half a dozen photos of the kids in a plastic wallet protector, many of them from when they were babies. There was his grandpa Glenn's wedding band. A pin from the Little League Softball World Series. Some of the kids' baby teeth. The key to an antique clock. Assorted coins.

And a postcard.

He picked it up a turned it over. There had been dozens of get-well cards sent to Teresa over the past two years.

This one was dated 7-1-99.

"Hi! We recently heard of the hardship and trying time that you all have endured during Teresa's illness, and we wanted to let you know that our thoughts and prayers are with you all! May

God bless you and your sweet family! Love Kellie and Kaysie (Brett's twin sisters)."

Dave had never seen the card before, and couldn't remember Teresa ever mentioning it to him. He wondered how it ended up there.

Friday, December 15, 2000

The phone rang and Dave knew who it was before picking up the receiver. Kellie Poulsen had called twice already, spending most of her time on the phone with Lauren. The two had clearly forged a bond during the week of the memorial, and Dave was glad that Lauren had someone that she could confide in.

Dave had already rebuffed inquiries and advice from friends about seeking counseling for the kids. He didn't think it would help, though his arguments didn't seem to persuade those that did.

He knew his kids still bore fresh scars from the loss of their mother. Christmas was approaching, yet holiday spirit was the furthest thing from their minds. Counseling, Dave thought, was just going to be an excuse to focus on their grief rather than on moving forward. Plus, he saw strength and resolve in all three children. If he thought they needed counseling, he would gladly have arranged for it.

Kellie had been sweet and energetic and was a nonstop talker, kind of like Lauren. He was glad that Kellie and Lauren were talking.

In the past few days, Dave had been kicking around the idea he had for a song. He thought the cowboy boots that he had bought while dating Teresa had become a strong symbol for his relationship with her. They had spanned his marriage, and it had seemed oddly appropriate that the seam had ripped apart as he kneeled down at her graveside.

He thought the song was a good idea, and it gave him something to think about at night besides how lonely he was.

He decided to talk over his ideas with Kellie.

Dave dialed her number.

"Well hello there!" Kellie was bubbly as ever. "How are you doing?"

"Oh, we're fine. Lauren told me about the poem you wrote for her," Dave said. "I really appreciate you taking the time to do that. I think she's taking it the roughest of the three kids."

"Oh, it's my pleasure," Kellie said. "She is such a sweetheart. And I love talking to her. We're both a couple of chatterboxes, so I hope it's been good to just keep her mind occupied with something else for a while."

"I'm sure it has," Dave said. "By the way . . . there's something I've been meaning to ask you about."

Kellie's eyes widened. She could feel her heart begin to beat against her ribs. "Yes? What is it?"

"Well, do you remember when you were here for the memorial and you said if I ever wanted to write a song to get my feelings about Teresa out, to give you a call?"

"Yes?" Kellie said.

"I've got an idea for a song I thought I might run by you," Dave said

"Oh. OK," Kellie inquired, growing more intrigued.

"Yes, well . . . I know that you're a songwriter, and I was wondering if you'd be interested in helping me out with it," Dave said. "I have this idea and I don't know whether it's any good or not."

"Sure! I'd love to!" Kellie said, unable to contain her excitement. "What's it about?"

"See, I had these boots. This pair of cowboy boots," Dave explained. "I bought them when I was dating Teresa. We were on a trip through Montana and on the way back we stopped in Jackson Hole. And that's where I saw them, in a store window. Teresa saw me looking at them and said, "If you buy those boots, I'll let you marry me in them."

Kellie was captivated instantly. It was a romantic moment that carried so much more weight coming from Dave's mouth.

"So I did," Dave said. "I bought them and ended up wearing them on the day we were married. And I wore them a lot over the past 15 years. They were my favorite pair. The day we went up to Dufur for the graveside service, I wore them. And when I squatted down to cover Teresa's ashes, all the stitching came loose on the right boot."

Kellie was momentarily flustered and at a loss for words. But she grabbed a pen and began scribbling notes down on a pad.

"Well, what do you think?" Dave asked. "Basically, the story goes, I married her in them, and I buried her in them."

Kellie's response was emphatic. "Oh my God, Dave, it's incredible. I can't believe it's a true story. Wow!"

"Good," Dave said, reassured. In his heart he knew it was a good idea, too

The doorbell rang. Dave knew that it was Keely and Dan Jacobson bringing the family dinner.

"I've got to go," Dave said. "But think it over and see what you can come up with, and let me know."

"Well, I have a few ideas already," Kellie said, enthusiastically. "I think I might work on it right now."

"Good. I'll talk to you later."

The next morning when Dave arrived at Metro Metals, there was a fax waiting for him. It was from Kellie:

Hey, Dave! Here is the lyric sheet to your cowboy boot song idea. All of this is subject to change (including the title).

I went ahead and fine tuned what I had but it still needs work. Take care! Kellie.

The song was called "These Boots and Me." Dave picked up the second page of the fax and read the lyrics to his song. Kellie must have written the song as soon as she hung up.

These boots and me we've seen some things
I never would have guessed
They walked me down the aisle
and much too soon I wore them as I laid that girl to rest
Now here we stand these boots and me
our soles have broken through
Feelin' lost and wonderin' now
What's this lonely cowboy supposed to do?

Chorus:
Guess it ain't for us to know
what life has in store
If we knew what was gonna happen
what would livin' be for?
Nobody knows about tomorrow,
so live for today
There will be sunshine, there will be sorrow
and that's just what we all have to face

Now walkin' down life's dusty road
just these boots and me
Heaven took my love from me, she was an angel here
     on earth
so I guess it's meant to be

She was the girl who stole my heart
and it's so hard to let her go
Walkin' off into the sunset
Feelin' lost and so alone

Dave was impressed. He sat down and sang the words softly to himself. She had captured his sentiment perfectly.

He picked up the phone and dialed Kellie.

"Hello?" she said, picking up on the first ring.

"Hey there!" Dave said, cheerfully. "I got your fax. I ... love ... this song. I don't think I would change one word. It's perfect. I can't wait to hear the melody."

Kellie was thrilled by Dave's words of approval.

"Well, it's the funniest thing," she said. "After we got off the phone last night, I just started writing. And believe it or not, I wrote that in 15 minutes! I'm not kidding. I have never written a song so fast in my whole life."

"Well, I think you nailed it," Dave said.

"Well, thank you! I'll let you get back to work."

They hung up. Dave read over the lyrics one more time, and began to imagine how they would sound with music. Kellie put the phone down and couldn't stop smiling for the next half hour. She was elated that Dave liked the song and couldn't wait for the next opportunity to talk to him.

∞

Kellie had just walked in the door after coming home from a church service when she heard the phone ring. She hustled to the living room to pick it up.

"Hello?"

"Hi, Kellie, it's Dave."

"Well, hello Mister! Merry Christmas!" Kellie said, excitedly. Suddenly, the loneliness she had felt at church all alone had evaporated.

"Merry Christmas to you too," Dave said. "Have you got big plans tomorrow?"

"Not too big," Kellie said. "Kaysie and Mark are in Missouri with his family, and I'm going to do presents and dinner with a friend and her family."

"Well, I'm actually in my truck on my way into work," Dave said. "I've got a Christmas present for my mother hidden for her there. But what I was really calling about was to ask you about another present that I'd like to give to the kids."

Kellie was bemused, but slightly puzzled. "What is it?"

"What do you think of me giving the kids a trip to Nashville for Spring Break?" Dave asked. "It would be a surprise, because they have no idea."

Dave and Teresa had talked about giving the kids a trip to Hawaii for almost a year. But Dave thought Nashville might fit the bill as well, or better.

"Sure!" Kellie said. "We would have so much fun here. I would love for you all to come visit!"

"Good," Dave said. "I just wanted to make sure before I went ahead and told them."

"Absolutely!" Kellie said, still processing the good news.

"I'll get a hold of you later to get more details," Dave said. "But thanks again. I hope you have a Merry Christmas."

"You too," Kellie said. "Merry Christmas!"

Kellie couldn't contain her excitement. Her Christmas wish had come true. She was one more step closer to making her life's wish come true as well. She called Brett to give him the good news.

Tuesday, December 26, 2000

Tamara had been adamant about the letter she had sent in the mail that week. Wait until after Christmas to open it, she had written on the envelope. And read it privately before you share it with the kids.

She had been vague about the letter's content but stressed the importance of her instructions for him to wait. Dave was curious to know what it could be.

He peeled the manila envelope open and took the letter out.

Dear Dave,

I hope I can find the words to express all that I wish to convey.

First and foremost, thank you for allowing me to participate (move in!) in your life during Teresa's last month. It was a profound and humbling experience for me.

I have such love and respect for you. I am awed by the skill with which you dealt with your children. Each update was full of love, respect and honesty. They are amazing children. They have amazing parents. You were so kind and tender to Teresa in every circumstance, always respecting her wishes, even when you doubted or disagreed. You loved her well. It was beautiful. I have never before stood in the center of such great love. Thank you for allowing me to witness and share in this.

I know the extent of my loss. It is staggering. At times I experience it as an adult, and take serious stock of my life—asking the difficult questions that an encounter with death demands. At times I am still a small child, and beyond words, and furious with the universe that I have lost my lifelong playmate and confidante—my best friend. I want my soul sister back. My heart breaks at the loss, and the fear that I let too many moments slip away without telling her how much she meant to me.

And so, feeling my own pain, I cannot begin to fathom yours. Know that I am thinking about you and praying for you. She was a source of great warmth and light. You must feel numb without her.

Her last words to me weigh heavily on me:

"Love my children."

"Take care of Dave. I know how much he loves me and this is tearing him apart."

Dave, I can't imagine how I can effectively do this from so far away. I wish I lived next door. Please let me be there for you and the kids in any way that feels right to you. You would be giving me a great gift in helping me fulfill my promise to Teresa. I do not want to butt into your life, and might err on the side of not being present enough. Don't be shy about helping me find the balance there.

I want to encourage your songwriting. Art is the voice of the heart and the one universal language. Teresa was gifted at expressing herself in words, as you are. If there is an opportunity to help you invest in this—please let me know. And finally, I am not a bad listener, so if you wish to talk, I'm here for you at any hour. Scott asked me to reiterate that if you wish to set up a living trust (with wills and guardianships within it) his office can do it long distance for you.

In her death, Teresa reconnected me to myself, my parents, my cousins and to you and your family. What a great gift. Her life was about love. And so was her death. Family was everything to her. Almost to her own detriment. And so as I sat with her on Thanksgiving Day, I was troubled that she did not have the opportunity to say goodbye to the kids. I knew this is not how she would've wanted it.

I know Teresa thought I was off the deep end with spirituality, fish oil, etc. The events of the past month (pink light, Grandma Clara on her bed) have convinced me that perception is reality, and mine is not far off the wall after all. I have hesitated in sending you this, for fear you will think me weird beyond words. Hopefully, if you think me a wacko, you will recognize I am a wacko with a good heart and right intentions.

On Thanksgiving Day, I held her hand and said,

"Teresa, I know you can hear me. I KNOW you can communicate with me by thought even though you can't speak. I am going to make my mind go totally blank, and write down everything you communicate to me. Say goodbye to your children."

Dave, with my left hand I held hers, and with my right hand I wrote as fast as I could. I could hardly keep up with her. I wrote it down verbatim, and it is attached. I honestly don't know if I was listening to Teresa or my own mind, but I was hearing her voice clearly and could barely keep up. I am passing it along. Save it, burn it, or share it if and when you feel it is appropriate.

I love you, and am truly here for you.

Wishing you a new year filled with love, joy, health and new beginnings,

Love, Tamara.

Dave felt goose bumps as he turned the page and read what came next. It was the letter, typed, that Tamara had dictated from

Teresa. He carefully read the words and was amazed. The language sounded precisely like Teresa, not merely the things he thought Tamara might have imagined.

He read the letter again, then a third time. He began to believe that they were, indeed, Teresa's words and her last communication to the kids.

He inserted the letter back into the envelope and put it in his bedroom. Yes, he concluded, there will be a time and place to reveal this to the kids. Just not right now.

He called Tamara to thank her.

Wednesday, January 10, 2001

The driving rain beat against the windows of the house and Kellie didn't even bother to look outside. She had learned over the years that rains like these were common in Tennessee. The whole day seemed dark gray and miserable.

Kellie's mood matched the weather. It had been nearly a week since arriving home from Salt Lake City, where she had spent New Year's with Brett and bought her new Dodge Durango.

Kellie cuddled up on her sofa to a cup of hot tea and began letting her mind wander to the place she really wanted to be: Oregon. She daydreamed that she was with the Grills, helping Dave and his kids through the winter. She considered her life and her ongoing commitments to work and to Kaysie, and for the first time, she felt out of place in her own home.

Kaysie tried talking to Kellie about all that was going through her mind, and tried to convince her that in time everything would work itself out for the best.

Kellie couldn't wait. She didn't know whether Wilma had told Dave anything yet about her feelings for him. She didn't know if

Dave was interested in any way besides platonically. And most of all, she didn't know how or when to make her next move.

The phone rang about 7:30 P.M. and Kellie looked at the caller ID. It was a 503 area code number. *Dave Grill!* She felt her heart suddenly beat to life and jolt her out of her stupor.

"Hello?" Kellie said, anxiously.

"Hey, it's Dave Grill," came the reply. He was stuck in traffic near the junction of Interstate 5 and the I-405 loop that swung around downtown Portland. Kellie couldn't help but feel the silliness of the greeting. Dave certainly didn't have to add his last name for her to know who it was.

"Hi!" Kellie said, trying to curb her enthusiasm. "How are ya? Whatcha doin?"

"I'm good," Dave said. It was 5:30 in Portland and he was on the interstate, moving at a snail's pace in the rush hour traffic. "I'm just sitting here in my truck. Traffic isn't moving very fast. I got caught right in the middle of it."

"So you decided you just needed someone to keep you company, eh?" Kellie said. "Well I'm honored!"

"That is exactly it," Dave said. "I figured if there was someone who wasn't shy about talking it would be you."

Kellie laughed at his joke. "Well I've never been accused of being the quiet one," she said. "People say if you're born with the gift of gab, find the receipt and take it back. But I can't find the receipt!"

Dave chuckled.

"I understand you got a new car," he said.

Kellie's mind went blank for a second. New car? Do I have a new car?

"Umm ... oh yes! The Durango!" Kellie said, remembering just in the nick of time. "Yes! I love it. Brett helped me with that. I got a great deal."

The conversation moved slowly, from the new car to small talk about the kids, and to the long-range plans for the Spring Break visit.

"The kids were thrilled when they got the package telling them about the trip to Nashville," Dave said. "I had written out the plan and then wrapped it like a present and put it under the tree."

"Oh that's cute," Kellie said. "And they are really excited about coming? Wow! I've been thinking of things to do and show everybody too. That's the week of the Horse Fair that Kaysie and I work at. It's so much fun."

Dave double-checked the dates to make sure they jived with Kellie's schedule. He told her he would book the airline tickets in the next few days.

It was the first time Dave and Kellie had talked since Christmas Eve, and only the fifth or sixth time since Teresa's memorial service.

All the while, Kellie could feel the desire to spill her guts begin to rise up and she wasn't sure if she could suppress it any longer. There had never been a better time than now. And after all, *Dave had called her.*

"Dave, I have something I really want to tell you," Kellie said.

"Sure, what is it," Dave replied, thinking back on what his mother had told him.

"I'm not sure if I know where to start, but I'm just going to come right out and say it," Kellie said, trying to remember all of the contents of that letter she had carefully composed on the plane but never sent.

Her hand was shaking so hard she held the receiver with both hands.

"I have had a crush on you since I was 12 years old. And I know you didn't know it then, and I know you don't know it now, but all of those feelings came flooding back to me when I came out there with Brett for Teresa's memorial."

Dave could tell Kellie was just getting started and didn't interrupt. Hearing it from his mother had been one thing. Hearing it straight from the source surprised him all over again. He could tell by the way Kellie expressed herself that she was sincere about her feelings.

"And I know it's still way too soon to even be saying things like this," Kellie continued. "But I just can't keep my feelings bottled up inside any longer. I have to tell you how much I've missed you and the kids since I've come back to Tennessee. And I know that sounds weird, but it's true."

Dave had no doubt that Kellie's words came straight from her heart. He was flattered by them and impressed by her gumption to tell him.

"I just want you to know that if a month, or a year, or five years from now, whenever you start to consider dating again, I want you to consider me," Kellie said.

There, Kellie thought. I've said it.

Dave processed all of this all over again as he idly watched out at the row of traffic ahead of him, alternately pressing the brake pedal and then tapping the gas.

"OK," Dave said. "I'll keep that in mind. This is all a little bit surprising to me. And I really haven't begun to even think about another relationship yet."

"Oh, and I know you wouldn't yet," Kellie said. "Teresa was wonderful and you two had a great marriage. I would never be disrespectful of that. But I just wanted to let you know that I've had these feelings for a long time."

Dave didn't let on that his mother had clued him in. And for a second, his mind flashed to the postcard in Teresa's little wooden box. Privately, he wondered, "OK, what else can blow my mind right now?"

He wasn't sure if he could live up to Kellie's 22 years of fascination.

"I think maybe you've put me on a pedestal," Dave said. "That's probably not who I really am. Maybe you've built me up to be something that I'm not."

"I don't think so," Kellie said. "You looked pretty wonderful to me when I came out there, and that's when you were grieving. Even at your lowest you are pretty amazing."

Dave thanked Kellie for her compliments, then said he needed some time to process it all.

"I'll call you back," Dave said. "OK?"

"OK," Kellie said. Her eyes were damp from the emotion that she put into her confession. But she felt a weight had lifted off her shoulders as well. "Talk to you soon."

Dave put his phone down and grabbed the steering wheel with both hands. He didn't really know how to feel but he began working the situation over in his head: The beautiful redheaded sister of his best friend had just confessed to having strong feelings for him. He was a 40-year-old widower. He was facing the prospect of raising three kids, two of them teenage girls.

Perhaps an opportunity is presenting itself. He has always been one to carefully consider opportunities.

Meanwhile, at the opposite end of the line in Tennessee, Kellie hung up the phone and began to panic. Had she made a mistake by gushing out her feelings to him so soon? Had she just flubbed it up?

She dialed Brett immediately.

"I told him," she blurted, as soon as her brother answered.

"You told who? What?" Brett asked.

"I just got off the phone with Dave and I told him all of my feelings for him and how I hoped to date him sometime and all of it!" Kellie said. "He called me just a few minutes ago, and —"

"What!?" Brett yelled back at her. "You told him!? Oh my God, Kell, you might have just blown it."

It wasn't the sympathetic reassurance that Kellie had hoped for. She needed her ally now more than ever.

"What were you thinking?" Brett said, beginning to scold her. "I mean, oh my God! It's too soon. Maybe not, but . . . I think it still may be too soon."

"Brett!" Kellie said, irritation mounting on top of her anxiety. "Don't say that! I couldn't hold out any longer. I'm going crazy here alone without them and I just had to say what I've been feeling!"

Brett began to calm down a little, but he didn't think Kellie's confession had been tactfully timed.

"I just hope he doesn't get scared off," Brett said. "I mean, Jeez, what's it been? Six weeks?"

Just then, Kellie's phone rang again.

"Brett!" Kellie said, cutting him off. "It's Dave again. Oh God. I've gotta go. I'll call ya back later and tell you what he says."

"OK, Kell. But be cautious!" Brett said.

Kellie clicked her phone over to answer Dave's call. In the last 10 minutes, Dave had come to the conclusion that he had nothing to be ashamed of and no reason not to consider exploring a new relationship. He had loved Teresa with all of his might. But she was gone. No amount of waiting was going to change either of those two facts. Dave had upheld his commitment of "'Til death do us part."

His conscience was clear.

"Hi," Kellie said, trying to act calm.

"OK. Here's what I can do," Dave said. "I am on my way to pick up Nikki and take her to a voice lesson. But I'll be in the parking lot for a half hour and we can talk more about this then. OK?"

"OK."

Another 20 minutes later, Dave was free to call and talk. He treated what he had to say as if it were a business proposition.

"I've thought about what you said. I think there is definitely some sort of attraction developing even though you're 2,500 miles away. I think we ought to get together and see, one on one, if there's attraction there. You might come out here and spend 10 minutes with me and decide 'What was I thinking all those years?' Or we can see if there is something there and we can deal with things as they come up."

Kellie listened intently, nodding with the phone pressed to her ear.

"Would you be willing to get together and see what happens?" Dave asked.

"Of course I would!" Kellie said. She had gone from the brink of despair to giddy excitement in a matter of minutes. "I'll go anywhere and do anything to meet with you. I'll follow you to the end of the Earth if I have to."

The words slipped out before Kellie even had time to edit the desperation out of them.

In the short time between phone calls, Dave let the new ideas marinate in his mind. He began to wonder: How could they do it? He couldn't leave to go that far away from the kids, even with his parents there. He felt like it needed to be a somewhat private meeting. Perhaps she would be willing to fly out and they could drive to the Oregon coast together. At least there, he might be able to avoid running into anyone he knew.

"Well, I've got an idea," he said. "Let me run it by you."

"OK, what have you come up with?"

"Would you be willing to fly out here, and I could pick you up from the airport and we could drive to the coast for the weekend? I think that we should spend some time together and see what happens. My mom could watch the kids."

"I absolutely would do that! I couldn't come out right away. I'd need a couple of weeks."

"Oh, I would too," Dave agreed.

"I've got a calendar here. How about the weekend of the 25th? That's the weekend of the Super Bowl, would that be alright?" Kellie asked.

"Super Bowl would not be a problem. I think that weekend would work out for me too. Give me a few days to work out some details and I'll make all the arrangements. In fact, I might even check airfares when I get home tonight."

"Great. Well, it sounds like we have a plan then," Kellie said.

"I think we do."

Dave went home that night and continued to consider his options. Where would they stay? How would he explain himself to his mom, whom he'd ask to watch the kids for the weekend? How could he keep the plan secret, and avoid running into anyone he knew?

Over the next several days, Dave began to put the plan in motion.

At first, he told his mother he needed to leave for that particular weekend for a business trip. And he didn't consider it much of a lie. For him, the trip was for business purposes. The business, in this case, didn't involve Metro Metals.

He also called Tamara, Teresa's sister. He wanted to explain himself, and how he had nothing to hide. Life is going to go on, he would tell her, whether now or later.

He picked Tamara, specifically, because she would be upfront and honest about her reaction to what he had to say. He was sensitive to feelings of disappointment or disapproval that she might harbor. Her response could serve as a barometer for the feelings held by the extended family, particularly Teresa's side.

But before Dave could explain the reason for calling, Tamara was eager to tell him something first.

"Well, Dave, I know I'm going to sound kooky, here," Tamara said. "But Teresa came to me while I was running the dogs in the park yesterday."

Dave paused a moment, processing this unexpected admission.

"What do you mean, she came to you?"

Ever since the Christmas letter, Dave's outlook on Tamara's alleged ability to communicate with Teresa was that it was something he couldn't take lightly.

"Well, I had finished running them and I sat down on a big rock next to the trail," Tamara said. "I was quiet and tired, and it was so beautiful and tranquil and I felt at peace for the first time since losing T.

"Anyway, while I was lost in thought and being quiet I felt Teresa's presence near. I spoke softly to her, and said we were all OK, but that we missed her terribly. Then . . . I heard her say that she was fine.

"I told her that I was worried about you and the kids and that I didn't know if you could handle everything alone, with such a busy lifestyle and three kids to look after. 'I'm worried he can't do it without someone. He may need to start dating,' I told her."

"Mmm hmm," Dave said.

"She said not to worry," Tamara said. Then she paused a moment, adding weight to what she said next.

"Then, Dave, she gave me that look. You know that smug, cute look that she always did when she was mischievous or being a know-it-all?"

"Yes, I know that look," Dave said.

"Well, she looked right at me with that face and said, 'Don't worry, Tamara. I have it all under control.'

"And so I said, 'What? What's all under control?'

"Teresa just gave me that smile again, that smug little grin of hers. And again, she said 'I have it covered.' Then she left.

"Can you believe that, Dave?"

Dave could barely believe the words, and he tried to imagine his wife reappearing to her sister. Before he could find a way to answer, Tamara continued.

"I think she's saying to keep alert. Maybe there's a new woman in your future. Teresa has it covered."

Dave swallowed hard and bit his lip slightly. Now it was his turn.

He spoke softly as he asked: "Do you remember Kellie Poulsen? Brett's little sister from the memorial?"

"Yes," Tamara said.

"Well, she and I are going to the Oregon coast together on the 25th," Dave said. "We set it up a few days ago. I guess she's always had this crush thing for me since she was a little girl, and now we're going to see what happens."

Dave kept going.

"Weird, huh? The kids don't know. No one knows except you now—and of course Teresa."

"Oh my God, Dave, that's it!" Tamara said. "That's what she was trying to tell me. Wow! Kellie is a beautiful woman, Dave. And she adores you and your kids, you know."

"Yes, I do know," Dave said.

"She's a little bit too talkative for me, but Makenna thinks she's God," Tamara said. "You'll have fun and I wish you all the best with her, Dave."

"Thanks, Tam," Dave said. "I'll tell you how it goes."

"Details, Mr. Grill," Tamara said, jokingly. "I'll want details!"

Dave chuckled.

"Bye Tam."

"Bye Dave. Love you."

Monday, January 15, 2001

Dave skied over to Keely and Dan and pulled his goggles off his face.

"What do you think about taking a go at Snapshot Alley?" Dave asked.

Keely preferred to stick to the groomed, intermediate slopes on Mt. Bachelor, leaving the runs labeled "Black Diamond" to the more courageous in the group.

"Come on," Dave said, pulling the blue bandanna out of his ski jacket. "This was Teresa's favorite. Let's go tie this on something over there."

Keely reflected on the importance of this. Teresa, after all, was the person who convinced her to even try putting skis on her feet. She had never approached her friend's artful grace on the slopes, but their families had turned Mt. Bachelor ski trips into an annual event.

Keely's husband, Dan, the five kids, and Dave, had been nudging her all weekend. Snapshot Alley was the only way to get to the part of the mountain that had been Teresa's favorite.

Keely swallowed hard, looked Dave in the eye, and mustered the determination that she knew Teresa would have demanded of her.

"Just follow me," Dan said.

Keely pulled on her gloves, grabbed her poles, and without saying a word, followed the men and the kids on the short trail that led to the lip of the precipice.

The kids gleefully launched themselves down the face of the steep grade covered in deep, dry Central Oregon snow. Dan and Keely started down next, and Dave paused a moment and watched them go.

He looked out across the steep run and smiled proudly as he watched Keely make the first two turns, carving a tentative, controlled line through the ungroomed snow. He knew Teresa would be smiling at the sight as well.

Dave also could hear that Keely was on the verge of terror. "Teresa! I'm doing it!" she screamed.

Dave moved out to the edge and hopped over the side, and let gravity do its work. As he accelerated into the run, it took all of three turns to descend almost half of the 900-foot drop. It was a quick rush, and the name—Snapshot Alley—came from the feeling that it was all through in the blink of a camera's shutter.

At the bottom of the run, Dave approached the others. Keely was grinning from ear to ear.

"Great job, Keels," Dave said.

"I'll never do that again!" Keely retorted.

They skied together on a gentler hill toward the kids and a sign that pointed in two directions, indicating options for the continuation of the run.

"How about that tree over there?" Dave asked.

"OK!" yelled Nikki.

They moved closer to a tree that stood up taller than the rest and sidestepped up a short slope to its base.

"Have you got the scarf, dad?" Johnny asked.

Dave pulled the blue bandana trimmed in white from the front pocket of his parka. It was the bandana that Teresa had used the previous year to cover her bald head underneath her ski hat.

"Here it is," Dave said.

He stepped out of his skis and reached up to pull a branch down lower, shaking the loose snow off of it. He handed the scarf to Nikki, who tied it around the branch. Then Lauren stepped up to it, and tied a second knot.

"OK, Johnny, now you tie one," Lauren said.

Johnny came forward, slid his hands out of his gloves, and added a third knot.

"Your mother may not be here on the mountain, but she's here with us in spirit," Dave said, adding spare, poignant words to the impromptu memorial.

Without another word, Dave snapped back into his skis, and then everyone else followed him toward the second half of Snapshot Alley.

At the base of the hill, they all decided to go into the main lodge and warm up. In the afternoon they sat on couches and reminisced on their day of skiing, and how it didn't feel the same without Teresa. The mountain had always held a special power over Teresa. Skiing had been her therapy.

Dinner was stewing in the crock pot back at their rented condo 20 miles away. They carried their ski gear out into the parking lot and started walking toward the Suburban.

Dave walked no more than five steps before glancing up to see the sun slip behind a veil of white, fluffy clouds. The light in the sky had changed from its afternoon shade of baby blue into neon pink. He stopped suddenly and pivoted back over his shoulder to look at the mountain. Bachelor seemed to be blushing.

Dave watched other people in the parking lot, all of them experiencing the same sense of wonder. Everyone, it seemed, had suddenly become dumbfounded by awe at the light display overhead. People began scrambling for their cameras, hoping to record the moment.

He noticed a man scramble for his video camera, put it up to his eye, and slowly turn 360 degrees to capture the panorama.

"I've never seen anything like this before," the man said, narrating for his tape.

Dave tilted his head back. It was the most beautiful shade of pink —with streaks of red, salmon-orange and even purple—he had ever seen. The colors seemed bled together like a water color painting. The pink glowed across the entire horizon and filled every part of the sky. His three kids and the Jacobsons were craning their necks to watch it too.

"Can you believe that?" Dave said, to no one in particular.

"It's mom saying 'Hi,'" Lauren said, still staring up, smiling.

"Your mother is definitely here," Keely said.

CHAPTER SIX

The Oregon Coast

Thursday, January 18, 2001

With their semi-secret rendezvous drawing ever nearer, Dave and Kellie were talking on the phone at least once a day, and usually more.

Dave's kids took the ringing phone in stride. They knew it was Kellie. And they knew that their father enjoyed talking to her. Talking, after all, was the one thing that could keep him from getting bored. And as a group, they were unthreatened by it. Kellie had made friends quickly with the girls. Only Johnny had been left out of the loop.

The phone calls rarely carried the weight of heavy romantic anticipation. Dave would call Kellie because of a new favorite song he heard on his favorite country station. Or Kellie would call Dave just because she had heard a joke he might like.

After their initial attempt at songwriting, "These Boots and Me," they also had new ideas about music and songs to discuss. And with each call, particularly since Kellie's confession, the fledgling relationship began to build.

Kellie usually called Dave's cell phone, but occasionally called the house. She loved talking to the girls, who were generally the first ones to pick up the ringing phone.

"You know, I have never really spoken more than a few words to Johnny," Kellie told Dave. "It makes me kind of sad that I don't know him very well."

Dave shrugged his shoulders and turned his head to scan the room before replying into the phone.

"Well . . ." he began. "Why don't you talk to him now? I'll go get him."

"Wait, Dave!" Kellie said. "What should I say?"

Kellie began to search for ideas to strike up a conversation with a 10-year-old boy that had recently lost his mom. She was caught, momentarily, at a rare loss for words.

"Tell him the deer story," Dave said, reassuring. "He'll love that one."

Kellie could hear Dave set the phone down and call to his son.

"John," Kellie could hear lightly in the background. "Kellie wants to talk to you."

She could imagine that those words had done little more than confuse the boy and she sensed his shy, tentative response when he picked up the phone.

"Hello?" Johnny said.

"Hi Johnny!" Kellie said, raising the enthusiasm in her voice. "How are you?"

"Fine," Johnny answered.

"How's school been goin'?" Kellie asked, scrambling to find some way to get past the one-word answers.

"Fine," Johnny answered.

Kellie knew this could be a tough nut to crack, and not because he was bitter or withdrawn, but just because of his youth and shyness.

"Well I'm excited that you guys are coming out to Nashville for Spring Break," Kellie said. "That'll be fun, huh?"

"Yup," Johnny said. He really felt no incentive to ask questions or offer more. To him, this was talking on the phone with an adult.

"Did your dad tell you that Nikki is going to sing the national anthem at the horse fair and rodeo that weekend here in Tennessee?" Kellie asked.

"Yup," Johnny said, again.

"You'll have to ride our horse named Boo when you're here. She's a real fun horse, but kinda fat. So she's great for a beginner. Does that sound like fun?"

Kellie braced for the same reply, and got it.

"Yup," Johnny said, beginning to sound a little bored.

"Hey! I have a cool deer story. Do you want to hear it?" Kellie said. This was her final chance to draw him out.

"Sure," Johnny said.

"Well, OK," Kellie said. "It's a neat one."

Kellie paused a moment to remember how it started before diving in, hoping that she would keep Johnny's attention.

"Well, let's see. Kaysie and I were coming home one early morning from house-sitting a house and cat in downtown Nashville a few summers ago.

"We left early. It was about 6:30 A.M. and we were headed out to our house, which is east of Nashville about 30 miles. We needed to stop and feed some other animals for friends that were at Disney World.

"As we took the road to their house, it was feeling like a real peaceful morning with the sun rising and the grass was all wet with dew.

"Just then, I said to my sister Kaysie, who was driving, 'This is the ideal situation for deer to be out grazing, so be careful.'"

Kellie broke away from the story for a moment to see if Johnny was still awake.

"Do you know what I mean, Johnny?" Kellie said, referring to the quiet morning.

"Yep," Johnny replied.

Kellie, convinced that Johnny was starting to get hooked, continued.

"Right after I said it, Kaysie slowed down from about 45 miles per hour to about 35 as we came around a bend, and sure enough, a doe jumped right out in front of us. She swerved, and I grabbed the dashboard, and said, 'Oh my God, where there's one, there's two!'

"Just as I said it, a huge, and I mean HUGE buck jumped out of some bushes right in front of us. Kaysie swerved again and hit the brakes. That buck was following the doe and it was a miracle that we didn't hit it."

"Wow," Johnny said. "You didn't hit it then?"

"No," Kellie answered. "It must have felt the momentum of the car and ducked back into wherever it had come from. We were frantic from almost hitting both deer and I told Kaysie to stop because I wanted to get out of the car.

"The big buck was thrashing around on the opposite side of the road and it looked like it had gotten caught in the fence. Kaysie drove down the road a bit and pulled into a driveway to park.

"I walked up to the big buck. He was laying on his side and breathing heavy but was no longer caught in the fence.

"Did he jump up and run when you got there, next to him?" Johnny asked, now completely engaged in the story.

"No!" Kellie replied. "That's the weird part. He didn't move except to breathe. His tongue was hanging out of his mouth and he was laid out as flat as a pancake. It was so odd. I slowly walked over to him and said, 'Easy boy, easy.' And I reached down to pet him.

"He was so beautiful and big. He almost seemed like an elk he was so big for a whitetail. Anyway, he didn't move and his eyes were sort of glazed. I started crying and I yelled for Kaysie to get a blanket and hurry. I guess I thought we'd take this deer to the vet! Duh! I wasn't thinking clearly."

Johnny laughed. "What happened next?"

"Well as Kaysie started walking over I could see the big guy was really struggling to breathe. As I cried, I sat down and took his big neck and head into my arms and held him on my lap. I stroked him and cried and he died right there in my arms!

"I screamed as Kaysie approached, 'He's dead! Oh my God, he died! He's dead!'"

"He died? Wow!" Johnny said. "That's weird. He must have broken his neck in all that thrashing in the fence, huh?"

"You're right, John," Kellie said. "You're so smart.

"We called the fish and game office and that's what they said too," Kellie said.

"What did you do with him? Leave him?" Johnny asked.

"Yeah," Kellie said. "We had to. He was too big to take and no one that we asked wanted his meat, and his horns were in velvet, so no one wanted them either."

"How big was his rack?" Johnny asked.

"He was an eight point. At least that's how they call it in the south, with four points on each side," Kellie answered. "I mean he was huge, Johnny. He was the biggest we had seen riding horses, or anywhere in Tennessee."

"Well that's a cool story that that big buck died in your arms like that," Johnny said.

"Yeah. And do you want to know the most interesting part?" Kellie asked.

"You mean there's more?"

Kellie could sense Johnny's interest picking up again. She had him eating out of the palm of her hand.

"Yes! You know how I help with that horse fair every year? The one Nikki will sing the national anthem at in March?" Kellie asked.

"Yeah."

"Well, I called this guy named John Sloan to let him know about this horse named Black Beauty coming to the horse fair. He's this newspaper writer who reports on hunting and fishing stories. When I had him on the phone I told him about the big deer and how huge he was and that he died in my arms.

"John Sloan said that he believed my story and that he was just about the biggest whitetail he'd ever heard about in these parts. He agreed because he had seen him, too!"

"He had? How?" Johnny asked.

"Well, you know the pasture on the other side of that fence that the deer got tangled up in?"

"Yes."

"Well that hay field was John Sloan's field. Kaysie had parked our SUV in his driveway that morning!"

"Weird!" Johnny exclaimed.

"He had a guy out cutting hay for him that day and found the big buck. The worker went to get John Sloan and brought him out to see it. And John Sloan said it was one of the biggest bucks he had ever seen in Tennessee or any other state in the south for that matter."

"Cool," Johnny said. "That was a cool story."

"Well, thanks," Kellie said, smiling proudly into the phone. "But can you believe it? I petted and loved on Tennessee's biggest deer and it died in my arms! Weird, huh?"

"Uh huh," Johnny said, agreeing.

The story was a success. Dave had been right.

"Well sweetie, I can let you get back to your homework again," Kellie said. "It was fun talking to you."

"Yeah," Johnny said. "Thanks for the story. It was nice talking to you, too."

"You're welcome," Kellie said. "Can I talk to your dad again?"

"Sure, here he is," Johnny said. "Bye, Kellie."

"Bye, Mr. J," Kellie said.

Thursday, January 25, 2001

Dave's phone rang as he hustled through the doors at Portland International Airport.

"Hi, Kellie!" Dave said, out of breath.

"Where are you?"

"I'm sorry! I got tied up in a meeting at work, but I'm here now. Where are you?"

"I'm at a pay phone by the Delta Airlines terminal."

Dave felt a little embarrassed to be late, but in the rush to get to the airport he didn't have time to get nervous. Events were scrolling by fast and he was merely rolling with them.

Already that morning, Dave had shepherded his kids over to his mother's, telling them all, "I'm going to be away for a couple days on business. I'll see you guys Sunday night."

Then he had stopped by Metro Metals for a half-day's work before heading over to PDX to meet Kellie. Her flight was due in at 1:15 P.M.

Kellie had rehearsed several versions of what she wanted to say when she met Dave. When the plane landed, however, she had a hard time standing up out of her seat.

"Oh, God," she thought to herself. "Please help me do this."

Kellie's trepidation was only overcome by the sheer force of her desire to make the weekend work out. It was, after all, the chance of her lifetime.

Kellie walked out of the jetway, eager for her first sight of Dave. She wore a purple silk jacket over a black tank top with a scooped neckline. Her purple and black chiffon skirt swayed over her black leather boots. She wore her long, blunt-cut, strawberry blond hair loose over her shoulders.

She emerged from the gate ready to impress. But when she looked around, Dave was nowhere to be seen. She scanned up and down the concourse, and couldn't find him.

Her adrenaline was replaced by a new surge of anxiety. "Where is he?" she wondered.

She found a pay phone next to the gate and called Dave.

Within minutes, he emerged.

"Kellie!" Dave said, spotting her hair as he approached the arriving passengers. "I'm sorry about that."

She saw him and couldn't contain her smile. She walked toward him, with long, animated strides. She was relieved and excited to see him.

"I stink and I have pit stains!" Kellie announced, catching Dave off guard. They met in an awkward hug and Dave turned his head to give her a nervous peck on the cheek. He let go before tilting his head a bit to laugh at her outburst. Kellie's self-effacing admission had momentarily disarmed him.

Kellie quickly threw aside her carefully memorized greeting. She had undermined her own intention of a romantic, Hollywood-type greeting.

They walked down to the baggage claim area together.

"How was your flight?" Dave asked.

"Horrible!" Kellie exclaimed.

"Why? What happened? Did you have some turbulence?" Dave inquired, concerned.

"No, the flight was fine," Kellie said. "I was so nervous I almost hyperventilated. And my legs were shaking so hard I almost couldn't stand up. You make me a nervous wreck!"

"Why?" he asked. "You have nothing to worry about. This is going to be OK. We're going to have a great weekend."

They walked out to the short-term parking garage, and Dave placed Kellie's suitcase in the back of the Suburban. Then he walked around to the passenger door to open it for her.

Dave unlocked the door, and then pulled Kellie into his arms, planting a spontaneous kiss on her mouth. It was an icebreaking kiss, sloppy in its execution but much-needed to erase the uncomfortable tension that enveloped them. As first kisses go, it was also a satisfying kiss, and one that was a harbinger of things to come.

"Thank you for doing that," Kellie said, as they released. "We needed that."

"I know," Dave said. "We definitely needed to get that out of the way."

They had no sooner pulled onto Airport Way, headed for the freeway that would begin their trip to the coast, when Kellie—feeling comfortable for the first time—turned and asked Dave, "Why am I here?"

It wasn't that she didn't want to be there, but she wanted to hear his answer to the question.

"Well," Dave said, chuckling nervously. He turned to Kellie and came up with a quick answer.

"Quite frankly, I don't have time to sit around and wonder about what to do next, or if this is something I should pursue. I'm not going to allow myself or the kids to wallow in this. We are going to move on. I don't have time for these long-distance phone calls and games if they're not going to go anywhere. So for me, I want to see if this works between us, so I know one way or the other."

"That's the perfect answer," Kellie said. "I feel the same way. I want to find out what it is really like to spend time alone with you. I mean, I can't even believe I'm actually here, in your car, driving to the coast with you. This seems like a dream, but I know it's real. I'm really here with Dave Grill, my secret crush. It's so amazing how life sometimes will come back around."

Kellie reached over and rubbed Dave's arm, lovingly. For the first time, she felt free to explore a love that she had only dared fantasize about.

"I know," Dave said. "It's weird for me to think that just two short months ago I buried Teresa and my life was totally shaken upside down. I was devastated. I didn't know what I would do. A father with three kids left behind. I never even thought of dating or seeing anyone else. Teresa and I were happy and in love and our relationship was still really good, even after being together for 16 years. You and your feelings for me were a complete surprise."

Dave suddenly felt a little self-conscious talking about his wife with Kellie in the seat next to him.

"Do you want me not to talk about her on this trip?" Dave asked. "I mean, we don't have to mention her if you don't want to. I don't want to make you feel awkward or anything."

Dave studied Kellie's reaction, trying to detect jealousy or discomfort.

"No, it's absolutely fine to talk about her," Kellie said. "We have to talk about her, don't we? She's the reason I'm here. She'll always be a part of you. I want to hear about her. I want to know all about the two of you together as man and wife, and her with the kids as a mom. All of it. It's fine to talk about her. Honest, it is."

Dave was relieved.

"It's true, we do need to talk about her," he said. "I just didn't want to upset you." He smiled, glad that she was confident and sure of herself. It was one of many small tests that Kellie passed. If the subject of Teresa had been off limits, Dave knew he would have struggled to get through the weekend.

Once they got out of metropolitan Portland, Dave stopped in Newberg, on Highway 99W, so they could get a cup of coffee and sit down for a few minutes. The weather was typical for Oregon at this time of year—cold and drizzly.

All the way to the coast, Dave maintained one conversation with Kellie and had another one ongoing in his head. Inside, nothing was clear. He told himself he was on a fact-finding mission.

"Teresa," he thought to himself, looking through the wet windshield and into the slate-gray sky. "I hope you can hear me. If this is not what you want me to do, show me some kind of sign, one way or the other. Let me know if you think this is the right thing."

Asking Teresa for guidance had seemed the natural thing to do for the 18 years they had known each other. Once again, Dave sought her input, though he was confident in his own feelings to make the right choice.

"Do you think I'm just a cold, calloused, heartless prick for being with you now, two months after Teresa died?" Dave asked, turning to Kellie. "It must seem strange to you that I can say we were so in love, and yet be here with you now so soon after her death."

Kellie carefully considered the question. But she had thought over every angle and perspective of the entire situation for two months. No, she thought to herself, Dave was anything but heartless for meeting her.

"Well, I must admit that was another question I was going to ask," Kellie replied. "Why are we doing this weekend at the coast so soon after her death? Most people say it takes years before they can even begin to heal or reach out for another person to share life with. Why are you so quick in trying this? I mean, don't get me wrong, I'm the person who really benefits from your accepting me so soon, and wanting to see where this leads. I'm not complaining."

Dave felt like elaborating. He was still sorting out answers to those very questions internally.

"I've searched my soul for answers," Dave said. "I know it sounds stupid, but I don't know why I'm doing this. I know it looks horrible. It's so soon, and it *is* totally out of character. I am *not* the type of guy who would jump right into another relationship. I would question anyone I know who would do what I'm doing right now. I can't explain it. I've asked Teresa to guide me and let me know if this is the right thing to be doing."

He smiled and gave Kellie a quick wink. They had just passed the Spirit Mountain Indian casino in Grande Ronde, about 18 miles from Lincoln City and the coast.

"I've asked Teresa to send me a sign to let me know if this is the wrong thing, and to let me know somehow, to hit me with a brick or something," Dave said, chuckling.

Kellie smiled back. "So, no bricks so far?"

"No nothing," Dave said. "I have tried to find anything to make me feel guilty or stop me from meeting you, but I haven't been able to. All I could do was be excited. I've been excited to start this, and meet, and try this trip to the coast with you. Who knows where it will lead? I'm a great believer in fate, and when opportunity knocks, you've got to open the door or you may miss out on some of the best things that life has to offer."

With every word, and every mile, Kellie could feel herself respecting and caring for Dave more and more. She felt the pressure of wanting everything to go right, and yet she felt the outcome of the weekend would be revealed naturally.

As they descended through the forests on the west slopes of the Coast Range, they could see broken clouds toward the coast. The late afternoon sun illuminated the clouds like multicolored spotlights, orange and yellow and pink. To Kellie the clouds looked filled with fire. But her own mind was set ablaze by the emotion that she felt for Dave, and the very thought of checking into a hotel room with him was enough to make her hands sweat.

They turned south onto the coast highway for the final leg of the trip, and Dave began to point out attractions along the way. He paused at the first stoplight in Lincoln City.

"So, are you sure you don't want separate rooms?" he said, turning to face her.

Kellie picked up Dave's right hand and held it up to her lips, and kissed it. She leaned over and whispered, "I'm positive."

Dave pulled into the guest registry parking lot at the Inn at Spanish Head, a resplendent stucco hotel with a red-tiled roof that is built into a bluff overlooking a stretch of Oregon coastline. Dave went into the lobby and checked in.

The unspoken attraction that had built over the past few weeks on the phone had only intensified during the two-hour ride to the coast. Once inside the room, Kellie threw her arms around Dave and they kissed again, deeper and with more hunger than at the airport.

"I need to take a shower," she said, beginning to peel out of her clothes. "Would you join me?"

"Uh . . ." Dave stammered. "I've got to go and move the car. It's only 15-minute parking."

Kellie raised her eyebrow at Dave.

"OK, mister," she said. "But hurry back. You know where to find me."

Kellie's confidence now brimmed. She brazenly stripped all the way and then playfully cupped her hands over her breasts and turned to go into the bathroom and start the water. She stepped into the tub and let the hot water begin to pour onto her skin.

Dave considered the moment, and made a beeline for the door. He dawdled toward the car, and picked up the conversation in his head again. "Oh my God. This is going to happen. Am I ready for this? Am I ready for someone else?"

Dave got nervous. He could feel the tension in his arms and chest as he walked back to the hotel room. He took a deep breath and opened the door. He could hear the water running in the bathroom. The door was open and steam was billowing out.

Dave sat on the bed.

"I'm back," Dave announced, over the sound of the shower.

"Come join me!" Kellie yelled back.

Dave took another deep breath and then gave in to the moment. Accepting her invitation, he pulled off his shirt. He set all modesty aside and stripped naked. He walked into the steaming bathroom and playfully pulled the shower curtain to the side, taking a peak at Kellie's pink body in the hot water.

"Come on in," Kellie said. "This feels great."

Dave stepped in, and suddenly soap and suds were all that separated him from Kellie. Kellie felt as if she were in the middle of a dream. Living her fantasy, she began exploring the body of the man she had idolized for two decades. Dave, meanwhile, allowed himself to touch back, finding pleasure and comfort in a woman with whom he could begin a new chapter of his life.

The shower was short, mere foreplay for what they both knew must come next. They stepped out of the shower and into dry terry cloth towels. Kellie took Dave's hand and led him to the bed. They made careful, passionate love to one another, the first of several such sessions that weekend.

Kellie lay in Dave's arms when they had finished, exhausted, satisfied and overwhelmed by the experience. She had never felt a sexual union like this one before, infused with love, heart and soul. She felt at home. She no longer had a shred of doubt that this was the man she was destined to be with. She never wanted to be without him again.

Dave, too, was pleasantly surprised. He had not come to the hotel room with Kellie with any expectation, other than to be prepared for any outcome. That it had happened like this, in a physical union that felt so complete to them both, had left him stunned. Maybe this was the turning point? Maybe the future, with Kellie, would be brighter than he could have imagined.

Yet still, he knew that sexual satisfaction wasn't the sign he was looking for. At some point that weekend, he still hoped for an indication of Teresa's approval.

"Wow," Kellie whispered, tracing Dave's jaw line with her finger. "That was incredible."

Kellie felt no inhibition telling him how she felt, and she was so overcome with her feelings there was no way for her to contain them.

"Dave, I love you," she said. "I know it's really soon to say. I hope it doesn't scare you."

Dave knew Kellie's feelings were still several steps ahead of his own, but was quick to show his acceptance.

"Nothing scares me, Kellie," he said.

"It's just that I have to say it, OK?" Kellie said, beginning to unravel all of the thoughts twisting through her mind. "You don't have to say it back or anything. I mean, I know it's going to take you a long time to heal and all of this stuff is happening so fast, so don't feel obligated to say it. It's just that I've never experienced anything like this. My heart is so happy. I can't believe this is happening."

Dave smiled back at her and touched her nose.

"I have no complaints," he said. "It was 'wow' for me, too."

Kellie began to feel hunger rumbling around in her stomach, reminding her that she had barely eaten all day.

"I'm starving," she said, getting up out of bed and walking naked to the window. She pulled open the curtains.

"Oh my God, Dave, come look!" Kellie said, delighted. The setting sun had painted the sky with even more brilliant hues than when they arrived. Rich pinks, yellows and burnt oranges layered on top of one another like oils on a canvas.

"Wow," Kellie said, again, with Dave now standing behind her. "I'm going to get my camera. Do you think it will take it with the glare of the window?"

"Try it, it should be OK," Dave said.

Kellie snapped two photos and then set her camera down to wrap her arms around Dave. They stood at the window as the sunset began to dim.

"It's so beautiful and peaceful," Kellie said.

"And kind of rare actually," Dave said, trying to remember the last time he saw a sunset like that on Oregon's usually gray coast in January. "I hope this means that we're in for good weather while we're here."

"Of course it does! Everything is so perfect, it has to mean perfect weather too. Teresa will see to that," she said.

They took another shower and then dressed for dinner. Dave and Kellie shared the elevator going down to the parking lot with a gray-haired man who looked about 70.

"Did you see that sunset?" the man asked. "That was something else."

"Yes," Kellie said. "We saw it. It was magical."

Dave put his arm around Kellie in the elevator and she looked up at him to share a smile.

They drove off into Lincoln City, prepared to stop when they saw a restaurant that captured their fancy. They finally settled on a small Italian place that oozed charm and romance.

Kellie and Dave sat down at a small table and looked around. They were the only customers in the place.

The owner and his wife began making small talk with them.

"Thank you for coming in," the woman said. "Where are you two from?"

Kellie, always eager to jump into a new conversation and make a new friend, answered the woman's questions. She was grinning from ear to ear, and for the first time felt the happiness of being on a "date" with Dave Grill.

They ate ravenously, but paused to talk as they did. The nervousness and anxiety of the ride to Lincoln City had been replaced with comfort and ease.

They returned to the Inn at Spanish Head and sat down in the lounge. Dave ordered a Bud, and Kellie asked for orange juice. They began to tell stories from the long period of time between their days as kids in Utah and the present day, filling in gaps in the timeline. Dave told her about his best memories of Brett and their wild teenage years together back at Brighton High School, and then moved forward to stories about Teresa and the kids.

They went back to their room, put on warmer clothes, then went out to walk on the beach. Dave held Kellie's gloved hand as they walked through the sand along the surf, both of them pausing from time to time to gaze at the stars scattered in the crisp, clear sky above.

The conversation shifted to Kellie's childhood.

"Did you know that my parents were miserable together back when you were in high school?" she asked.

"No. Really? I mean, obviously I know they got divorced. But back then they seemed pretty happy to me," Dave said.

"Well, it wasn't as happy as it seemed," Kellie said. "It was all an act."

Dave stopped walking to turn to look at her. He thought he knew her family better than that. "How so?"

"When Kaysie and I were about Johnny's age," Kellie said, "My mom confided in us that she didn't love our dad any more. I mean she told us like we were her girlfriends and yet she wanted us to keep it a secret."

"Why do you think she did that?" Dave asked.

"I don't know. To ease her guilty conscience, I guess. I don't really know why. All I know is that it screwed us up for many years. I mean, neither Kaysie nor I ever dated in high school. Never! It's almost like the thought of our mom not loving our dad made us suspicious of relationships in general. I mean, it's strange to think about that now, and I'm not trying to lay blame on her for our lack of boyfriends, but I think it's because of the unhappiness we saw at home that we held out the way we did."

"Well, so . . . how do you feel about your mom now?" Dave asked.

"My mom is our biggest supporter and cheerleader, and really always has been our best friend. I mean, that's partly why she told us," Kellie said.

"Well, what about your dad?"

"Oh, I love him. He kind of reminds me of John Wayne — straightforward and tough. My relationship with him is a lot better now and I think he and my mom are just better off apart," Kellie explained. "They both had their problems. But I guess we all do."

Kellie continued.

"In the long run it was probably great for you and me, because I have never dated much, and I've only had four serious relationships—meaning I had sex with them—in all my 34 years."

"Well, hold on a minute," Dave said, pretending to be serious. "I can't be with you if you've had a whole four relationships with men!"

Kellie laughed, and they both cracked up.

"Well, no need to worry," she said. "Brett made me get an AIDS test a few weeks ago. He didn't want me to take any chances with you. I was so mad at him. It made me feel like such a slut! I know he was trying to be safe, after all that you and the kids have been through in losing Teresa. He didn't want anything to go wrong, but it was a weird thing for him to ask of me. I decided to do it, though, because I figured it couldn't hurt to know everything was OK and it is. Oh, the things I do for you!"

Kellie smiled and raised Dave's hand up to kiss it. Having come to the edge of Siletz Bay, they had run out of beach. They turned and began walking back toward the hotel.

"Thank you for doing that, but you didn't have to," Dave said.

"I know, but after giving it some thought, I wanted to," she said.

"Well, thanks," Dave replied. "I hope you know that I don't want this whole weekend to be nothing but sex. I mean don't get me wrong, what we did a few hours ago was great, but it doesn't have to happen again this whole weekend. I mean I want us to really talk and get to know each other, and if we happen to have sex again well that's OK too, but I don't want this whole weekend to be about sex, sex, sex. You mean more to me than that."

For the first time, Dave felt that it was he who was rambling.

"I feel the same way," Kellie said.

They continued to talk as they strolled all the way back to their hotel.

Once inside their room, Dave turned on the gas fireplace. It had been cold outside, and it felt good to them to place their hands near the fan blowing warm air into the room. They removed their coats and sat together on a couch facing the fireplace.

The conversation continued to flow, from Kellie's ex-boyfriends to favorite foods to their childhood pets. It was comfortable and relaxed. Kellie felt the same sensation of security talking to Dave as she did with her twin sister. He listened intently as she gushed forth everything on her mind.

Dave was struck by the way his own feelings were gravitating.

"I've had every out in the world to stay away from this, but something is right here," Dave kept thinking. Kellie was so completely different than Teresa, almost to the point that they were opposites.

Teresa was bossy, brassy and exuded confidence in a cool, self-assured way. Kellie, meanwhile, was a lightning bolt of energy and a nonstop talker who could drive people unused to such a barrage up a wall. But there was no mistaking Kellie's genuine heart and her obvious affection for both him and the kids.

Kellie sat up from the couch and moved over to the window, trying to see the darkened ocean. She leaned close and breathed on the window, steaming it up. Then she wrote in the moisture with her fingertip: Kellie Poulsen-Grill.

Kellie smiled as she came back to the couch and wrapped one of Dave's arms around her waist. "That's what I used to write on my PeeChee folders at school when I was 12."

"You did?" Dave said, smiling in amazement.

"Pretty cocky, huh?"

"Very. But maybe it was foreshadowing."

"I hope so," Kellie said, leaning in once again for a taste of Dave's mouth in a slow, warm kiss.

They talked until 1 A.M. before fatigue began to overtake them both. They brushed their teeth in the same sink, and then Kellie took off all of her clothes.

"It's OK, isn't it?" she asked.

"Sure," he said, eying her lean body.

"There's just one hitch," Kellie said.

"What's that?"

"You have to get naked too. I love to sleep naked, and I want you to, also."

"You won't get any argument from me," Dave said, beginning to undress.

Kellie noticed how Dave had been hesitant to reveal himself at first, but had warmed up to the idea of loosening his modesty around her.

They crawled into bed together, and surprisingly, only talked into the early hours of the morning.

At 5 A.M., they both noticed the time.

"I know I said I didn't want this weekend to be all about sex, but I've just got to have you again," Dave whispered to her.

They melted into one another yet again, making love for the second time.

Dave dozed peacefully, while Kellie got up and took another shower. The sound of her hair dryer woke Dave. He joined her in the bathroom and took his own shower.

Despite the short night's sleep, they both felt invigorated and ready to start the new day. They drove to an unimpressive-looking building that looked vaguely like a double-wide mobile home, with a sign that read "The Pines." Inside, they found a hearty breakfast. As they ate, they began to plan their day.

Dave had it in mind to drive south, where he could show her the Yaquina Head Lighthouse, and then farther, to Newport and the Oregon Coast Aquarium. Kellie had little knowledge of the Oregon coast, so agreed with all of Dave's suggestions. She just wanted to be near him.

The day was warming up, and by 11 A.M., the cloud cover had lifted to reveal a warm, blue sky overhead. It was an unusually bright, balmy day for January. The thermometer in Dave's Suburban read 60 degrees.

Driving south on Highway 101 they came upon the small, touristy town of Depoe Bay, lined with gift stores, saltwater taffy confectionaries and charter boat offers. Kellie asked Dave to stop. The town's claim to fame, according to a road sign, was the "World's Smallest Harbor."

Dave and Kellie strolled along the sidewalk on the ocean side of the highway and watched as waves beat against the rocks below them. Kellie took her camera out of her jacket pocket and asked Dave to take a picture of her the next time a wave crashed in.

Dave took the camera, and as he held it up to his eye a breaking wave slapped into a pile of boulders beneath them. An arc of spray shot into the air and vivid rainbow appeared in the midst of a clear blue sky.

"You'll never believe it, but there was a rainbow over your head as I took that photo," Dave said. "I wonder if it will show up on the film."

Even as he said the words, Dave began to wonder about what he had just witnessed. A rainbow? On a day like this, without a cloud in the sky? He had never seen such a thing. Could this be the sign from Teresa that he had been looking for?

Kellie took the camera, and the two switched positions. Aiming the camera at him, she noticed the same rainbow and snapped another picture of it.

"Wow," Kellie said, "I saw it too!"

Dave asked a man standing nearby to take a photo of the two of them, together, in the same spot.

"It was strange," the man commented. "But as I took that picture I could see a rainbow right over the two of you."

Dave and Kellie thanked the man, and began to wonder if that photo, too, would reveal the rainbow. When they looked for it again, though, the rainbow was gone.

"I asked Teresa for a sign on the way over here yesterday," Dave said. "I was hoping she would let me know, one way or the other, whether this was the right thing for me to be doing, or if this is all a mistake. I think that rainbow was the sign I was looking for."

Kellie tingled at Dave's words. As much as she wanted the weekend to go perfectly, the way it was going was beyond her wildest imagination. She had no control over the outcome, and shook her head. A higher power was in charge, she believed. There was nothing left for her to do but let go and let events unfold.

They couldn't wait to see the photos, but they would have to.

They resumed their drive south, and the first stop they made was at the lighthouse.

Dave pulled out his cell phone and dialed Brett in Salt Lake City.

Brett answered. "Hey buddy, what's going on?"

"Well, I'm sitting here staring at a gorgeous redhead, it's 60 degrees and I'm about to go into a lighthouse," Dave said. "I just wanted to call and say thanks for being a Stupid Cupid."

Stupid Cupid, Kellie had told Dave, was the term Brett had used for himself since the week of the memorial.

"Not a problem," Brett said, elated to hear that things were going so well. He took a personal satisfaction in knowing that his efforts had not been in vain. "Don't do anything I wouldn't do."

"Guess that means I can do just about anything, huh?"

"You got that right."

Dave winked at Kellie and handed her the phone.

"Hi, big brother," Kellie said.

"So . . ." Brett said, smugly. "Was I right or what?"

"Oh my God, Brett, it has been incredible," she said. "You were right. We've had sunsets and rainbows, and everything has been wonderful. I'll tell you all about it later, but we're about to go into the lighthouse."

The day moved along with more sightseeing.

After touring the aquarium, Dave and Kellie drove back into Newport and stopped at Sizzler Steakhouse for dinner, and then moved on to the Embarcadero Hotel lounge for a drink. They continued to talk easily about anything and everything: Kellie's aversion to alcohol, more about each of Dave's kids, politics, songwriting, sports and even jokes.

Dave learned that with Kellie, there is seldom a pause.

Dave paid the bill and they walked hand-in-hand outside toward the Suburban. They were giddy over the overwhelming success of the day.

"Well, there was this baby Polar bear," Kellie began.

Dave turned to her, smiling. "Yes?"

"Dave this is my favorite joke," Kellie said.

"Go on, I'm listening," Dave said, opening her door and then moving around to the driver's side.

"Well he went up to his mom, who was doing the dishes, and said 'Mom, am I 100 percent Polar bear? I mean, could there be any chance that I have some Koala bear or Black bear or Grizzly bear in me?'

"'No dear, you are 100 percent Polar bear and don't you ever doubt that. Now run along and leave me alone. I'm busy.'

"So the little polar bear went to his dad, who was working on the car, and said, 'Dad, am I 100 percent Polar bear? Could I possibly have any Kodiak or Panda or Brown bear in me?'

"'The dad looked up and said, 'No, son, you're 100 percent Polar bear. Why do you ask?'

"Because I'm fuckin' freezing!"

Kellie dropped the punchline and Dave burst out laughing.

Dave put the Suburban into gear and began to back out of the parking space.

"Can I tell you something?" Dave asked.

"Of course, anything," Kellie said, still giggling at her joke.

"I don't quite know how to say this and have it come out like I mean it," Dave said.

"Just say it!"

"Well, it just . . . it's just you're so much fun being around. It's like . . . well . . . it's like being with Brett, but I get to have sex with you!" Dave said, beginning to laugh again. "Does that sound bad?"

"Oh, Dave, no!" Kellie said. "That's one of the nicest compliments anyone has ever given me."

Dave turned the Suburban north onto Highway 101 and began the 30 miles back to the Inn at Spanish Head in Lincoln City. Kellie could feel exhaustion beginning to catch up to her. She lay across the front seat, with her head in Dave's lap and her feet against the passenger window. Dave stroked Kellie's long, red hair as he drove. She dozed on and off.

Back at the hotel, they were both ready for sleep. They got under the covers, once again naked, and their touching soon turned into another passionate interlude. It left them physically exhausted. Thirty-six hours had begun to seem like a lifetime of happiness.

"I love you, Dave," Kellie said.

"I love you too," Dave said. "I don't know why I deserve this much luck. To have had Teresa, who was the most wonderful woman in the world . . . and now you. You are so wonderful too."

The words moved Kellie to tears.

"Oh, Dave, how can you say you're lucky?" Kellie asked. "You have been through so much losing Teresa and being left with three kids. I think you are just getting your due. You're a great person who has endured so much. God knows that you deserve happiness now, after all you've been through. You're finally getting some more good because you've had so much bad lately."

Dave could feel his emotions begin to rise, but kept them in check. He began to talk about the loneliness since Teresa had died, and the hardship of watching her slip away before his eyes. He admitted how hard it had been to get through the memorial service.

Tears rolled down Kellie's cheeks as she listened, silently rubbing Dave's back and shoulders as he talked.

"When I carried Teresa's cremated remains out of the funeral home, I thought to myself, 'Now let's see you come back, you fucking cancer!'" Dave hadn't admitted that to anyone.

Kellie began to cry even harder.

"Dave that is so hard," she said. "I'm so sorry."

Dave wanted Kellie to know where he stood. "The thing is, I loved her and I still love her so much," he said. "I will always love her, Kellie.

"Our relationship and marriage was good, really good, unlike a lot of couples who have been married for 16 years. Our love was still alive, and I miss her so much."

Kellie hugged Dave tighter.

"I know. I am so sorry," she said. The conversation continued, again, until 5 in the morning.

They slept in until about 10, and woke up ready to greet a new day. One of the first things that came to Dave's mind was the film. He wanted to see if the rainbow had been captured.

Dave walked into the bathroom, where Kellie was brushing her hair.

"I want to take the film in and get it developed at a one-hour," Dave said. "Kellie, do you know where that roll is?"

"Yeah, it's in my purse, right over there on the nightstand."

Dave walked over to it, and looked inside. It wasn't there.

"Well, I don't see it. Is there anyplace else you think it might be?"

Kellie had a puzzled look on her face. "I know I put it in my purse. It's got to be in there."

But she couldn't find it, either. She started to search the room, and Dave left to go hunt for it in the Suburban.

Ten minutes went by, and they still couldn't find it.

Dave returned to the room, frustrated but focused. He was on a mission to find that roll, which contained proof of Teresa's sign of approval. To lose the film was unacceptable. What sort of sign would that be? "OK," he said. "Let's think about this for a minute. Where could we have left it yesterday? We need to retrace our steps because I want that film found."

Dave and Kellie frantically tried to remember yesterday's details. Kellie had changed the film once, at the aquarium. Where had the finished roll gone?

Dave pulled open the phone book and found the number for Sizzler. Maybe they had left it on the table?

"Has anyone, by chance, found a roll of undeveloped film since last evening?" Dave inquired.

"Not to my knowledge," the manager replied.

Dave tried the lighthouse and the aquarium. No film.

They drove 30 miles back to Newport, anxiously retracing every step of the previous day's path.

Dave went into the Sizzler and walked to the booth that he had shared with Kellie the day before, running his hand between the seat cushions and kneeling to look under the table.

Dave searched the sidewalk and curb near where Kellie had taken a picture of a whale mural. He got on his hands and knees and peered into a storm drain. Nothing.

Then they drove across the Yaquina Bridge and returned to the aquarium. Dave explained to the staff that he had switched film inside and was eager to look for the lost roll. He was allowed in, and went to the exact spot where Kellie had reloaded the camera. It wasn't there either.

Back out in the parking lot, Dave was beginning to feel discouraged. Kellie had scanned the surface of the parking lot and also come up empty.

"Well, shit," Dave said. "Do we dare try to search the Embarcadero, too?"

"I don't know, Dave," Kellie said, shrugging her shoulders. "I don't think I took my purse in there. But I guess we could give it a try."

"At the very least, we can have another drink," Dave said glumly.

They re-entered the lounge and sat down.

"How are you guys today?" an approaching waiter asked.

"We're fine, but we'd be doing a whole lot better if we could find this roll of film we lost yesterday," Kellie said.

"That's too bad," the waiter said, sympathetically. "Can I get you something to drink?"

Dave ordered a beer for himself, and an orange juice for Kellie.

Two minutes passed and the waiter returned and put their drinks down. Then he reached into his pocket and pulled out a roll of K-Mart brand film. He set it down in front of them.

"This wouldn't be what you're looking for, is it?"

Dave was stunned. Kellie leapt to her feet and threw her arms around the waiter.

"Thank you! Where did you find it?" Kellie exclaimed.

"I came in this afternoon for my shift and it was sitting on the bar," the waiter said. "I almost threw it away but I set it on the back counter thinking someone might have lost it."

Dave grabbed the film and inspected it. Sure enough, it was the roll they had been searching for all day.

"You will never know how valuable this roll of film is to us," Dave said to the waiter.

"I'm glad to help," the waiter said, smiling. He turned and left.

Dave and Kellie looked at each other, smiled and broke into laughter.

Kellie raised her glass.

"To the three of us," she said. "You, me and Teresa!"

"I'll drink to that."

They wasted little time at the lounge.

"I want to get these developed right now," Dave said.

Dave drove to the Newport Fred Meyer store and submitted the film for developing at the one-hour finishing desk.

They began to kill time by idly wandering the aisles of the store, sitting down on a futon that was on display.

Dave thought of something he had been meaning to ask.

"Do the numbers 333 mean anything to you?" Dave asked.

"What do you mean? The time, or the date or something?"

Dave had noticed the clock because he wanted to check on the film in one hour. The time on his watch was 3:33 P.M.

"I don't know," Dave said. "I've just had that time pop up a lot lately. In the middle of the night, or when I look at my watch at work. It happens a lot. In fact, right after the memorial, when I was getting used to being alone at night, I had a string of four or five nights in a row where I woke up suddenly, turned to my nightstand and my alarm clock showed 3:33 A.M. I keep having 333s show up, whether it's on my odometer, on license plates, or billboards. For some reason, I keep noticing them. The odd thing is, they usually happen when I've been thinking about Teresa."

Kellie listened intently but couldn't think of any explanation for the phenomenon.

"Well, maybe that's supposed to be our wedding date— March 3, 2003? That would be three, three, three," Kellie said, teasing him.

Dave pondered it some more. "Maybe," he said, smiling back at her.

An hour later, Dave eagerly stepped to the counter and paid for his pictures. Before they left the store, Dave flipped through the pictures quickly, as Kellie peered around his arm.

"There they are," Dave said proudly, coming across the first one. He pulled it from the stack and examined it.

It was a portrait of Kellie, smiling in her sunglasses in the direction of the surf below the walkway. And there, over Kellie's head, was the rainbow from the day before. He could barely believe his own eyes: A rainbow on a cloudless day.

Curious, Dave thought. Was it, indeed, a sign?

Dave considered the question carefully. He wasn't the type to get caught up in flights of fancy. But he had asked, and then received.

Now he simply wondered.

He looked at the next picture, of himself. The rainbow was still there. It looked so close that he could have reached up and grabbed it. He shook his head, trying to wrap his mind around an explanation.

And then he looked at the third picture, the one with both of them standing and smiling. The rainbow had a spectral quality to it. A shroud of white lingered over the water.

More importantly, it was right there in Dave's hands. And he couldn't imagine a more obvious sign. This rainbow hit him over the head like a truckload of bricks.

In an instant, Dave knew that he had the answer to his silent prayer. Teresa approved. The best part of it was that Teresa's signal also pointed in the same direction as his heart. With each passing hour, he could begin to feel the importance of Kellie's presence in his life.

Dave felt a spiritual awakening. The last of his doubts disappeared as he studied those photos and considered their deeper meaning. The future, suddenly, was bright again.

And he would keep his promise.

PART TWO

"Sail On"

CHAPTER SEVEN

At First Sight

Thursday, August 24, 1978

Brett's two-tone brown 1974 Chevy pick-up rumbled up Old Wasatch Boulevard and turned onto the long, gravel driveway that led to the house. Following the pickup was a blue Camaro. In the front yard, the 12-year-old redheaded twins, Kellie and Kaysie, were playing with the dogs—large Samoyed/husky mixes named Reggie and Barretta.

Brett hopped out of his truck and the dogs rushed over to greet him. The girls looked up to see whom their brother had brought home.

The car door swung open, and a muscular, brown-haired 17-year-old stepped out.

"Well, this is the house," Brett said casually. He grabbed the front of the damp T-shirt he was wearing and began flapping it to fan his torso. "I am boiling hot. How about you? Let's go in and get something cold to drink."

"Sounds good," Brett's friend said.

Kellie and Kaysie approached, trying to corral the excited dogs away from the newcomer.

"Reggie! Barretta! Get down you big mutts!" Brett snapped. His friend didn't mind them.

"Grill," Brett said. "These are my sisters, Kellie and Kaysie. They're twins. Can you tell? Girls, this is Dave Grill."

Dave stuck out his hand to shake, and did a double take. He wasn't sure which one was which. All he saw was bright red pigtails and freckles.

"Hi," he said.

The two boys, just back from a sweltering football practice at Brighton High School, were still covered in sweat despite having changed into fresh T-shirts and cut-offs. They proceeded into the house and Brett began another introduction, this time to his mom.

Back outside, Kellie was mesmerized.

"Kaysie!" she whispered excitedly. "Oh my gosh, that is the cutest boy I've ever seen! Who is he? Where did he come from?"

Kaysie had already turned her attention back to the dogs.

"I don't know. Who cares? Just some friend of Brett's," Kaysie said. "Let's put the dogs away and go jump on the trampoline."

"No," Kellie said. "I want to go see that boy again. Let's go spy on him and Brett!"

Kellie had been struck by the boy Brett called "Grill." He had dark features and green eyes. His voice was deep and his chin was chiseled. His hair was long in back and was still damp from sweat, and it was sleek and dark brown. She wondered if he was partly Ute Indian. He seemed so mature, much more so than her brother. His muscles seemed to pop out of his arms and legs. There was something else about him that she couldn't quite pinpoint. But she wanted to go watch the boy until she figured out what it was.

Kaysie wasn't excited about a covert mission but when Kellie was adamant about something, she usually went along with it.

They shooed the dogs back around the house and locked them behind a fence.

Kellie led Kaysie slowly through the side garage door and then into the kitchen. Brett and his friend were drinking Gatorade in glasses filled with ice. They talked idly about getting together with some of their friends and going out later.

The girls got glasses and filled them with water. Kellie tried to act cool, but cast a side-glance in the direction of Brett's friend, continuing to size him up. The boys acted as though the girls weren't even in the kitchen. There was hardly a reason to conceal her interest but Kellie didn't want her sudden crush to be noticed.

The boys left the kitchen and moved to Brett's room down in the basement.

Kellie moved down the stairs behind them and dragged Kaysie with her. She went as far down the corridor to Brett's room as she could without being seen and crouched down to listen.

Brett and Dave talked about where and when they would meet up again that evening.

"Why don't you go home and get showered and we'll meet over at Pick's at 7," Kellie heard Brett say.

"Sounds good," Dave said.

Kellie, sensing that they were coming out of the room again, scurried into her own room so that she wouldn't be seen. Kaysie slipped in behind her.

The boys walked down the hall and up the stairs, and outside.

Kellie followed them, unnoticed. She kneeled in front of the window facing out to the driveway. She watched Dave open the car door and slide into his seat. She watched him back the car out, turn around and drive away.

Saturday, October 23, 1982

Kellie stood with her mom, dad, Kaysie and Brett in the stands of the football stadium, with a stocking cap pulled down over her long red hair and knit gloves on her hands.

Her eyes were riveted on the player wearing the white jersey with the burnt orange number 7. It was Dave Grill. Each time he touched the ball, Kellie's heart began to beat faster. She hoped she'd get to see him score a touchdown. She hoped he wouldn't get hurt.

It was the first time Kellie had seen Brett's friend Dave since their days playing high school football together. The two friends had gone their separate ways off to college. When her mom and dad made plans for the trip to Oregon, their intention was to go to Ashland and watch Brett play for his Southern Oregon team. But after they purchased the airline tickets, Brett injured his back and was forced to miss that game.

As an alternative, they came north to see Dave Grill's Lewis and Clark team play at Willamette University in Salem.

The change of plans had brought a sense of excitement to Kellie. She hadn't forgotten her infatuation with Dave. Now a 16-year-old high school junior, she had begun to think of herself as nearly worthy of his attention. She and Kaysie had started modeling at 14, appearing in newspaper ads for Salt Lake City department stores. Modeling gave her confidence. And she looked older than her age.

And today, she told herself, she might even have enough confidence to tell Dave that she was interested in him. Or at least flirt a little more openly.

All that anticipation came to an abrupt halt when they found their seats next to Gary and Wilma Grill, and Dave's grandpa Glenn. There was someone else there with them. It was Teresa O'Brien, Dave's new girlfriend.

Kellie smiled and shook Teresa's hand as they were introduced. She was a beautiful brunette with short hair, porcelain skin and alluring hazel eyes. She wore a Levi's jean jacket, 501's and cowboy boots.

In a heartbeat, Kellie knew she wouldn't even try to compete. When the game was over, the group of them moved down next to the field, and Dave came over to greet everyone and thank them for coming. Teresa, however, captured Dave's immediate attention. He gave her a quick kiss.

Kellie winced at the sight before resuming her smile. Dave Grill had a girlfriend, and she was a knockout. Kellie quickly surmised that she wouldn't get her chance with Dave after all. She knew Teresa would marry him.

Kellie's heart sunk.

After all, what chance would she have had with a junior in college who was the star of his football team?

"I guess I can cross him off my list," Kellie whispered to Kaysie in the backseat of the car.

By the time she returned home, Kellie decided it had been silly to pine for a boy who barely knew she existed.

CHAPTER EIGHT

Tentative Beginnings

Monday, January 29, 2001: Oregon

Wilma answered the door and Dave walked in.

She cut right to the chase.

"So? How did things go?" Wilma asked.

Dave smiled and paused before answering.

"Well, let me put it like this. I think my life just got a lot more complicated," Dave said.

Wilma had been the only family member, other than Tamara, in whom Dave had confided before he left for the coast with Kellie. He knew that she must be curious about the outcome of the weekend.

"Complicated? How so?" she asked.

"In a good way," Dave said. "There is definitely something brewing between Kellie and me."

Wilma smiled. She had been hoping for good news to come out of the trip.

Dave recounted the details and explained the photos in which the rainbow had appeared.

"It was the strangest thing," Dave said. "I literally felt like it was a sign from Teresa that this is something that I need to be pursuing."

Wilma listened to the story, astonished. The pieces might fit together once again after all. She could see in Dave's face that there was some renewed vigor.

Wilma gave Dave his house key back.

"Well it's nice to see that there is some hope again in you," she said.

Dave nodded.

He was still trying to make sense of it all. Would he move the kids to Tennessee? Would Kellie eventually move to Oregon? All of those questions and their ramifications were beginning to surface. But for now they were unresolved.

Dave left, and Wilma paused to pray a silent "thank you" to whoever was listening.

Later that night, Wilma slept through the night—free of worry—for the first time since early November.

Monday, January 29, 2001: Tennessee

When the white van pulled up in front of Kellie's house, she looked out a window to see who it was.

"Who could that be?" Kellie asked Kaysie as the vehicle came to a stop in the driveway. The noise had set their dogs to barking in the backyard. They weren't used to strangers pulling up to the house.

Kellie held the curtains to the side as she watched a man come around the front end of the van, holding an armful of red roses in a glass vase.

"Oh my God! They're roses! Dave!" Kellie shouted gleefully.

Kaysie eagerly opened the door and took a closer look.

"Wow," Kaysie said as the deliveryman walked up to the porch.

"Are you Kellie?" the man asked.

"Nope, but she's right here," Kaysie said, smiling broadly.

Kellie sheepishly poked her head around the corner. "I'm Kellie," she said.

The man did a double take, noticing the redhead's mirror image.

"Well these are for you," he said.

"Wow," Kellie said, agreeing with her sister. "Thank you."

Kellie took the vase into her hands and quickly turned back into the house to set them on the dining room table.

The small white envelope said, "Kelli." She didn't care that it was misspelled.

She peeled open the seal and pulled out the card.

" I love you. V."

Kellie read the words out loud to her sister.

"V" was the nickname that Kellie had given Dave after their first night together. It stood for "Victory." Kellie's long wait to find love had come full circle, and for her, finding her white knight felt like the biggest win of her life.

"That is the first time you've ever gotten red roses," Kaysie said. There were no secrets between them.

"It is," Kellie said.

"Well you must have impressed him," Kaysie said, grinning. "Those are really beautiful."

"I know," Kellie said, beaming. "I can't believe this is happening. I can't believe he sent me roses! I'm going to call him."

Kellie went to the phone and immediately dialed Dave.

"This is Dave," Dave said into his cell phone.

"Hi. I've got roses and they're red. I've never gotten red roses before. They're beautiful and they're so big," Kellie said, beginning to ramble.

Dave smiled, knowing that his gesture had been well received. Kellie continued to search for eloquence but the words came spilling through the phone.

"I love the card and how you signed it 'V'," Kellie said.

"I'm glad you like them," Dave said.

"I love them," Kellie said. "And I love you. I'm missing you."

"Well, I told the kids last night," Dave said.

"Oh," Kellie said, beginning to slow down. "How did that go over?"

"It was fine. Lauren didn't like that I said I was at the coast for business. But I knew that if I told them you were coming out here they'd have wanted to see you and we wouldn't have our time alone."

Kellie listened. She was more than curious about how the kids would react to the news that she had been out to visit.

"How did you tell them?" she asked.

"After I dropped you off at the airport on Sunday, I went back home and as soon as I walked in the door the kids were full of questions."

"What did they ask?" Kellie said.

"They wanted to know exactly where I had gone and what I had done and why," Dave explained. "So I told them. And I showed them our photos."

"I want more details!" Kellie exclaimed. "Tell me how you told them."

"We sat down at the kitchen table and Lauren asked me, 'Where did you go?'" Dave said. "And that's when I said, 'If you must know, I went to Lincoln City and I didn't go on business-business. I had Kellie fly into town and we went there together.'"

Kellie was surprised at Dave's blunt delivery of the news.

"Did their jaws just drop open?" she asked.

"Nikki sort of giggled and said 'What?' And Lauren got kind of quiet. Johnny's eyes got kind of big," Dave said.

"Then what?" Kellie asked, impatiently.

"Well, basically I told them the truth," Dave said. "I told them about how you told me you had a crush on me. And I told them that we made a plan to spend a weekend together to see if there were any feelings there, other than you just being Brett's little sister."

"Uh huh," Kellie said, listening intently.

"And that's when Lauren spoke up and said, 'Well, was there any feelings?' I said 'Well, I think there might be something there.' Then I told them to hold on for a second, and I went and got the photos and showed them."

"What did they think of the rainbows?" Kellie asked.

"I think the photos helped them to realize and accept that something special happened between us."

"How did they react to all of this?" Kellie asked, curiously.

"They were all surprised, needless to say. But Nikki seemed to be the most accepting of it. And I think Lauren was a little bit upset about it. I'm not sure if that was because we were together or because I didn't bring you here to see them. Johnny was kind of nonchalant about it."

"Well, that sounds about as good as you could expect, right? I mean, probably even better than that," Kellie said.

"Yeah," Dave said. "I thought it went OK. I just told them that we are going to go on, and I'm going to go on. And it's just an opportunity that I needed to pursue. Who knows? Maybe this will work out for the best for all of us."

Dave's office phone began to ring.

"Uh . . . I need to catch this," Dave said. "I'll call you back tonight."

"OK," Kellie said. "Thanks again for the roses. Bye."

Saturday, February 3, 2001

The oven was pre-heating to 350 degrees when Keely Jacobson arrived, carrying a platter of chicken enchiladas covered in cellophane.

"Come on in," Dave said, opening the door.

Keely had been dutiful about making a dinner entrée for the Grills about once every other week and dropping it by. It gave her peace of mind that she was helping a family that she still perceived to be in crisis. It was not three weeks since her family and theirs had made the ski trip to Bend. She had felt Teresa's presence there, and it made her feel protective of Dave and his family.

"Hi Dave," Keely said, cheerfully. "How are you doing? Where are the kids?"

"Everything's just fine," Dave said. "Lauren's off to a movie, Nikki is over at Michelle's house and Johnny's hanging out with Taylor. They should all be getting back before too long. They know you're bringing enchiladas and they're excited about it."

Keely set the dish down on the counter and pulled off the plastic.

"How are things with you?" she asked.

Dave could tell she had something on her mind.

"Fine," Dave said. "Can I get you something? A glass of wine?"

"That would be great, Dave, thanks."

Dave walked to the cupboard and reached up to take a glass down. He poured Keely a glass of Merlot, and cracked open a Hamm's for himself.

"Dan tells me that you had a visitor last weekend," Keely said, feigning a weak smile.

"Well . . . as a matter of fact I did," Dave said. "What else did he tell you?"

"Oh, he just told me that you had been to the coast with Brett's sister and that you showed him some pictures with rainbows in them."

Dave nodded.

"He's right. Would you like to see them? They're pretty amazing."

Keely said, "Sure, I'd love to see them."

Dave could sense that there was something measured and unsure in the tone of her voice. He pulled the pictures out from a stack of paperwork on the dining room table.

"These were taken at Depoe Bay. You know, right there next to that bridge, across the highway from all the shops?"

Keely nodded.

Dave showed her the photos, one by one, as he began to formulate how he was going to tell Keely about the trip.

"How do you feel about her?" Keely said. "She lives awfully far away, doesn't she?"

"Only a couple thousand miles," Dave responded, smiling. He was trying to lighten what he could tell was a heavy load for Teresa's closest friend.

Keely wasn't biting. She went straight to her concern.

"When Brett told me during the week of the memorial that he was going to set you up with her, I told him it was too soon," Keely said. "Dave, I still think it's too soon."

Dave was bemused by Keely's words. Too soon? For what? He smiled at her, with his eyebrows raised.

"Too soon for who?" Dave said, inquisitively. "You?"

Dave could feel himself start to get defensive. But Keely seemed intent to say what was on her mind.

"There is a one-year rule," Keely said.

"A one-year rule?"

"Yes, Dave. You need to let some time pass to grieve before moving on. That should be at least one year. Everyone wants you to be happy, Dave. Don't get me wrong. But it's just too fast. Think of the kids. Think of Teresa's parents and Tamara. They've been through so much already."

"OK, now stop right there," Dave said. "First of all, let's get one thing straight. I don't give a shit about your one-year rule. I loved Teresa more than anything, but the reality is she's gone, and our lives are moving on. Kellie is a family friend who confided in me that she has had a crush on me for a very long time. And when I found out about it, I was flattered. I think I owe it to myself, and my kids, to look into this opportunity. I didn't go looking for this. It just fell into my lap."

Keely took another sip of wine and set her glass down.

"I know it's an unusual situation. I just wish you would consider what I've said," she protested. "I don't think people are ready to see you with someone new so soon. What's it been, three months?"

Dave's hackles continued to rise.

"Keely, I know this is going to be hard for you, and for a lot of people around here who loved Teresa and still miss her. But I made a promise to move on, and I intend to keep it. Kellie isn't going away. She's going to be involved in our lives. I'm not sure yet to what extent. But I'm not waiting any longer for the sake of waiting. And I really don't care about what society's rules say about that."

Keely nodded. She could see that the wise course of action was to back down and reconsider her position. The last thing she wanted was a dispute that would jeopardize her closeness with Dave and the kids.

The oven light clicked off. It was hot enough for Dave to put the enchiladas in.

Nikki walked in, smiling, and greeted Keely.

"Hi," Nikki said, reaching out to hug Keely.

"Hi, hon," Keely said. "I was just about to go. I've got some more errands to run."

And with that, she prepared to retreat.

Dave approached Keely, hugged her, and offered his thanks. "I appreciate your concern," he said.

She looked up to meet his eyes, and then looked away.

Friday, February 16, 2001

Kellie slowly sank all the way down into her tub and let the hot water envelope her.

She had put herself through a hard day, frantically trying to take care of as many housecleaning clients as possible to make extra money for her trip to Portland. In addition, she had cleaned all of the horses' water troughs, draining them with five-gallon buckets before scrubbing them with bleach.

Her shoulder was paying the price. She had fought with a vacuum cleaner earlier in the day that kept catching on a shag carpet. Her right arm was sore, from her fingers to her shoulder. It felt good to soak.

She was beginning to relax, leisurely washing with a soapy washcloth when she was suddenly startled to find an abnormal hard spot along her right breast. She pitched forward, splashing water onto the floor as she sat up straight. She felt it again, startled. It was the size of a pea, and she continued to rub it, hoping it would disappear if she changed positions. It didn't.

"Kiz! Come in here!" Kellie called out. In the next room, Kaysie had the stereo turned up loud, and didn't here her nickname being called.

"KIZ!" Kellie yelled louder, standing up in the tub. "KAY-SIE!"

"What is it?" Kaysie said, finally entering the bathroom. She could see her sister was concerned. "What's wrong?"

Kellie was still rubbing the strange spot under her right armpit. "Come here and feel this. It's a lump. Oh my God, it's so weird. It's a lump. I swear, Kiz, it's a lump!"

Kaysie walked over to the tub, which Kellie began to step out of. She could sense her sister's sudden panic. "Where?"

Kellie grabbed Kaysie's hand and placed it on the offending spot. "Right here. Do you feel it?"

"Oh my God, Kell, there is a lump." Kaysie was alarmed but tried to soothe her sister's worry. She knew exactly where Kellie's mind would go.

Together, they quietly began to discuss the possibilities, and none of them seemed acceptable. Kellie finished drying off and pulled on a sweatshirt and a pair of sweat pants.

They were both nervous. Kaysie grabbed Kellie's hand and led her into the room they used for an office.

How could this be happening? The question produced a surge of anxiety that screamed through Kellie's head. "Not now! Not to us!" she thought.

The future with Dave that she had been visualizing for the past three months seemed, in an instant, to be on the verge of collapsing.

Kellie pressed her eyes shut and clutched her hands together. "Please, God, don't let this happen to me, too. It's so unfair!"

Kellie recalled a statistic she had heard on *Oprah*, about how one in eight women are diagnosed with breast cancer.

She got on the phone with her mom, Brett, Chad and her father and told them what she feared.

Brett implored her not to tell Dave, at least not yet. Kellie didn't have to be reminded what sort of emotional wound this might inflict.

The next morning, Kellie called her doctor and made an appointment to have the lump examined. The doctor scheduled a mammogram.

Three nearly sleepless days later, with emotions taut with stress and worry, Kellie got a call from her doctor. It was good news.

The lump was not a tumor of any sort. It was merely a swollen lymph node, a result of Kellie's day of heavy lifting and wrestling with the vacuum cleaner.

The words sunk in quickly. Kellie was overcome with emotion. After hanging up, she collapsed on her bed and cried uncontrollably, clutching a photo of her and Dave at the coast.

She looked at the collage of photos that she had made of Dave, the kids, and Teresa, that she hung on her bedroom wall. Her tears dripped off her face and onto the picture frame. She was relieved beyond words. And she felt pangs of guilt, too, because when Teresa Grill got her phone call there was no good news.

It made Kellie cry even harder.

Thursday, February 22, 2001

Kellie arrived at Dave's house just as the Grills were gearing up for the weekend. Nikki and Lauren arrived home from school first, and Kellie volunteered to go with them to their haircut appointments while Dave waited for Johnny.

Kellie was eager to pick up where she had left off three months earlier with the girls. They laughed and talked easily and emphatically about everything. Kellie's hyperactive personality was in overdrive and the girls loved it.

Nikki, who recently had attained her driver's permit, drove Kellie and Lauren in the Olds Cutlass that Dave and Teresa had gotten from Ron and Jean. They took a meandering route back home through a new subdivision so that Nikki could have more driving practice.

"Nikki," Kellie said. "Have you thought of any good ideas for a song yet?"

Over the past week, Kellie and Nikki had talked on the phone about writing a song together. Kellie saw it as a way to forge a bond with Dave's oldest child.

"Well, I do have one idea but I'm not sure how good it is," Nikki said. "I wrote some words to a song I call 'Sail On,' about when life gives you hardship and you have to get past it."

"Oh, that sounds like a great idea!" Kellie said. "What have you got so far?"

"Not very much," Nikki said. "Just a chorus."

"Can you remember it enough to sing it?"

Nikki thought for a second, then hummed to find her pitch before beginning to sing:

> *"Sail high, above the tallest mountain,*
> *Try to fly and reach the brightest star.*
> *Don't let go of your dreams, keep sailing higher.*
> *When it seems like all hope is gone—sail on."*

"Nikki, that is really good," Lauren said from the backseat.

"Thanks."

"Lauren is right," Kellie agreed. "That is an amazing start. I know we can work with that and turn it into a great song. Are you sure you've never written a song before?"

"No. That's the first one," Nikki said, smiling proudly.

Back home, Kellie continued to visit throughout the evening. When it was time for bed, she retired to an air mattress in the family room. She was, after all, playing "friend" and nothing more.

Kellie tossed and turned, and the lyrics that Nikki had sung rolled through her head. She began to think of verses that would stick to the theme laid out by Nikki's chorus. Sail boats. Hang gliders. Moving on after suffering a loss. She let the tune play in her head and began to think of verses that might fit.

At 4:30 A.M., Kellie got up and silently grabbed a tape recorder and a legal pad out of her bag and walked out into the garage. She came up with the bridge first, jotting the words down and then softly singing them into the tape recorder.

Then she wrote down verses that went along with the theme of the song. She sang them into the recorder, and went through a process of rewinding the tape and recording better lyrics as she improved her ideas.

By 6 A.M., she had it. She sung the words into the tape recorder one final time, then set it down and crawled back into her bed for a little sleep.

When the kids got up an hour later, Kellie got up with them. She was eager to tell Nikki what she had been up to.

"I got up at 4:30 and worked on the song," Kellie said. "I think I about got it."

"Wow," Nikki said, impressed.

Kellie sang a few lines of the bridge to give Nikki an idea of where she had steered the song.

"Maybe we can work on it a little more when you get home from school and then you can sing it for everybody at dinner," Kellie suggested.

"Cool," Nikki said, "I'd love that."

Friday, February 23, 2001

While the kids were at school, Kellie made plans for the dinner she had been organizing since before she left Tennessee. She made a trip to the grocery store and checked off each item that she needed for the 15 guests that would be coming over. Once back at Dave's house, she quickly assembled trays of lasagna so that they were ready for the oven.

She had gotten phone numbers from Dave and invited some of his closest friends to the dinner. Her goal was that it would be a fun event, and that she would get to know some of the people she had met only briefly at the memorial.

When Nikki arrived home, Kellie played the tape recording of the song she had written. Kellie played it in sections so that Nikki could memorize the words and the melody.

"I love it!" Nikki said.

"Well, what do you think about singing it tonight?" Kellie asked.

"I may need to practice it a couple more times, but yeah, I want to give it a try," Nikki replied.

Nikki sat down at the computer and typed the lyrics:

> No one ever said life was gonna be easy
> I just never thought it could be this hard
> Livin' and learnin' we give love and get burned and
> Now it's time to mend my broken heart
>
> I know there's hope over that horizon
> I know hard times can only last so long
> I know someday the tides gonna go my way
> And it's the day to move on . . . It's time to sail on
> Sail on
>
> (Chorus)
> Sail high above the tallest mountain
> Try to fly and reach the brightest star
> Don't let go of your dreams, keep sailin' higher

When you feel like all hope is gone
Sail on

Life is bound to be full of surprises
Can lift us up just to let us down
Move us and shake us, bend us and break us
The sun's still shinin' even if there's clouds

Trust yourself you know the right direction
Through life's hardships we must stay strong
Don't get pushed around, fight back, stand your ground
Believe in you and you can't go wrong . . . It's time to sail on
Sail on

(Bridge)
Sail on til you see your bright tomorrow
Sail on til you're all that you can be
Sail on overcome your sorrow
Life can be all you dare to dream . . . Sail on

(Repeat chorus)

Nikki printed seven copies of the lyrics. Kellie went back to the kitchen and resumed preparing dinner.

Wilma and Gary showed up first. Kellie felt comfortable with them already. The Jacobsons came too, as well as two other couples that were longtime friends of Dave and Teresa. There were curious eyes at the dinner table, as the visitors observed Dave and the kids with a new woman. Dave and Kellie were a united front, and the kids were unfazed. Kellie appeared genuinely happy to let the dinner serve as a peek into their possible future together.

When everyone was finished eating, Nikki handed out the copies of "Sail On" and told everybody how the song had come together in the last 24 hours.

Then she sang it, beautifully.

The poignant lyrics sent several of the adults to tears. The simplicity in the words held a determined sense of heartfelt resolve and hope. Teresa's death was still a fresh wound for all of them. There was bravery in Nikki's delivery of the new song.

When Nikki finished singing, the party started to wind down. The guests left, and Kellie thanked each one profusely for coming. Gary and Wilma stayed the longest. Kellie and Wilma gravitated to the kitchen to clean up, and the girls chatted away with them. The girls began to tell Kellie about their childhoods, and Wilma filled in some of the pieces that they couldn't remember. The details of the girls' lives started to paint a more complete picture.

"Oh, I wish I could have seen what you girls looked like when you were little," Kellie said.

"We can show you," Lauren said.

Nikki and Lauren went to their rooms and dug out the scrapbooks that Wilma had made for them. They were filled with photos, stretching back all the way to when they were newborns.

The girls competed for Kellie's attention as they found their favorite pictures and showed them to her. Kellie gushed over them and coaxed the girls to tell her the stories that went along with the pictures.

Dave, Gary and Johnny heard the laughter and joined in on the stories being told in the kitchen.

Meanwhile, Johnny quietly disappeared from the room.

He returned a few minutes later with his scrapbook.

"I want to show you mine," Johnny said.

Without waiting for a response, he set the book down on the countertop and squeezed between the edge of the counter and the stool that Kellie was sitting on. He moved onto Kellie's lap and began to open the book.

Kellie's eyes widened. She turned and caught a glimpse of Wilma, who smiled and gave her a wink.

Sitting at the kitchen table, Dave noticed what had just happened as well. He caught his mother's glance too, and was pleasantly surprised himself.

Johnny flipped open the first page and began to explain to Kellie what he knew about each photo, stretching back to his earliest days. He turned each page and continued showing Kellie the pictures of birthdays, fishing trips, Christmas mornings, school and sports.

Kellie listened intently, holding Johnny in place on her lap by wrapping her arms around his waist. She asked questions about who was in the photos with him and Johnny patiently explained each one.

Kellie was struck by how eager Johnny was to bring her up to speed on his life and let her know who he was.

Saturday, February 24, 2001

Dave had the kids up earlier than usual on a Saturday so they would be ready in time to meet Doug Hart.

Dave had set up the visit with Doug and Kathy Hart—the parents of Johnny's best friend, Taylor—so that Kellie and the kids could have a "horse fix." The Harts had polo horses and acreage in Lake Oswego.

Dave pulled the Suburban up to the Harts' Tualatin home, where he had arranged to meet Doug.

"Doug's car isn't here. I know he said he'd meet us here at nine.

I'll go see if he's here," Dave said, putting the Suburban into park and opening the door to get out. He walked over to the front door and pressed on the doorbell. He waited nearly two minutes before Kathy cracked open the door and peered out into the daylight.

She was still in her white bathrobe. Her hair was tousled. It looked like she'd just woken up.

"Yes?" Kathy said, blinking her eyes to wake before noticing it was Dave. She raise her eyes a little further out the door and saw Kellie and the kids in the Suburban. She smiled hesitantly, but she was clearly thrown off by their arrival.

"Doug told us to meet him here," Dave started to explain.

Kathy's face bore no indication that she knew anything about it. The conversation after that was brief. Dave apologized for waking her and walked back to the Suburban. Kathy waved to Kellie and the kids as she closed the door.

Dave pulled open his driver's side door, chuckling.

"Oh, Doug is going to be in *trouble*," he said.

"Why? Where is he?" Kellie asked.

"I guess he's working out at the club this morning and is just going to meet us over at his parents' house," Dave explained. "I just woke up Kathy and she is so embarrassed. She said the boys are with Doug at the club. She is pissed. She hates to be put on the spot like that."

Dave continued toward Lake Oswego.

"Well I feel bad," Kellie said, feeling sympathetic to Kathy. "I wish Doug would have called us."

"Oh, it'll be fine," Dave said. "I think it's kind of funny."

He picked up his cell phone to dial Doug.

"Hey, are you working out?" he asked into the phone. "Oh, OK. Yeah, I woke up Kathy. She's not happy but she did say that when we're done riding to call her and she'll meet us wherever we want to do lunch."

Dave pulled to the side of the road near the corner of Borland and Stafford roads—commonly called Wanker's Corner. He still needed directions from Doug.

From there, the morning moved more quickly. The kids all helped to brush and groom the two horses and a little black pony. They took turns riding the horses in the covered arena.

Kellie took a short turn after Doug on a chestnut thoroughbred mare named Cindy. Kellie was impressed as she watched Doug saddle and ride the horses. He definitely knew his way around the animals, much like she did.

Doug's parents, snowbirds, were still in California, so they had the horses to themselves.

Kellie vaguely remembered a brief introduction to Doug and Kathy Hart, and their two young boys, at Teresa's memorial service. She remembered how Johnny and Taylor had seemed fastened at the hip that weekend.

Doug told Kellie how his family had been in Hawaii during Thanksgiving the week that Teresa died. After Johnny's phone call with Taylor, Doug and Kathy had decided to come back early. They had been heartbroken at the news, and saw how Taylor had been affected by the call.

"My mom is dead and my best friend is gone," Johnny had said, near tears, into the phone to Kathy. The Harts booked a flight and made it back in time for the memorial service. "Friends" didn't seem like a strong enough word for the bond forged between the two families. Kellie could see that it felt more like extended family.

After the horses were put away and turned out to pasture, Kathy pulled up the driveway in a black Ford Expedition. She got out and walked up to meet Kellie.

"Hi," Kathy said warmly, extending a hand to shake Kellie's. "I'm Kathy."

She was dressed now, in blue jeans with a harvest orange-colored sweater. Her shoulder-length blond hair and makeup were now perfectly done.

"Hi," Kellie said eagerly. "I'm Kellie. It's nice to meet you."

"Likewise," Kathy said. She gave her youngest boy, Connor, a hug, and asked, to no one in particular: "Did you have fun riding?"

"It was really fun," Kellie said. "Thanks for letting us do it."

"Well don't thank me," Kathy said. "Thank Doug for that."

Doug approached and greeted his wife.

"Hey honey," Doug said. "Are you going to go to eat with us?"

"Yes. Where are you going?"

"How about Billigan's Road House?" Dave suggested, entering the conversation.

"Yum, they have great steaks," Nikki said, turning to share her knowledge with Kellie.

"And you can throw your peanut shells on the floor," Lauren added. "I'm starving. Let's go!"

The three vehicles rolled single file toward lunch.

The five kids took up the end of the big table, while the adults sat across from one another and chatted. They laughed and told stories and Dave or Doug occasionally reprimanded the boys for throwing peanut shells across the restaurant.

Dave and Kellie did their best to try to act like amiable friends and nothing more. There was nothing romantic between them, no touching or ogling eyes. It still felt too early to be openly public with their affection for one another.

That night, at the Harts' house, Kathy and Doug talked briefly of their day with the Grill family and Kellie.

"They're a couple, you know," Kathy said matter-of-factly as she was getting ready for bed.

"Who are a couple?" Doug asked, puzzled as he brushed his teeth.

"Kellie and Dave," Kathy said. "They are trying to fake it but I saw the way they looked at each other. They are a couple and I think this is really serious stuff. I can just tell they are both really into each other, and she just loves those kids."

"Oh, Kathy, I don't think so," Doug said. "I think she's just Brett's little sister. She's known Dave and his family forever."

"No," Kathy said, insistently. "Mark my words. It's more than that. A woman knows. And I just know it."

She was eager to show him she was right.

"Watch this," she said. She turned toward the door to her bedroom and called out for Taylor.

Seconds later, the tall 10-year-old appeared at the door.

"Yeah mom?" he said.

"Tell me about Kellie and Dave," Kathy said. "What does Johnny say about her?"

The boy was suddenly a little nervous. "Well. . . ."

"Is Dave dating her?" his mom asked.

"How do you know? Did Johnny tell you?" Taylor replied.

"No, it's just a feeling I had," Kathy said. "So it's true? They are a couple?"

"Yeah," Taylor admitted. "But no one is supposed to know yet. They know it's too soon and Johnny said not to tell anyone. You can't tell, mom, OK?"

"I won't," Kathy said, reassuring her son. She turned to catch her husband's reaction.

"I'll be damned," Doug said, shaking his head. "I would have never thought of it."

"We women know these things," Kathy said, smiling.

Kathy considered this new information. She liked Kellie, and also how Dave's family radiated happiness and contentment around her.

There was a new spark, and its name was Kellie.

Monday, February 26, 2001

Dave was at work and the kids were at school, leaving Kellie inside the family's home alone for the first time.

She took a sip of her hot black tea and rubbed the top of Hannah's furry head. As she took her hand away she noticed the loose strands of black fur that fell to the kitchen floor.

"Oh, girl, you are shedding something awful," Kellie said softly to the dog.

Kellie had made an effort to clean the house—swept, mopped, vacuumed and dusted—before Friday's lasagna dinner. But the kitchen was a mess once again. The basset hound, Gideon, and the greyhound/lab mix, Lucy, only added to the problem. The dogs were tracking in mud from outside. Kellie noticed cobwebs and dust on the curtains and drapes. The comforters and sheets on the beds all needed to be washed.

She decided to spend her morning giving the house an early spring-cleaning.

After finishing her tea, Kellie got to work. She went upstairs and stripped off all the bedding, including blankets and bed spreads. She brought the heavy laundry downstairs and started the first load in the washer.

She took all of the curtains and drapes off their rods and took them into the backyard to beat and shake the dust out of them. She took the window coverings in the garage and piled them next to the mountain of bedding.

She found a bottle of Windex under the sink and began to wash the insides of all of the windows in the two-story house. She paused only to rotate loads of laundry through the washer and dryer.

It was mid-afternoon by the time Kellie finished mopping the kitchen floor, and she was exhausted. The washer and dryer were still working on curtains, but she had remade all of the beds in the house with clean sheets, blankets and comforters. It felt like quite an accomplishment to see it all done.

Kellie talked with Dave on the phone and told him all that she had been up to.

He was impressed, and thanked her, but insisted that she didn't have to work on her vacation.

"I don't mind," Kellie told Dave. "In fact, I feel a great satisfaction helping you guys out. Honestly, it makes me feel good to do this for you."

Dave knew that some of the household upkeep had fallen behind in recent months and he was glad to have Kellie's energy to tackle it.

"OK," Dave said. "We'll take you out to a delicious Italian dinner at Caro Amicos tonight as payment for services rendered."

Kellie was invigorated by the sound of Dave's voice. It made all the work seem worth it.

"It's a deal, mister," she said.

Wilma stopped by soon after she hung up with Dave. She knew Kellie was alone and she wanted to visit. She was surprised by Kellie's progress.

"Oh, this house has needed a deep cleaning for so long, it looks great!" Wilma said, hugging Kellie. "Thank you. You've gotten so much done today."

"Yeah, Kaysie says I'm a tornado when I clean," Kellie said. "I plan on doing the laundry room tomorrow and getting all of the dirty clothes washed and folded and put away—even the socks."

Kellie was referring to the chair in the family room that had become the unofficial home of unmatched socks, and there were dozens of scattered singles.

"Well, let us know if we can help," Wilma said, including Gary in the offer.

"It's really OK," Kellie assured her. "I can do it."

Kellie told Wilma about their dinner plans and invited her and Gary to join them. Another look at the clock convinced Kellie to get moving again.

"I'd better get in the shower," Kellie said. "The kids will be home any minute." She stashed the mop and bucket.

"Okay, well we'll see you tonight," Wilma said. "Thanks again Kellie. You're a sweetheart."

"Oh, you're welcome," Kellie said. "What can I say? I love this crazy bunch! Love will make you do crazy things."

"You're right about that," Wilma said, reaching out to give Kellie a hug before leaving. "Just don't work too hard. You know this is your vacation."

"I know, but I'll get to party and vacation soon enough in Salt Lake for Brett's birthday."

Wilma left and Kellie rushed up the stairs to get in the shower. She wanted to be fresh and ready again to greet the three kids and Dave when they got home. She was eager to see their reaction to what she had been up to all day.

Even though he had been on the phone with her three times already, Dave was a little unprepared by the difference Kellie had made in his house. The last four months, he and the kids had tackled the necessities. Most everything else had fallen by the wayside.

Dave had stacks of unpaid bills, and although he had been diligent about rotating dirty laundry through the washer and dryer, he was usually a couple of piles behind. Dishes got cleaned, but usually on an every-other-day cycle. Sometimes it was more like two or three days.

But Kellie had brought a new energy to the house. She had the ability to see things that needed attention, prioritize them, and then complete the tasks in short order. It was clear to Dave, and his kids, that it was something they had been sorely lacking.

CHAPTER NINE

Put To The Test

Wednesday, February 28, 2001

Kellie had all three kids up early, and took them out to breakfast at the Pig 'N Pancake. There was excitement buzzing around all of them. The kids were looking forward to leaving in the afternoon for the warm weather in Arizona, where they would see the Ralston family—Aunt Tami, Uncle Scott and the cousins, Makenna and Al.

Meanwhile, Kellie was anxiously awaiting her trip with Dave to Salt Lake City for Brett's 40th birthday bash. And she was just one day from her own birthday. It would be her first birthday with Dave. Kellie was happy for the kids, and they were happy for her. It felt like everyone was going to come out a winner.

On the way home, Kellie took the passenger seat and let Nikki drive. They took a meandering route through the green rolling hills of Stafford, a prime real estate area where mansions sprouted up next to old stands of Douglas fir, surrounded by lush, manicured lawns.

Jean and Ron arrived at Dave's house about 10 minutes early. They pulled up in their platinum Tahoe. Nikki, driving the Oldsmobile, was right behind them.

"Well, where did you come from?" Jean said, smiling as she watched her grandchildren emerge from the car.

"We were right behind you coming from breakfast, and I was driving," Nikki said excitedly, approaching "Gigi" to give her a hug.

"You guys are early," Lauren noted. "How are you? It's so good to see you." She too raced forward, hugging her grandfather.

Johnny was right behind them. "Hi Gigi! Hi Papa!"

"Well hello you darling kiddos," Gigi said, embracing one at a time. "We got here early because the roads were so clear through the Santiam Pass."

"Not an ounce of snow on the roads," Ron said. "Clear as a bell." The grandparents then turned their attention to the woman behind the kids.

"Hello," Jean said. "How are you doing, Kellie?"

"Fine thanks," Kellie said, cheerfully as ever. "How are you guys? You look great."

Kellie approached and gave Jean a hug.

"Good," Jean replied. "We're doing pretty well all things considered."

Kellie let go and greeted Ron, who was already walking toward the front door of the house.

"Hi Ron," Kellie said.

"Hi," Ron said, barely turning to look at her.

"Are you kids ready?" Jean asked.

"Yep," Lauren answered. "We're all packed. Our bags are in the front entry."

"Good," Jean said, following her husband into the house. Kellie followed them in.

"This house is so clean," Jean said, blurting out the words with some astonishment.

"Yeah," Nikki said, agreeing. "Kellie gave it a spring cleaning. She even washed all of the curtains and windows."

"It looks good," Jean said, pivoting in the living room to notice a spotlessness that hadn't even existed when Teresa was healthy. Ron wandered through the first floor, from the kitchen to the family room, noticing the same thing. Yellow daffodils brightened up the kitchen table in a small vase.

"Thanks," Kellie said, self-consciously. "I've had a few days to do some things before we fly down to Salt Lake for Brett's birthday. I thought I'd make myself useful."

"You did a nice job," Jean said.

"Oh, thanks," Kellie said, feeling slightly awkward. "I do it for a living so I'd better be good at it, right? The songwriting doesn't seem to pay the bills. I'm proudest of the laundry room. Do you want to see it?"

"Sure," Jean said, still wide-eyed. "Come on Pops, let's go see the laundry room."

Kellie led Jean and Ron into the garage and turned on the light. The once impossibly messy corner of the garage was suddenly neat and organized.

"I found lots of food that had expired so I tossed it out, and I got all of the laundry caught up," Kellie explained, smiling. "Gary even helped me match the socks up."

"Well that's good," Jean said, doing her best to remain pleasant. Ron started talking to Johnny about a fishing article he had been reading.

"What did you do with any clothes that you found of Teresa's?" Jean asked with some seriousness in her tone.

"I only found a yellow sweater," Kellie replied. "I just washed it and hung it up in her closet."

"Good," Jean said, satisfied. She moved back through the door leading to the family room. "Well ... We'd better get your bags loaded and get going. We don't want to be late and there's no telling how traffic will be."

The kids grabbed their bags and started to carry them outside. Kellie had bought each of the kids gum and candy, magazines and batteries for their Walkmans for the trip. Jean paused and returned her attention to Kellie. Ron remained quiet.

"So when will David be home?" Jean asked.

"He's supposed to be here in about two hours," Kellie responded. "Our flight to Salt Lake is at three o'clock."

"Well good," Jean said. "Have a safe flight and tell that big brother of yours to have a wonderful birthday for us, OK?"

"I will," Kellie said, smiling.

Ron stacked the kids' bags in the back of the SUV.

"Bye, Kellie," Lauren squealed, rushing over to give her a hug and a kiss on the cheek. "Thanks for everything. I'll read my magazine on the plane. Tell uncle Brett 'Hi' and 'Happy birthday' and have fun, and happy birthday to you tomorrow, too."

"Thanks, sweetie," Kellie said. "You have fun too."

"Bye, Kell," Nikki said. "Thanks for everything, especially the song." Nikki reached out to hug Kellie.

"We wrote a song together while she's been here," Nikki informed her grandparents.

"That's great," Jean said.

"I'll sing it to you on the way to the airport. It's called 'Sail On,'" Nikki said.

"OK," Jean said.

"Bye Kellie," Johnny chimed in. "Have fun and tell Brett 'Hi' from me, OK?"

"I will," Kellie assured him. "Have fun with your cousin Al. See you later Mr. J. It sure has been fun being here with you these past few days."

"Yeah, it has," Johnny said, nodding his approval.

Jean and Ron watched and listened to the kids gush over Kellie as they said their good-byes. They weren't sure what to make of it.

"We'll see you in Nashville!" Lauren shouted, excitedly from her window in the back seat of the SUV.

"Yeah! It won't be long and you'll be in my territory. It will be a blast," Kellie said, waving to them as Ron turned on the ignition.

"Bye, Ron and Jean," Kellie said, standing near Jean's open window. "Have a safe flight and have fun with Tamara, Scott and the kids. Please tell them 'Hi' from Dave and me."

So she was speaking for Dave, now, too? Jean smiled back at Kellie but clenched her jaw as she did.

With one final attempt at cheer, Jean said, "We will." And then she pushed the button to raise the window.

Kellie went back into the empty house where she was greeted by the three dogs, panting, licking and wagging their tails.

"I wish everyone was as accepting of me as you three," Kellie told them as she kneeled to pet the dogs. This was the first of many mountains Kellie knew she would need to climb in order to gain favor from people that still held Teresa's memory close to their hearts. Jean and Ron represented the steepest, toughest mountain of all. Kellie, for the first time, saw that winning over Teresa's parents wasn't going to be easy. She was going to have to earn it.

The Delta Airlines flight to Salt Lake City was crowded and the boarding was slow. Dave and Kellie inched their way toward the back of the plane and squeezed into two seats next to one other.

Kellie held Dave's hand as she thought about the last few days with the Grill family. It had been a whirlwind of activities and events. The one weighing on her mind, though, was the slightly uncomfortable meeting with Teresa's parents, Jean and Ron.

It had gone fine, Kellie told herself. But as she relayed the events to Dave she grew worried that they were going to present an obstacle she couldn't overcome.

"Oh, it will all work out," Dave said, consoling her. "They don't hate you. They just hate what you represent: A new woman in the place where their daughter used to be. It's not you. They would feel this way about anyone who was stepping in."

"I guess you're right," Kellie said. "It's just that they made me feel so awkward, when all I've done is tried to help you guys and . . ."

Kellie was stopped short.

"You have helped us, Kell, tremendously," Dave said. "And soon they will see that. It's just going to take time. I'm sorry if they hurt your feelings. Just don't take it personal. They really are wonderful people, and they will soon come around. It's just going to take a while."

"Oh, I know," Kellie said. "And I know they're wonderful. I feel so bad for them, and I just want them to know how sincere I really am."

"They will," Dave said. "Everyone eventually will figure it out. You're pretty special, young lady."

With that, Dave leaned over the armrest and kissed Kellie lightly on her lips.

"I love ya," he said. "Thanks for being here."

"I know I'm probably overreacting," Kellie said sheepishly. "I love you too. It's just . . . I'm such a softie, I hate for anybody to hurt, or act weird toward me."

"Let's not dwell on it," Dave said, reassuringly. "It will be fine. They have the kids, and we are going to celebrate two birthdays."

Dave's good mood eased Kellie's worries. He was clearly looking forward to seeing his old high school friends again.

"It will be fun, and I get to spend my birthday with you," Kellie reminded him. "That's the best present of all."

Kellie raised Dave's hand and kissed it.

The flight went quickly as they talked about the plans for Brett's 40th on Saturday.

Dave felt as loose and relaxed as he could remember. Away from Tualatin and around his old buddies he felt free to bask in Kellie's warmth and love, and he returned those feelings to her openly. He was in love. Life felt good that weekend.

Dave and Kellie had some time alone at Brett's while he was at work, and they made use of it. They made love in the guest bedroom, allowing their passion for one another to boil to the surface.

With time to kill in the afternoon before Brett was due home, they spent the lazy hours in bed.

"Sometimes when I think of how I used to not be able to look into your beautiful green eyes I can't believe I was ever that scared of you," Kellie said.

"Well, you weren't ever *scared* of me, were you?" Dave asked.

"OK, maybe not scared but definitely nervous. Or maybe I was a little bit scared by the power I felt you had over me," Kellie said.

She continued to let her mind wander, lying comfortably in the crook of Dave's arm.

"I mean your eyes, your body, your voice," Kellie said. "It's just . . . there is nothing sexy about you."

Dave listened to Kellie's misspoken words and pretended to take offense.

"Nothing?"

"What?" Kellie asked.

"You said that there is nothing sexy about me. I just wondered if you really meant nothing," Dave said, dryly.

"Wait a minute. Did I say that?" Kellie said, trying to remember her words.

"You said there's nothing sexy about me," Dave said, still pretending to be serious.

Kellie began to stammer. "I . . . I did? Well . . . I didn't mean to. I meant to say there is nothing that isn't sexy about you. I meant to say 'isn't.' I'm sorry."

"No," Dave said, feigning some disappointment. "You definitely said 'nothing.' I'm going to have to go with what you said first."

"Oh, Dave, stop it!" Kellie said, beginning to giggle. "You know I didn't mean that. Now you better quit teasing me, mister! You're ruthless!"

Kellie began to bite his shoulder, playfully.

"I meant nothing that isn't sexy. You better believe me," she pleaded.

"Well I think everything about you is sexy," Dave said, continuing to play. "I just wish you liked something about me."

Kellie snuggled closer.

"OK," she said. "You got me. It's hopeless isn't it? I know you'll never let me live this down."

"Nope," Dave said, smiling. He tilted Kellie's chin up and kissed her softly.

"You're too fun to tease," he said.

Monday, March 5, 2001

Dave checked his watch and estimated that the plane carrying Jean and Ron had probably just touched down. He waited at his desk at Metro Metals for their phone call. The kids weren't due back for a few more days.

Dave's cell phone rang, on cue.

"David, this is Jean."

The words were terse and to the point.

"We just landed. We're going to take a cab to Metro Metals to pick up the car. Just leave our keys at the front desk and we will pick them up there."

Dave was at a loss for words. The airport was no more than 10 minutes from his office. Jean's words didn't make sense.

"Uh, well . . . that's alright. I can come and get you," he replied.

Jean reiterated her instructions, only there was more emphasis in her voice. Dave could tell by her tone that she wasn't happy. He didn't immediately understand.

"No, I think it would be best if you leave them at the front desk," she said sternly. "We'll get them there."

Dave furrowed his brow, wondering what the problem was, but chose not to argue.

"Sure," Dave said, after a pause. "I'll leave them at the front desk."

"Thank you."

Jean hung up and Dave set his phone down. He pulled open his desk drawer and picked up their car keys, and started to walk toward the reception area. The wheels began to turn in Dave's head. Why the frosty reception? Did the kids say something that startled their grandparents? Something about Kellie? Or the trip to the coast?

Dave handed the keys to the receptionist.

"My in-laws are coming to pick these up and they should be here in about 15 minutes," Dave said. "Let me know when they've picked them up, OK?" He decided to retreat to his office, wanting to make sure he didn't accidentally run into them.

"Sure, Dave," the receptionist said.

Back in his office, Dave was still trying to guess what had caused this new problem. Clearly, the last person Jean and Ron wanted to see was him. But why?

He dialed Tamara.

"Tamara, what is going on? Your mom just called and told me not to pick them up. They are taking a cab to my work to pick up the keys to their car from the front desk. They obviously don't want to see me," Dave informed her.

This news didn't come as any surprise to Tamara.

"Dave," she said. "The shit has hit the fan."

"Why? What happened down there? Did the kids say something?"

"No," Tamara said. "Apparently when they came to your house Kellie was there and it surprised them. She had cleaned, she had packed the kids' suitcases and mom and dad felt like she had taken over. It looked to them like a new woman had taken charge of Teresa's home."

Dave paused briefly while he considered that.

Tamara continued.

"As soon as they got here, they backed me into a corner and wanted to know everything that I knew about you and Kellie, and what's going on. So I told them. *Everything.*"

"OK," Dave said. "That's fine. I'm not sure I get why that's such a huge problem."

"Dave, in their minds this is way too soon. And I'm sure it was just a difficult situation for them to face."

Dave's mind reeled back across the weeks and he recalled telling Jean that Kellie would be at the house when they arrived.

"They knew she was going to be there," Dave protested. "I still don't understand what's got them so pissed."

"You've got to try and understand," Tamara said. "They've lost a daughter. And even if they knew Kellie was going to be there, when they were faced with her, it was more than they could handle."

Dave sighed.

"What happened the rest of the time?" Dave asked.

"Dave, it was maybe the worst week I've ever had with them," Tamara said. "They were irritable with me, irritable with the kids. Everyone was walking on eggshells all week."

"What did the kids say? Did they know their grandparents were so angry?" Dave asked.

"Oh yeah," Tamara said. "They knew it. I'm not sure if they fully understood why. The kids showed up so excited they were all bouncing off the walls. Actually, I think mom was expecting them to be a little more subdued and solemn. That just fed into the aggravation."

Dave began to see the picture a little clearer, but he didn't like it.

"Well, Tam," he said. "I'm sorry that I put everyone in that position. But I'm not sorry that Kellie was here. Yes, she has been an incredible help around here, and I'm sorry that Jean and Ron got so upset about it. I'm sorry you had to take the brunt of it. Do you think I should call and talk to them?"

"Honestly, I think I'd let it rest for a few days," Tamara said.

Internally, Dave could feel himself beginning to fume.

"OK," Dave said. "The reality is I don't owe anyone an explanation of what I'm doing."

"I know you don't," Tamara said. "Just try to be empathetic to their feelings."

"Tam, I am very empathetic, but people have to understand that I've lost my wife, and the kids have lost their mother and we're just beginning to figure out how we're going to go on with our lives." Dave said emphatically. "The decisions I make are no one's business but mine, and I don't need to be second guessed or take any shit over what I decide to do."

"I know you don't," Tamara said. "This is just a difficult situation for everybody. Please try to be understanding of their feelings."

"OK," Dave said. "Thanks again for having everybody. I guess I'll see the kids on Wednesday, huh?"

"Yeah."

"I'll talk to you soon then," Dave said. "Bye."

"Bye, Dave."

Dave hung up the phone feeling stunned. The more he thought about it, the more defensive he became. He knew that Jean and Ron were three hours from home and that it wasn't a good time to try and reach them. He knew it would be an ugly conversation.

Dave left work and went home to his empty house, still grasping with this new, unpleasant information. All through Dave's marriage to Teresa he had felt uncommonly close to his mother- and father-in-law. He had spent countless holidays with them both, and been hunting and fishing with Ron at least a dozen times. Never in his wildest dreams had he expected a situation to come along where his relationship with them could be eroded.

However, he felt this issue might put all that to the test. He was in no mood to answer to anybody about how to move on with his life, especially his new relationship. The one exception would have been a veto from the kids. But all three of them had seemingly bonded with Kellie and not only approved, but encouraged, the match.

Dave didn't have an appetite for dinner. Instead he sat down at his desk and began to type a letter on the computer. In it, he outlined his frustration with Jean and Ron's reaction to Kellie and their sullen behavior in Arizona. He felt like they were judging him and he was in no mood to feel guilty. The letter was direct and made no attempt at diplomacy. His thoughts streamed out through his fingers.

He paused to read the letter and it summed up perfectly the way he felt. Ron and Jean could either accept his decisions concerning himself and the kids, or they could detach themselves. At that moment, he didn't care. The choice was theirs.

It was 11 P.M. by the time he stopped and printed the letter.

He dialed Kellie, hoping she was still awake in Tennessee.

"Hi," Kellie whispered excitedly. She was in bed but not yet asleep. She knew that a call this late must be from Dave.

"Did I wake ya?" Dave asked.

"No, I was just laying here thinking about you," Kellie said.

Dave quickly reset the tone of the call.

"The shit has hit the fan," Dave said, remembering Tamara's apt phrase.

Kellie sat up. "What do you mean? What's the matter?"

Dave led Kellie through the day's events and the conversation he had earlier with Tamara.

Kellie cringed as she heard how the new problem had unfolded.

"I wrote a letter to them and I was wondering if I could read it to you first," Dave said.

"Sure, go ahead."

Dave picked up the letter and read it, emphasizing the points that he intended to hammer home.

"Oh my God, Dave," Kellie implored. "You can't send that to them!"

"Why?" Dave said. "I'm not going to kowtow to them."

"But Dave," Kellie said, "they're the grandparents. And this has all got to be extremely difficult for them. That letter is too vicious. It will drive a wedge between you and them."

"They need to understand where I'm coming from," Dave said. "I'm giving them the choice. They can either accept what's going on, or they can choose not to be a part of our life."

"Oh, Dave you can't!" Kellie said, adamantly. "They've just lost a daughter. You know how much she meant to them. It's going to take them some time. I don't think you can give them an ultimatum like that."

Dave continued to make his points and Kellie tried to get him to soften them. Over the next several hours, Kellie persuaded Dave to reconsider and compose a less hostile version of the letter.

"Let them hate me but don't let this destroy your relationship with them," Kellie said. "You guys are so close and the kids adore them. You can't lose them. They're too important. At least sleep on it and see how you feel tomorrow. Will you do that?"

Dave finally agreed.

"Thanks for listening," he said. "I better let you get to bed. I love you."

"I love you too," Kellie said. "I'm sorry having me in your life is putting you through all this."

"Don't be," Dave replied.

"OK. Goodnight. Call me tomorrow and let me know what you're going to do."

Dave considered all that Kellie had to say. He put the letter in a desk drawer.

Maybe the need to send it would blow over.

Saturday, March 10, 2001

Dave rolled out of bed and took another look at his letter.

The last few days had done little to calm him down. A short, icy phone conversation with Jean on Wednesday night after the kids had gotten home had only intensified the fracture he felt was growing between him and his in-laws. Dave had talked with the kids upon their arrival, and he didn't like what he heard from them, either.

The rest of the week, Dave's mind had strayed to how to resolve this new problem.

He sat down at the computer again and began to chip away at some of the jagged edge that he knew would cut a little too deep.

It still contained the basics. This time, he decided to try it out on Tamara.

"Hi Tam. It's Dave," he said as she picked up the phone.

"How are you this morning?" Tamara asked.

"Well, I'm still a little agitated about what's going on with Ron and Jean, and how they treated you and the kids in Arizona," Dave said. "I've had a conversation with your mom, and we still have some issues to deal with. I have written a letter to them and I thought I would read it to you before I send it to them."

"OK," she said.

"First of all, Tamara, I was so pissed after I got off the phone with you Monday," Dave said. "I wrote a pretty scathing letter when I got home that night. But I called Kellie and read it to her and she said it was too harsh. I've just revised it and tried to tone it down some, and I was hoping you'd tell me what you think."

"OK," she said again.

Dave recited the new version of the letter, never pausing until the end.

When he was finished, he asked, "So, what did you think?"

"I don't blame you at all for what you're feeling," Tamara began. "The only thing I can say is remember what a great relationship you've had with my parents and how important their relationship is with your kids. Try to put yourself in their shoes when you re-read it, knowing the grief that they're still going through. They're both still very raw, emotionally. I think you make some very valid points and concerns, but you'll need to decide if one more revision is in order. If you decide to send that letter, I think you're justified in doing so."

Dave thought about the content of his letter once again.

"I hope that they can accept it," Dave said. "I'll continue to work with the wording. I know it still has some hostility in it."

"I know you'll decide what's right," Tamara said. Her gentle persuasion coaxed another re-write out of Dave.

He sat at the computer once again, and attempted to calm some of the storm that raged in the language of the letter.

Monday, March 12, 2001

Dave sat in front of his computer for a third time and tried to articulate his feelings again, hoping to eliminate some more of the hard edge. He was much more diplomatic in his approach this time.

He had nothing to hide and nothing to be ashamed of. He had no patience for anyone, even Teresa's parents, who would take offense with Kellie or his own decision-making. This time he was careful and tactful, though still in no mood for apologies.

Dear Ron and Jean,

First and foremost, I want to remind you that I respect, admire and love the two of you very much. I sincerely hope you remain actively involved in my life and the lives of your grandchildren. That is a choice the two of you have total control over. You will always be welcome in our home with one condition. The kids, myself and anyone else that may venture into our lives are a package deal. All-inclusive. Let me also remind you, as a forty-year-old father of three, I really don't owe you any explanation about anything I have done in the past, or what I may do in the future. However, because I respect and care for you and because you are the grandparents of Teresa's children, I will give you the courtesy of explaining what seems to be a major source of aggravation and confusion for you.

Before I begin, if you have any doubt about the love I had and continue to have for Teresa, the devotion, the commitment, as well as the sorrow and pain I feel having lost her, stop reading now. If you feel that way, you have become so blinded by your sorrow that nothing I say will ever be heard or accepted. Because I want there to be nothing misconstrued, I am choosing to write rather than call you on the phone. Let me address two issues I understand are specifically bothering you.

1. Is there a relationship developing with Kellie Poulsen? Yes. I have known Kellie and her family for over 22 years. Brett is my all-time best friend. I know the quality of their family. What I didn't know was the fact that she has had feelings for me since she was 12 years old. A short time ago, Kellie put her heart on the line and confessed her feelings for me. She conveyed those feelings knowing full well it was "too soon," but if I ever felt ready to see other people, she would like to be considered. As Ron has continually reminded me, "always keep your lateral options open." Well, I did. I called Kellie the next day and suggested she come out to Oregon. I wanted to find out if this was anything we wanted to pursue or if she should just remain "Brett's

little sister." The long and short of it is, yes, there is a relationship developing. Where it ends up remains to be seen. The only thing I know for certain is I will continue to pursue her and my children are very accepting of that. They are my one and only concern.

2. You felt "blindsided" because you didn't know she'd be here? If that is true, I apologize. Jean, I know we specifically discussed her visit, including where she was going to stay. I went so far as to tell you that she would be staying with us and, just like when Susan visits, John would move in with me, Lauren would use John's room and Kellie would use Lauren's room. Ron, I do believe you were in the garage during that conversation, but even so, I had no doubt you knew she would be here. We discussed logistics of how she and I were leaving for Salt Lake after the kids' departure to Arizona. If I were trying to hide anything, believe me, she would have been nowhere in sight when you arrived.

The last thing I want to do is hurt either of you. We have been through more than I would wish for my worst enemy. The day we lost Teresa I could have easily laid down and died myself. I can only imagine how difficult it was and is to lose a child. God forbid any parent should have to go through that. Although I didn't hear her voice, I felt Teresa urging me not to lie around crying and asking why God took her from the kids and me. I vowed at that moment that if anyone expected me to lie down and surrender, they could forget it! For the kids' sake, that will never happen.

For the record, there will never be a day I don't think about Teresa. There is not a waking moment that she is not in my thoughts. As I move ahead with my life without her, it is because of her that I am able to move ahead. She and I discussed things that I will never share with anyone else. One thing I will say: Teresa and I will be together for eternity. Whether or not anyone believes this is of no concern to me. Only Teresa and I truly know the bond we had. Somehow our children understand that bond as well. They are moving on with their lives and they are supporting me in moving ahead with mine. If only you could feel a fraction of the comfort I feel from that bond, then and only then could you begin to understand how I can move on. I have no guilt, no regrets, and no remorse. Any unanswered questions Teresa may have had for me before she died have certainly been answered as she searched my heart.

Jean and Ron, I pray that somehow you can find peace and comfort soon. There is comfort in family. Don't take out your frustrations on Tamara or the grandkids. If you are feeling guilty about anything you said or didn't say to Teresa, tell her, she will understand. She will hear you. If you ever have questions about what I am doing or what the kids or doing, just call and ask. We have nothing to hide from you. The love we felt as a family the last days and hours of Teresa's life were as real as it gets. As difficult as it was to go through, find strength from the love that filled that room. If you don't, you will become bitter, broken, old people. Don't let that happen. As I said, my door will always be open to you, but you will have to accept whoever and whatever is on the other side of it. The choice is entirely up to you.

As for the kids and me, we are moving ahead with our lives. We have no idea what is ahead for us, but we have vowed to move on and face every challenge head on. We know that if we don't we will have to answer to "mom." She is a part of our daily conversation. We will forever cherish the memories we have of her and she will always be a part of our lives. I will do everything in my power to make sure her memory stays fresh in their minds. I sincerely hope you will be around to help me do this. The ball is in your court. Let me know what you're going to do with it.

With utmost respect and sincerity,

Dave signed the bottom of the letter. Then he folded it and mailed it. His position had been stated clearly and confidently. He was unwavering.

∞

Dave picked through a short stack of envelopes he had pulled out of his mailbox.

When he saw Jean's handwriting, he immediately set the other letters down and opened hers. It was dated March 18.

Dear David,

Thank you very much for your kind and straightforward letter, we really appreciate it. You and I talked about a lot of things on the telephone but I will respond to your letter in writing.

We know you did not intentionally mean to hurt us but when we arrived at your home and found another woman "in charge" less than three months after our daughter died— that was very difficult for us. In all reality I think most Moms and Dads would have felt the same way. It seemed to us that a lot of people knew about this but we did not and it was hard to figure out and understand. Were we hurt? Yes, very much so. Are we healing? Yes, very much so.

Please know that we want to always be involved with you and the kids. They are the only living part of Teresa that we have left. We love and adore each one of them. You and Teresa did a great job raising them, and David, you have done a wonderful job with them through Teresa's illness and since her passing. We commend you for a job well done. They are bright, well adjusted, poised and well mannered and that only comes by good parenting. They have been surrounded by loving parents, grandparents and even great grandparents that have all gotten along together. We want it to remain that way. We love you and your family and want our relationship to continue and grow.

Are we bitter and do we feel guilty and frustrated as mentioned in your letter—absolutely NO. We do not doubt your love for Teresa; that has always been very evident. Teresa was our dear and much loved daughter and the loss of her is very, very great. Her two-plus years of cancer suffering took its toll on us but we are so thankful for all the good times. We wish for you Peace and Happiness and Good Health. The next person you bring into your life will be accepted by us as part of our family. We love you, Nicole, Lauren and John, and hope to grow older enjoying our special relationship.

Our love,

Jean and Ron had both signed the typed letter.

Friday, March 23, 2001

Kellie watched the digital clock on the radio of her silver Durango and tried to calculate how late she was going to be. Despite the rainy road conditions, she sped on Interstate 40, heading west into Nashville. Dave and the kids were waiting there for her at the airport.

The day had already been hectic. Kellie had been in Murfreesboro trying to tie up loose ends before the Volunteer Horse Fair got into full swing.

The three-day event drew in 10,000 people for equine seminars, shows and shopping. Kellie served the event as its media coordinator and also was in charge of the Breed and Stallion Show.

She tore herself away just in time to scramble to meet the Grills. Kellie called the airline to check their flight and discovered it had left Minneapolis early. She called Dave's cell phone and left him a message apologizing that she was on the way but unlikely to greet them at the gate. They were due in around 6 P.M.

The last thing Kellie wanted to be was late. After all, she had barely stopped thinking about Dave and his kids since the last time she had seen them. She could hardly believe that after all of the build up over their arrival that she would be wasting precious minutes and seconds of the visit.

Kellie had made a list of all the things she had planned for them. She had arranged for Nikki to sing the national anthem twice—at the Horse Fair "Mane" Event on Saturday and the rodeo on Sunday. She had also set up studio time on Music Row for Nikki to record the vocal track for her song, "Sail On."

The to-do list included horseback riding on the farm she shared with Kaysie, a visit to the Grand Ole Opry, fishing, and dinner at the Cherokee Steak House. And that was just for starters.

Kellie hurried into the airport and was relieved to find Dave and the kids waiting near the baggage carousel. Lauren was the first to spot her and the greeting was emphatic. Lauren dropped her bag and ran into Kellie's arms.

"Oh my gosh," Lauren squealed. "It's so great to see you. We've missed you so much—this is going to be so much fun!"

Lauren's excitement boiled over and was infectious.

"My people!" Kellie replied. She hugged Lauren back and they spun each other around like long-lost best friends. "I'm so glad you're here. I'm so sorry I wasn't able to get you at the gate. This day has just been nuts!"

With Kellie, every sentence was loud and boisterous, punctuated by her waving hands.

"That's OK," Lauren said.

Johnny and Nikki greeted Kellie warmly as well. All the kids, like Dave, were fans of country music and they were excited to be in Music City.

Dave made his way to Kellie and hugged her too.

They had become accustomed to keeping their romance low key around the kids. They waited until they were out of sight to kiss.

"Oh, it's good to be here," Dave said, stretching his arms up over his head. "That's a long flight."

"I know," Kellie agreed. "We live about as far away from each other as we can get."

After loading their bags into Kellie's car, Johnny told her about what he had been up to lately. Baseball season was starting up soon and he was excited about it. Kellie listened, noticing how far the boy had come out of his shell since she first met him.

Dave noticed it too, and gave Kellie a wink on the sly.

Kellie began playing tour guide and led her visitors into Nashville. The rain had stopped and the moon and stars were visible overhead. She brought them by the Bell South Building, dubbed "The Batman Building" and Music Row, 16th and 17th Avenues, and Broadway with all of the small clubs lining both sides of the street.

After explaining her way through the heart of Nashville, Kellie moved onto the freeway and headed 30 miles east to her home near Lebanon. They reached her home at 7 P.M. Dave and the kids unloaded their bags and took them to their designated rooms.

Kellie continued the tour for Dave and the kids, introducing them to all of her pets: two horses, four cats and four dogs, including a wolf named Timber. These were the animals that lived at her house on nine acres. There were more, but they lived on the 36-acre farm where Kaysie lived.

Kellie took them out to dinner at a nearby family restaurant in Lebanon before bringing the tired foursome back home.

The next morning, Kellie took them over to Kaysie's to show her guests the rest of the property and the animals. Dave wandered into the front yard with his cup of coffee and watched a black lab named Blackjack laying on the ground, studying something.

"What's he doing?" Dave asked, turning to Kaysie.

"He's looking at the ticks. We're getting warmer weather and they're starting to hatch," Kaysie said. "That reminds me, all you kids need to spray your ankles with Off so you don't get ticks or flea bites."

Dave wandered over next to the dog and kneeled down. What he saw almost made him spill his coffee. The ground looked like it was moving as the tiny insects crawled everywhere.

He backed away.

In an instant, he knew the answer to one of the questions that had been burning for months: Would he move the kids to Tennessee and make a new life in the South with Kellie? No.

Dave was glad to live in the Northwest and he didn't think he could uproot his kids anyway. His job and his family were there. The idea of getting used to ticks and chiggers was the final straw.

Dave and Kellie discussed their possibilities for a future together. It would be easiest, they both agreed, if Kellie came west.

The rest of the vacation in Tennessee seemed to fly by at a frenetic pace with Kellie leading Dave and the kids from one adventure to the next.

As they departed, Dave kissed Kellie in the airport. It was a first in front of the kids. They didn't seem bothered by it in the slightest.

In the span of a week, Kellie began to feel the beginnings of something new. She felt like part of the family.

Friday, April 20, 2001

Kellie nervously waited for the plane to land at the Portland airport. She paid attention to how anxious she felt about seeing Dave and the kids again. It was just three weeks since she had seen them all in Nashville for Spring Break, but each day since then had seemed to drag on, long and boring and pointless.

With the Grills, she felt whole again.

This trip to Portland would be a productive one, filled with the tiny steps that she knew would move her closer to a permanent spot in Dave's life. She would meet some of Dave and Teresa's friends for the first time, bravely testing the waters. In their eyes, she knew she would be viewed as Teresa's replacement.

But there was even more to be concerned with. The momentum of the relationship had brought them to this point. Kellie hoped to secure a place to rent nearby, with every intention of moving from Tennessee so that she could be close enough to date Dave and continue moving toward their eventual goal: Marriage.

Danelle and Mark Wiese were hosting a wine-tasting fundraiser for Lauren's softball team, the Tualatin Twins.

Kellie thought about the conversation Dave had told her about over the phone.

As he purchased tickets to the wine tasting, Dave had asked Danelle if he could bring a date.

She had laughed. "Sure . . . If she drinks a lot of wine!" She was sure he must be joking.

But Dave wasn't kidding. He was ready for his friends to meet Kellie.

After picking her up from the airport, Dave brought Kellie back to his house and their emotions quickly led them to the bedroom. After their passionate reunion, Dave started to fill her in on the latest news in the family and the next day's wine-tasting party. He knew that this was going to be a difficult situation to bring Kellie into, but he felt it was necessary.

"Are you nervous about this? Because I don't want you to be. I'll be right there with you," Dave said. "My mom and dad will be there too."

"Well, to be honest, I am a little nervous," Kellie admitted. "I know how much these people loved Teresa, and I hope they aren't too mean to me."

"I won't let them be," Dave said.

Saturday, April 21, 2001

Dave and Kellie arrived on the Wiese's doorstep ready to step into the shark tank.

The event called for semi-formal attire and Kellie chose her outfit carefully so that she wouldn't call too much attention to herself. Little did she know she was about to become the center of attention.

Danelle greeted them first, welcoming Dave and Kellie into the house.

"Well, I must admit Dave," she said, forcing a smile, "I thought you were kidding about bringing a date, but this is a pleasant surprise."

"Danelle, this is Kellie," Dave said. "Kellie, this is Danelle, the owner of this brand-new, beautiful home."

As they exchanged small talk with Danelle, Dave could tell that his entrance with Kellie was causing heads to turn.

"Can I get you a glass of wine?" Danelle asked sweetly.

"Oh. No thanks. I don't drink." Kellie said. "I'll just have a glass of water."

"You got it," Danelle said.

Wilma and Gary began to circulate among the guests. Kellie kept her eye on them, knowing they were a safe harbor if the seas got too rough.

Dave made no effort to conceal the fact that he had a date. He nonchalantly introduced Kellie as he moved through the crowded living room.

The greetings followed a similar pattern.

"Nice to meet you, Kellie," they would say. "Where are you from? How did you meet Dave? How long are you in town?"

Some of them had heard of Kellie already. Their kids knew of the Grills' spring break vacation to Nashville. A few others had seen her at Lauren's softball game earlier that afternoon.

Then, after the brief introduction was over, they would casually approach Dave's parents seeking more information: *Who* was *she*?

Wilma and Gary spent much of their evening softening the blow.

"Known her forever," they said, time and again. "Comes from a great family. Dave played football with her brother."

There were more than 80 people at the party and nearly all of them met Kellie face to face.

Dave could tell that their reactions ran from curious to suspicious to downright shocked. He easily picked up on the nuance and body language and could tell that the animosity was right under the surface. Several times he caught the expression of someone after Kellie had turned her attention away. The rolling of the eyes, the disgusted looks, the raised eyebrows—it spoke volumes.

They were in the midst of some of Teresa's most loyal friends and they were still feeling raw from their loss months later. The end of their friend's life had come so abruptly. Most of them never had a chance to say good-bye.

"I wish I could take a year off my life and put it onto hers," one of the softball moms said. "I'd do it in a heartbeat."

After leading Kellie around the home for introductions, Dave broke off to chat with Tom Re.

"Are you going to be OK if I leave you for a minute?" Dave asked Kellie.

"Yeah, I'm fine."

A pair of sisters approached Kellie.

"You're the bravest person we know to show up here tonight," one of them said.

"Really? I don't think I'm so brave," Kellie said, smiling.

"Believe me," the other sister said. "To face all these people, *believe* me, it takes courage."

"Well, I'm here tonight because I know how much I love Dave and the kids and how much they all love me," Kellie replied.

"I hope that everyone will accept me and like me, but if they don't, I really don't care."

Kellie was blunt, but it was the way she felt.

"That's a great way to be," the first sister said. "Good luck."

"Thanks," Kellie said. "I'm sure I'll need it."

Feeling a little isolated on an island, Kellie gravitated back toward Dave.

CHAPTER TEN

A New Home

Sunday, April 22, 2001

"That's him over there," Dave said, pulling the Suburban to the side of the road. "We call him Sonny D."

Dave was eager to show Kellie the horse that he and the kids had nicknamed, and occasionally fed carrots to, over the past few months.

Kellie quickly opened the door and hopped out. She began surveying the red sorrel quarter horse as it approached. He was limping badly and Kellie winced as she watched the horse struggle with each step.

"My God, Dave, what's happened to him?" Kellie asked. The sight of the animal's pain made her queasy.

"I don't know," Dave replied, beginning to share Kellie's concern. "He was fine when we were here last week to see him."

Kellie could tell there was neglect involved in the animal's condition. She didn't like what she suspected.

"I think he's foundered," Kellie said. That wasn't good. Foundering, as Kellie knew, was a crippling affliction caused by eating the wrong foods. It causes the connective tissues in a horse's hooves to break down. Seldom can the condition be completely cured.

The horse was alone on the lot and a for-sale sign indicated that the small home was vacant.

Kellie reached over the fence and petted the horse on his muzzle and neck.

"Easy boy," she said, soothingly. She looked him over closely and bent down to lift up one of his front hooves. The very touch was enough to almost knock the horse down and he recoiled in pain.

"Dave, he's foundered! He's crippled. He needs a vet," Kellie said, alarmed. She could feel herself beginning to panic. "We've got to find his owner."

Dave walked next door to seek information while Kellie stayed with the horse, petting him.

The owner lived on this same street, Dave learned, and he and Kellie went to pay the man a visit.

It was a dilapidated mobile home with half a dozen hogs and two more horses in the front yard.

Dave walked up to the porch and pressed the doorbell. That set off barking by a large, unfriendly dog in the house. A heavy-set man wearing nothing but a pair of white cotton briefs pulled the front door open.

"Yeah?" the man said.

"Hi," Dave replied. "We're trying to find the owner of a red horse at the yellow house that's for sale."

"That would be me," the man grunted. "Excuse the underwear. One of my hogs gored me in the butt two days ago. I just got out of the hospital. It got infected. Give me a minute and I'll put some pants on."

"Thanks," Dave said. The man closed the door and Dave turned to Kellie, who was standing behind him. They didn't say a word, but their eyes told each other that they were trying very hard not to pass judgment on the distasteful squalor of the man's home.

"C'mon in," the man said when he returned. He motioned for the dog to be quiet.

Kellie followed Dave through the front door and they took a seat next to one another on a dirty, broken couch. The man eased himself slowly into a recliner on the other side of the room.

"I'm Dave Grill and this is Kellie," Dave began. "We saw your horse out there. It looks like he's foundered."

"I know," the man said, shaking his head. "That stupid son of a bitch."

The man identified himself as Darrell, and continued to elaborate.

"Some dumbass realtor left the stall open and the damn horse ate 50 pounds of grain," he said.

"Oh, my God," Kellie gasped. "That's horrible!"

"He was down for three days," the man continued. "I thought he was going to die. But he's doin' better now."

"Well, he's real sick," Kellie said. "Have you had him looked at by a vet?"

"Nope," Darrell said. "I don't believe in 'em."

"What?" Kellie said, exasperated.

"I don't believe in them," the man said again. "I think they're a crock."

"He's going to die if you don't do something for him," Dave said.

"Aww, he's fine," the man said. "He's tough."

Kellie clenched her fist inside her coat pocket and tried to suppress the anger that she felt from showing in her face.

"Well you should at least have a horse shoer look at his hooves to see if he needs corrective shoes," Kellie said.

"Nope," Darrell replied. "Don't believe in them neither. They're all full of bullshit."

Kellie grew pale at the man's response. He clearly didn't care for the animal.

"Your horse is suffering," she said, trying one more time. "He needs to be helped."

"He's fine," Darrell said. "But I'm going to sue that goddamned realtor for that horse."

"Your horse needs some help," Dave said, repeating Kellie's words. "My kids lost their mom to breast cancer last Thanksgiving and they have been really sad. They found your horse when we bought a Christmas tree across from his pasture. They've grown to love him, and I'd like to buy him from you if you would let me. I'll get him the medical attention he needs."

"Do you know he's a stud?" Darrell asked, incredulously.

"Yes," Dave replied.

"Do you have horses?"

"No."

"I ain't sellin' no one with kids a stallion," Darrell said. "Plus, he's real valuable. He's a son of the famous cuttin' horse Peppy's Badger Chex."

Kellie knew their chance of liberating the sick horse for 100 bucks had just slipped from slim to zilch.

"Well, he ain't a valuable cutting horse if he's crippled," Kellie said. "How about you sell him to me? I have eight horses and I've raised and broke three studs."

The man considered Kellie's words a moment, rubbing his stubbly chin.

"OK, I'd sell him to you," he said.

Kellie quickly ran the situation over in her mind. Dave, the kids and Wilma and Gary would have to care for the horse until she moved out. But this horse needed her help.

"OK, how much?" Kellie asked.

"Let me show you his papers," Darrell said. "I mean, he's the real deal. He has lots of training and . . ."

Kellie was losing her patience with the chubby man, whom she took for a heartless prick.

"His training and blood aren't worth much if he's crippled," Dave said.

"But he's a stud, you could breed him," Darrell boasted.

"If he lives and if he can mount on those crippled feet," Kellie chimed in.

"How much?" Darrell said.

"Two hundred," Kellie said, aware that she was starting low.

"Hell no!" Darrell fumed, insulted. "I'd have to have a lot more than that. I could take him to the auction and get double that for him."

"He's going to cost us tons of vet and farrier bills. How much more?" Dave asked.

Darrell knew he was getting backed into a corner.

"Five hundred. That's our top offer. And we're getting screwed because that horse will probably never walk again, let alone breed or do cutting," Dave said.

Dave stood up, as if he were ready to walk out. Kellie stood to go with him.

"OK, OK," Darrell agreed. "Five hundred is OK. Let me sign his papers."

The horse's registered name was Peppy's Boogie Man, but Darrell had taken to calling him Booger.

Kellie wrote Darrell a check and took Sonny D's American Quarter Horse Association Registration. The registration number caught her eye. The first numbers, she noticed, were a sequence of three threes.

Dave and Kellie walked from the smelly, dirty trailer back to the Suburban. Dave already had his phone out, dialing information.

"I need the number for Willamette Valley Equine Vet Clinic and I need it quick," Dave said.

Monday, April 23, 2001

Kellie sat in the passenger seat of the burgundy Oldsmobile cutlass next to Nikki, who had the wheel, driving to her voice lesson in Tigard.

It was the first time since writing "Sail On" together that Kellie had spent much time alone with Nikki.

The 15-year-old mused as she drove, talking easily with Kellie.

"You know, I've been thinking about something," Nikki began.

Kellie reached to turn down the volume on the radio to give the girl her undivided attention.

"What is it, sweetie?"

"This might sound a little weird, but it's been on my mind and I just wanted to tell you," Nikki said. "I've been thinking about how everyone says it's so devastating and awful and tragic that my mom died. And they're right. It is."

Kellie nodded.

"But when I think about you and your relationship with my dad now, I realize that even though it's so terrible, it's not so terrible, devastating or tragic for you, is it?"

Kellie was impressed. Little of what was transpiring had escaped the kids.

"You're right," Kellie said, feeling the slightest bit guilty.

"I mean, like, it's so sad but there's also some happiness that can come out of sadness. So there is good that comes out of bad," Nikki said.

"That's true, Nik," Kellie said. "You amaze me the way you think. Sometimes, I swear you act more like you're 30 than only 15."

"Well, it's just what I've been thinking," Nikki said, turning her eyes back to the road.

"It's kind of like the saying, 'When God closes a door, he opens a window'," Kellie said.

"Yeah," Nikki agreed. "Kind of like that."

Tuesday, April 24, 2001

Lauren leaned over the bathroom sink, applying mascara to her eyelashes. She was getting ready for school. Kellie stood next to her, chatting freely.

"I had a conversation with Carlyn yesterday at school and she might be kind of mad at me today, I don't know," Lauren said.

"Why? What happened?" Kellie asked.

"Well, she was saying that she didn't think it was right that you've come into our lives so soon after mom died. She thinks my dad's really making a mistake by moving on so fast," Lauren said.

Kellie knew it was a view that was held not only by Carlyn, but many others as well.

"So what did you say?" she asked Lauren.

"I just told her to think about when her mom goes out of town for work and how hard it is on her dad to do the cooking and laundry and getting the kids to school and do his work and everything else," Lauren said. "I said, 'Now think how hard that is, Car. And your mom comes back and is able to get it all done again. Well my mom's gone and she's never coming back. And we like having Kellie here. It helps us to feel like a family again. She does the things that our mom used to do. And we really love her.'"

"Oh, thank you," Kellie said, near tears. "I love you, too."

Lauren paused, fearful that her tears were going to ruin her fresh makeup. She set the applicator down, turned and gave Kellie a hug.

Kellie released Lauren.

"You know, Lauren, a lot of people are going to judge our situation and not understand," Kellie said. "We just have to have thick skin and not let it upset us. We know the truth and what this is all about. And we know your mom is guiding us through all of this."

"I know," Lauren said.

A horn honked outside. The carpool had arrived.

Lauren grabbed her backpack and hustled down the stairs.

∞

Kellie wiped the perspiration from her forehead with her right forearm and grunted. The frustration only made her more persistent.

The grass in the backyard had grown ankle deep and Kellie was determined to cut it. But with each pass across the yard, the blade kept getting caught, and when it did, the engine died. She was reviewing her options for a more efficient plan when the phone rang.

She peeled her work gloves off and ran in the house, thinking it must be Dave calling to check in. She almost tripped over Hannah, who was lying on the rug by the sliding glass door.

"Sorry, girl!" Kellie said as she stumbled to miss the nearly blind dog.

"Hello?" Kellie said, almost out of breath.

It was a woman's voice. She didn't recognize it.

"Who is this?" the voice inquired.

"This is Kellie."

"Kellie who?" The question didn't sound pleasant. Obviously, this caller wasn't expecting anyone to pick up the phone at the Grill house in the middle of the day.

"Kellie Poulsen."

"Are you related to the Grills?"

Kellie was already quite sure that this was none of the woman's business. But she played along.

"No, actually, I'm Dave's girlfriend." Kellie said the words proudly. She was put off by the woman's tone.

"His *what*?" the woman asked, shocked.

"His girlfriend," Kellie repeated. "I'm here visiting Dave and the kids. I live in Nashville, Tennessee." She was getting perturbed by the questioning and was losing her patience with it.

"Oh . . . well . . ." the woman stammered. "I . . . I am a friend, and I was wanting to give, uh, Dave and the kids, uh, a house cleaner. I talked to him a while ago, and I have this cleaner who is really good and I figured that with Teresa gone they are probably in need of some help, and uh . . ."

Kellie cut her short.

"Well, they won't be needing one," Kellie informed her. "I've been getting a lot of it done myself. And I plan on moving here soon."

"Oh, *really*?" the woman replied.

Kellie had the suspicion that some plans had been blown by her sudden emergence into Dave's life. This woman had an agenda, and she probably wasn't alone. Now that a half-year had gone by since Teresa's death, this was probably just the first one brave enough to come forward. Kellie recalled Brett's term: The casserole women.

This one wasn't backing down easy.

"Well, tell Dave I'll call him in a few weeks to see how things are going."

Kellie knew that the woman meant things more than just cleaning. She also meant Dave's relationship.

"OK," Kellie said. "I don't believe I got your name."

"Uh . . ." the woman started sputtering again. "You know what, that's OK. I'll just call back another time."

"OK," Kellie said, her patience worn through. "Bye now."

She didn't wait for the anonymous woman to say anything else. Click.

Kellie called Dave at work and told him about the odd phone call. Dave laughed, knowing instantly who it was. He thought it was funny that the catty woman had challenged Kellie.

Dave teased Kellie and told her he'd be waiting eagerly for the woman's next call.

"Maybe I can get a date out of it," he said, smiling into the phone.

Kellie vowed some revenge when he got home later, and then said she needed to get back to her mowing and laundry.

Dave's playful tone changed.

"Thanks for all you're doing. I love you," Dave said. "Thanks for fighting for me."

"You're welcome," Kellie said, at ease again. "I love you too. I'm just glad I acted when I did or I'd have to take a number."

"Oh, I seriously doubt that," Dave said. "I think you've got me pretty high up on a pedestal."

"No, I don't!" Kellie said. "Bye, hon. I'll see you tonight. I'm making the trout you and Johnny caught for dinner."

"Mmm," Dave said. "Sounds good. OK, I'll see you soon. Bye."

Kellie petted the dogs for a few minutes as her mind continued to process the phone call from the woman. Then she went into the laundry room and shifted towels from the washer to the dryer.

Wednesday, April 25, 2001

The quest for new homes was now a top priority.

Kellie was weighing her options for moving out to Oregon so that she could see Dave on a more regular basis. As much as she wanted to move in right away, she decided the proper thing to do would be to rent a place to live in a for a while, and then move in when they were married. By now, that was beginning to seem inevitable. Or at least she hoped so.

She found a small, two-bedroom cottage with 20 acres and a barn for horses in Sherwood, about 10 miles west of Tualatin. She put money down to hold it. She could bring a few of her horses out from Tennessee, and move Sonny D there as well.

Dave, also, was looking to move. He wanted a fresh start for himself and the kids, and was scanning the real estate in Wilsonville, about five miles south of Tualatin. He wanted more space and a few acres. He knew it wouldn't be long before Kellie joined them.

His search began early in the year but had intensified in recent weeks. Dave took the kids and Kellie out to take a look at a five-acre place with a running creek and barn next to a big house. He put an offer on it, but was second in line. An earlier offer had already come in.

He didn't get the house.

Slightly discouraged, Dave and Kellie discussed their options.

"What if we offer them like twenty or thirty thousand to just walk away?" Kellie suggested. She wanted the place badly enough to make the bold move.

"No way," Dave said. "Before I'd do that I'd just look for a more expensive house."

"OK," Kellie agreed. She knew he was right.

"Let's go check out that for sale by owner over on Frog Pond Lane then," she said.

That place also had five acres but it was priced out of Dave's range. Kellie hadn't sold her house and Dave hadn't sold his, either.

"Can't we just go and take a look?" she asked. "I have the flyer in my suitcase. It's in Lauren's room. The girls and I picked it up when we were cruisin' one day."

Kellie retrieved the flyer and brought it to Dave, who was standing in the kitchen. It was $100,000 more than the house Dave had just made an offer on.

"I don't know," Dave said. "This is really expensive."

"I know," Kellie said. "But what harm would there be in just seeing it?"

"I guess we could do that."

"Would you just call on it Dave? Please, oh please, oh . . ."

"OK," Dave said. "But no guarantees, Kell. This is really out of our range."

Dave called and talked with the owner. The man was just about to leave town and Dave had caught him in the nick of time. He said he could show it to them right now. The man said he was in the middle of a divorce and he needed to sell the house soon.

"Just give us five minutes," Dave said. "I'll be able to tell you in five minutes whether I'm interested. And if I'm not I won't waste your time."

Dave and Kellie quickly left and arrived at the house on Frog Pond Lane about 10 minutes later.

The home was even better than the flyer had let on. Shortly after walking upstairs, Dave saw Kellie's excited expression.

"Bob, I like what I see," Dave said. "We want to see it all."

There was a horse in the back field and Kellie quickly bonded with it, running with it and playing tag. It was a lonely Arabian named Dancer. After touring the barn and shop, the owner led them back to the house. He went inside. Kellie pulled Dave close and gave him a kiss.

"Dave, we just have to get this beautiful place," she said. "It is just perfect. I mean *this has to be our place*! I have to have this to be our home together when we get married. I want to live here."

"What about your rental?" Dave asked.

"I'll give it up," she said.

"OK, but you've put more than two thousand dollars down on it, remember? What if you can't get your money back?"

"I think I can," Kellie said. "That landlord lady had more than eighty phone calls in one weekend. I'm sure she can fill it again."

"What about living with us?" Dave asked. "I thought you were concerned about doing that from the start for fear of what some people might think of you."

"Actually, I think I should live with you so that I can help you more with the kids, and cook and clean and drive them places and stuff. The kids already told me they were sad that I wasn't going to be living with you. They don't want me to have my own place."

"Well . . . we'll see," Dave said. He was still noncommittal about meeting the seller's price.

They went back home, and Dave went on to work. He called his mom and dad to see if they would come over and see a new home that interested him. Dave set up an appointment to see the house again with the owner's ex-wife. The kids came too.

The next day, Dave made an offer on the home.

"Bob, it's Dave Grill," Dave said into the phone. "I wanted to call and let you know that we would like to make an offer on your place. We are prepared to give you your price, but there are a few things extra we want. We want the trampoline, the refrigerator, and I want the horse for Kellie."

Bob and his wife quickly agreed to Dave's terms.

Saturday, April 28, 2001

A year after making it to the Little League World Series, Lauren resumed playing softball with most of her same teammates from the previous summer. They were no longer little leaguers. Instead, they played on an American Softball Association team: The Tualatin Twins.

Lauren's dedication to the game was intensifying. She was eager for another season of games and camaraderie with her friends. Sports dominated the weekends in the Grill household. It was a new wrinkle for Kellie. She didn't know the first thing about softball, but found out in a hurry that she needed to become a quick study. These games were important.

All of the softball regulars were there—the Weises, the Res, the Johnsons, the Colgans and others.

Kellie made herself comfortable in a lawn chair and nibbled on sunflower seeds as she watched the game.

A blonde woman and her daughter approached and set their chairs near Kellie's. They talked about Lauren's team and seemed to know many of the players.

When it was Lauren's turn at the plate, Kellie cheered: "Come on, Loe! Let's go, double-oh!"

The blonde mother turned in her seat.

"Are you here with Lauren?" she asked.

"Yes, I am," Kellie answered, proudly.

"Oh. Are you her aunt?"

"No, I'm her dad's girlfriend," Kellie said, smiling under her sunglasses.

"Who? *Dave*?" the woman asked. She seemed confused.

"Yes, I'm with Dave and the kids," Kellie said.

"Oh," the woman said. "I didn't know he was dating already."

"Yeah, well I've known him forever," Kellie said, confidently. "He's my brother's best friend."

"Oh," the woman replied. Kellie noticed some disappointment in her expression.

Kellie turned back to the game, and the blonde woman did too. In a few minutes, the two began some small talk again, and Kellie took an interest in the girl, who was about 10. Kellie asked the girl about her softball team.

The conversation came around to a trip that the mother and daughter were soon taking to Utah. That got Kellie talking to them about her home state and the discussion turned friendly once more.

Lauren's game came to an end with a win.

"Well that sure was a sweet win," Kellie said excitedly.

"It was," the 10-year old agreed.

"It was nice talking to you both," Kellie said, standing up to fold her chair. "I hope you have a fun trip to Utah."

"Thank you," the woman replied. "You know . . . I have to tell you something."

"You do? What is it?" Kellie asked, curiously.

"Well to be honest, when you said that you are dating Dave and that you're now with him and the kids . . . I was a little bit mad. To be honest, I've had him in my sights. He's a wonderful man, and with my being single I thought that I might pursue him some day."

"Oh," Kellie said. She didn't know what else to say.

"But now, after spending time with you, I can see what Dave sees in you. You are so beautiful and friendly and nice."

"Well *thank you*." Kellie said. The stranger's compliments made her blush.

"I should hate you but I don't," the woman said. "In fact, I really like you and wish you all the best."

Kellie thanked the woman again. She was amazed by her honesty.

"Take care. I'm sure we'll see you around," the woman said. She turned, took her daughter by the hand, and began to walk toward the parking lot.

Dave and Lauren walked up as the mother and daughter left. Kellie told them briefly about her conversation. Once again, Kellie was confronted with the knowledge that Brett had been right. Dave Grill was a hot item. Kellie was glad she hadn't waited to make her move.

Sunday, May 20, 2001

Tom Re held the corner of a white sheet as he spoke to about a hundred people gathered along a paved path in the middle of Tualatin's Ibach Park.

"We're here today to celebrate the memory of Teresa," Tom said, his voice wavering with emotion. "Thanks to all of you for coming out and making this dedication a reality. There was a lot of hard work and coordination among many people to make this happen."

He pulled the sheet back to reveal a bronze drinking fountain. It was shaped like a clover, with three spigots. The crowd applauded, seeing it for the first time.

"Dave, would you and your kids like to come up and be the first to try this out?" Tom asked.

Dave, standing a few feet away, stepped forward. He was touched by the community's thoughtful gesture. His Little League World Series coaching partners, Tom and Mark Wiese, spearheaded the effort to commemorate his wife's legacy. Tom had coached soccer with Teresa and was hit hard by her death. Shortly after her memorial service he began putting his idea for a tribute into action.

He presented his plan for a drinking fountain to the City of Tualatin. It was accepted. Mark helped Tom pitch the idea to local businesses and the close-knit group of friends that had raised their kids together on the community's softball and baseball diamonds, football and soccer fields, and basketball courts. The money flowed in quickly. Two schools in Tualatin—Hazelbrook and Bridgeport —raised more than a thousand dollars combined with a themed fundraiser called "Pennies from Heaven."

Teresa's memory remained strong in the lives that she had touched. She had been a champion of kids, as a teacher, coach and mother, and treated all of them as if they were her own.

The shiny fountain included a knee-high faucet, and a basin for dogs to drink from.

Dave had come to the dedication ceremony directly from coaching one of Johnny's baseball games. Nikki, Lauren, and most everyone involved with the previous summer's little league team was there. Ron and Jean came also. For some in the crowd, the fountain brought a sense of closure that had been missing since Teresa's rapid deterioration and death in November.

Dave leaned over and pressed the shiny metal button. The water arched up to meet his lips. He took a sip and moved to the side. One by one, his kids followed.

At the foot of the fountain, a bronze plaque was inscribed with one of Teresa's poems. It was one she had written for Keely as a birthday gift several years earlier.

It was titled, "A Time in Every Woman's Life."

There comes a time
In every woman's life
When she must judge
The true value of her self-worth.
Some will use their social status,
Others their quality of life.
And still, a few will judge
Themselves by their closest friends.
It is by the latter that I chose to judge myself.
For by this measure,
I am truly the world's
Richest woman.

∽

Kellie pulled onto Tater Peeler Road in her Durango, pulling the U-Haul trailer behind her. Nearly 2,500 miles separated her from her new life with Dave and the kids.

It was a beautiful, sunny day. The dogwood trees were bright pink with their new blossoms. Green buds popped open on the hackberry trees. Kellie felt pangs of sadness as she drove away from the countryside that had become so familiar. She thought about the neighbor's horses and wondered if she'd ever see them again. She imagined that the valley where she had ridden horses would be encroached upon by new development after she left.

She wondered when she would come back. She thought about her friends—in the music business, from her house cleaning, and from her volunteer work.

Kellie's home wasn't yet sold, but she was weary of waiting. She missed Dave and the kids too much, and she was eager to begin her life with them full time. She hired a real estate agent to sell her house and had signed over power of attorney to Kaysie so that she could sign the paperwork when the time came to close.

Kaysie agreed to ride with Kellie as far as Salt Lake City. Brett would ride with her the rest of the way.

Separating from her twin felt a little like a divorce. Kellie and Kaysie had been side by side for all of their 35 years. The longest they had ever been apart in their entire lives was three weeks.

Kellie and Kaysie had done almost everything as a duo. They both got real estate licenses out of high school and for a short time ran their first business, a modeling school and agency that served southern Utah.

At 19, they moved from Utah to Los Angeles, pursuing their modeling and taking acting lessons. But their stay was short. In 10 months, they found little work, although they were offered the centerfold of *Playboy* if they would agree to pose as twins. They couldn't bring themselves to do it.

All the while, they were writing songs, and the show business dreams that they harbored seemed better suited for Nashville. But first, they returned to Utah and went to college for a year, taking music courses to guide their composing. At 21 they went east to Tennessee, where they lived for 14 years.

They poured their energy into writing songs, and had six album cuts. The most prominent artist to use one of their songs was Marie Osmond. Two more of their songs were put on hold by stars—George Strait and Garth Brooks—but never made it onto their albums.

In the early fall months of 2000, Kellie was at her wits' end over another romantic failure. Despite her sister's constant companionship, she felt lonely, even desperate.

She had so much energy, and yet felt unfulfilled.

She prayed in her bed at night, sometimes with so much frustration and emotion it led to tears.

"Dear God, what do you want me to do? What do you want me to be?" she would whisper. She begged for guidance.

Then an unforeseen set of circumstances started the wheels turning. In a matter of months, she had been thrust into a bold new adventure with her original girlhood crush. She now knew that she had loved him since the moment she laid eyes on him.

As Kellie prepared to move west, she knew that her other half was staying behind. The sisters went through both of their houses, deciding who owned what. So much of what they had accumulated was shared equally between them.

They went through everything, realizing that even the smallest things, like earrings and silverware, were difficult to separate. Kellie came across a cowboy painting that hung in Kaysie's farmhouse. They both wanted it. Kellie acquiesced. Kaysie relented with their grandpa's cowboy hats. For a week, the sisters compromised their way through the separation.

All eight horses, they decided, would stay behind in Tennessee. Kellie pained over the idea of leaving them all, but she knew that more animals awaited her in Oregon. Already, they had Sonny D. And soon, they would have Dancer, the Arabian at Frog Pond Lane.

"Can you believe this is happening?" Kellie said, shaking her head as she gazed ahead at the interstate.

"Actually, no," Kaysie said, sitting in the passenger seat flipping idly through a case of CDs. "It feels like a dream. And it's scary, yet it's not. I think we both knew that some day we might have to do this. Don't you think?"

"Yes," Kellie said. "I guess so. We have to grow up some-time, right?"

The sisters talked about how they would do it. Kaysie had Mark, her boyfriend of five years. Kellie knew that it was merely a matter of time before they got married.

And Kellie had Dave and the kids. She couldn't imagine any other person on Earth that could pull her away from Kaysie and the life she had in Tennessee.

The thing they would miss the most was riding horses together. It was the activity that bound them the tightest, and it was the love that they had shared the longest.

The miles melted away. They traveled across the Mississippi River and into the Great Plains. They drove all day, switching turns at the wheel occasionally at rest stops. When evening came, they found a motel and stopped.

They reached the western outskirts of Cheyenne, Wyoming and saw dark, foreboding clouds on the horizon. Sure enough, it was a snowstorm and they drove right into it.

Snowflakes began to drift down onto them, and the further they went, the more intense the snow became. Before they knew it, they were driving into a blizzard.

"Do you think we should stop?" Kaysie said.

"I don't think so," Kellie said. "We've got to get through this and get to Salt Lake. I'm afraid if we stop we could get snowed in somewhere."

"OK," Kaysie said. "But just be careful. We need to get you there in one piece."

At times through the Rocky Mountain pass, it seemed like that objective would be easier said than done. A tractor trailer, sliding precariously on the icy freeway as it tried to pass the Durango, sprayed a blinding wake of snow and ice onto their windshield, tilting the trailer out of balance and nearly forcing them to stop.

Kellie gripped the steering wheel hard and slowed to keep her SUV and trailer moving straight ahead. Kellie whispered words of prayer as they continued through the storm.

It seemed like one final test for the twins before they went their separate ways.

They were relieved to finally reach Salt Lake City late on Wednesday night.

Thursday, May 24, 2001

Brett and Kellie were on their way early, around 6 A.M. They had a schedule to keep. They needed to be in Portland by Friday because they were going to go to Johnny's baseball tournament over Memorial Day weekend.

Kellie gave her sister a hug good-bye, and they fought back tears.

Pulling away from Kaysie made the gravity of the move seem that much more real. There was no turning back.

The sisters would no longer be simply "The Twins." They would now each have their own individual identities, independent of one another for the first time.

Brett, aware of Kellie's separation anxiety, tried to keep her mind focused on what lay ahead.

"Well, can you believe you've come this far?" Brett asked. "I mean, another 800 miles and you'll be there. You'll be an Oregonian soon."

"I know, Brett. It seems like a dream," Kellie said. "I feel like I'm destined to do this. It's like I don't have a choice. I felt it from the moment I heard that Teresa had died."

"Well, I don't think any of us had a choice," Brett said. "I didn't feel like I had any choice but to take you to the memorial. And I didn't feel like I had any choice but to plug you into Dave's family."

"I'm so glad you did," Kellie said.

"As I recall, you weren't so eager to go at first," Brett reminded Kellie.

"I know," she said. "But deep down . . . it's weird . . . this all seems like fate."

"I'll tell you what it is," Brett said. "It's Teresa."

Kellie nodded.

The trip between Salt Lake City and Boise, Idaho went smoothly. They simply cranked up the radio and sang along with the music. They reached Baker City, Oregon—a prominent spot on the old Oregon Trail—by nightfall.

Friday, May 25, 2001

Shortly after noon, Brett and Kellie emerged from the west end of the Columbia Gorge on Interstate 84 and entered Portland's eastern suburbs. Kellie tried Dave on her cell phone and made arrangements with him to meet for lunch.

Dave and Kellie were excited to see each other. Brett was thrilled to have brought them together, figuratively, and now literally. The early matchmaking seemed worth it.

At the restaurant, a waitress approached to take their drink order. She sensed Kellie's happiness and commented on it.

"Are you rich?" the woman asked.

Kellie was momentarily startled.

"Pardon me?"

"Are you rich?" the woman asked again. "You just seem like you're so happy and you have a glow about you. It just seems like you've won the lottery or something."

"Yeah," Kellie said, beaming with pride. Dave was seated next to her with his arm around her shoulders. "I guess you could say I am rich. I'm rich in love. I just moved here from Tennessee to be with him and his kids. I'm very happy."

"Well you look it," the waitress said. "Congratulations and good luck."

When the drinks came, Dave lifted his glass of Bud and proposed a toast.

"Here's to good friends, and to Kellie moving here," Dave said.

"I'll drink to that," Brett said.

Kellie smiled. She was nervous and tired, but mostly ecstatic.

After unloading Kellie's U-haul into the vacant Frog Pond Lane house's garage, the three of them returned to the house on 70th.

When they returned, they found a family that was ready to go.

Kellie stepped into the fast-paced life immediately. First up was a trip over the Cascades to Oregon's dry side, to LaPine for a baseball tournament.

Jean and Ron also made the short trip from Bend to see Johnny's games.

They were cordial but still cool to Kellie. News that she had pulled up stakes and moved to Oregon to be with Dave and the kids was met with skepticism. They turned their affection to their grandkids.

Doug and Kathy Hart were there, watching Taylor, who was on Johnny's team.

Kellie was glad to have them around. The Harts felt like allies. The tournament lasted through Monday, and Brett flew home on Tuesday.

Kellie's life with the Grills was now in full swing.

Saturday, July 21, 2001

Kellie felt her spirits sagging with a scratchy throat, stuffy nose and headache.

Dave and the kids were at home and Kellie could hear Nikki and Lauren race up and down the stairs and giggle behind their bedroom doors.

Kellie felt uncharacteristically bad. She lay in bed, coughing and shivering. It was almost more than she could bear. She couldn't remember feeling more miserable. On top of everything, Kellie was wiped out from the move to the new house. For three weeks, Kellie had been packing and unpacking boxes and getting the new house up to speed. It was sapping her usually limitless energy.

Every so often, Dave or the girls would come in and check on her and see if she needed anything. Hot tea? Soup? Cough drops? Kellie politely declined them and curled up into a fetal position under the covers, trying to wish away the pounding sinus headache that Tylenol didn't seem to help.

Kellie guessed that it must be afternoon and the clock on her nightstand confirmed it. It was 1 P.M.

In the silent room she fell asleep.

She awakened to more sounds of giggling and laughter coming from upstairs. Kellie heard Dave's low voice in the mix. She sat up and pushed the covers aside and stood up out of bed. She felt only slightly better despite the nap.

She put on her robe and wandered up the stairs, holding her empty tea cup. In the kitchen, she filled the cup with water and put it in the microwave, setting the timer for 90 seconds.

While she waited for the water to warm, she looked out the window to the front yard. They had been moved into their new house for less than a month. Johnny threw a football to Lauren, and Dave, playing defense, carefully tackled her to the ground. Lauren squealed with laughter. Johnny saw a chance to surprise them and ran up and flopped down on both his dad and sister. Dave wrestled briefly with Johnny, secured the ball and threw it to Nikki, who was standing nearby and laughing at her silly siblings, and even sillier dad.

Kellie smiled as she watched them from the window. The affection that the four displayed for one another was humbling. Their bond was the tightest she had ever seen in a father and his kids.

Kellie felt the tickle return to her throat and coughed. She reached for a fresh tissue and blew her nose. She wished that she felt well enough to be out in the sunshine and join the fun on the front lawn.

But Kellie was focused on her misery and how much it aggravated her. She opened a bottle of vitamin C and shook three of the tablets into her hand and set them down.

She walked back to the edge of the sink and looked out the window. Dave and the kids had resumed their game, though she couldn't tell whether it had any rules. They seemed too happy to care.

Kellie caught herself moping.

"Quit feeling sorry for yourself you big fool!" Kellie said out loud. "If you think you're sick, imagine how Teresa felt. At least you will get better. You have a cold. She had cancer. She watched her family play and knew she wasn't going to get any better. How do you think she felt? How dare you act and think this way. Get a grip! It's a cold!"

It was rare for Kellie to give herself a pep talk like that. But the words, as she said them, carried some gravity. No matter how bad she felt, Teresa's suffering was exponentially worse. She vowed to snap herself out of her funk.

The microwave dinged and the timer flashed.

She opened the door and took her hot water out.

Then the digital display reverted back to the clock.

It was 3:33 P.M.

Kellie stared at the microwave, startled by the numbers.

"My God," Kellie said, softly. She turned to look at the clock on the stove: 3:33.

Kellie felt as though Teresa were speaking to her. The number had become significant for the entire family. It reminded them that Teresa was watching, like their own personal guardian angel, and in some cases they took it as a sign that she was smiling down upon them.

In the kitchen, Kellie took the 333s as just such a sign.

She took a deep breath and thought about what Teresa might say to her in that instant.

Everything is OK.

Calm down.

It's just a cold.

You're going to be fine.

Saturday, August 4, 2001

Kellie had her eye on Johnny as he approached his fishing pole, leaning against a tree. He was headed to the dock to join the other boys who were trying to catch crappie out of Foster Lake.

"Hold it, Mr. J," Kellie said, breaking off her conversation with Kathy Re. "I want to see another bite of that hamburger before you go running off. All I've seen you eat today is Skittles and chips!"

Johnny stopped in his tracks, turned and went back to the paper plate sitting on the picnic bench. He picked up his half-eaten burger and took another bite. Then he took one more, stuffing the remainder in his mouth.

"Hmmff?" Johnny asked, his mouth full.

Kellie nodded her approval, and the boy was off.

The other mothers in the camp—Kathy Re, Danelle Weise and Joanne Johnson—glanced over to watch the interaction between Kellie and Teresa's youngest child. They were impressed.

"Nice job," Danelle said. "You've got that boy trained."

"Thanks," Kellie said, not intentionally trying to display her authority over Dave's kids. "It's just that he's had nothing but sugar today."

Lauren approached.

"Kellie, will you come into the tent with us? We're braiding each other's hair and Carlyn wants to hear the Timber story."

Kellie excused herself from the other women and followed Lauren. Inside, she sat cross-legged with six teenage girls. After Kellie related the story of her wolf, Timber, she continued to listen to the hot topics of the day with them—boys, softball and new school clothes.

At the campfire later that night, Kellie felt like she had begun to earn some respect from the other moms. She knew they were still scrutinizing her.

But the consensus was building among the women: Kellie is making their life better. There is not a devious thought in her mind. She's a nice person. How can we hate her?

Lauren came and sat down on Kellie's lap as the conversations around the fire began to thin out. They watched the embers glow red. Johnny and a few of the boys roasted marshmallows.

Kellie rubbed Lauren's shoulders and admired her French braids. Sitting next to the fire, they both got warm and sleepy.

Lauren stood up to stretch her legs, turned and kissed Kellie on the lips, then moved to her dad, and kissed him as well, before wishing everyone good night.

Once again, the adults all noticed. Kellie was clearly loved and accepted by Dave and all three kids.

Thursday, August 9, 2001

Tamara and her kids, Makenna and Al, arrived in town for the family reunion, planned for Cove Palisades State Park in Central Oregon. More camping, more water skiing. More fun.

It was the first time Tamara and her kids had seen the new house. Kellie, Nikki, Lauren and Johnny gave them a tour, paying special attention to the growing number of pets—horses, dogs and cats.

The kids all went out to jump on the trampoline. Soon, they would be loading up to head off on another outing.

Tamara was taking the Suburban, filled with kids, to the O'Brien reunion.

Kellie was struck by the warmth and friendliness of Teresa's sister. It was the first time she had seen her since December. She was tall, with dark features and a quick, sharp wit. Kellie thought of how many times she had supported Dave—before and after Teresa's death.

"This is quite the place, Kellie, my dear," Tamara said. "You and Dave have done good finding it."

She was clearly impressed.

"Well thank you," Kellie replied. "We do love it."

"And so do the kids," Tamara said, finishing Kellie's sentence. They stood together and watched all five kids jumping on the trampoline, cracking each other up as they tried to bounce one another off kilter.

"I'm so proud of all that you and Dave have accomplished in your short time being together," Tamara said. "The kids are doing great. They look wonderful. You both should be very proud."

"Oh, that's nice of you to say that," Kellie said. "They are such great kids. It's been fun. Hard sometimes. But fun."

"I know," Tamara said. "I don't know how you do it, Kellie. You're amazing. How you just stepped into three kids and all of this land, and moving Dave and the kids, and yourself all the way from Tennessee, and these horses, and everything else, you must be exhausted."

"Well, I do fall into bed at night, there's no doubt about that," Kellie said.

"I just say it because it's true," Tamara said. "And I want to tell you something. I know what I'm about to say because I'm a mom."

Kellie listened intently as they walked toward the patio table on the deck and sat down.

"I want you to promise me that you won't let these kids and Dave suck every bit of energy out of you," Tamara said, smiling. "Because they will, you know. Parenting is so demanding and I want you to promise me that you will always find time for yourself in all of this craziness. You need to ride your horses, and, especially continue your songwriting. It is so important not to lose yourself in all of this. Stay strong and take some time for yourself, OK?"

It was some of the first parenting advice Kellie had ever been offered.

"I promise," she said. She considered Tamara's words to be golden.

∞

For three nights, the O'Brien family camped and waterskied on Lake Billy Chinook, a reservoir formed near the junction of three rivers— the Crooked, the Metolius and the Deschutes—in Central Oregon.

On Sunday, the family reunion picnic took place at Dufur City Park.

Dave, who drove out to join the festivities and retrieve the kids, brought Tamara's letter with him. He felt they were ready to hear their mom's final words.

Johnny and Al were playing down at the creek when Dave produced the letter and asked the girls to come and listen. Teresa's parents were there. Her cousin Bobbi was there. And of course, Tamara was there.

Dave explained how he had received the letter from Tamara around Christmas, but had decided to hold onto it. Now, with Teresa's family around, Dave decided to let his children hear their mother's final words to them.

He pulled the envelope out of his jean jacket pocket and then carefully slid the typed page out, unfolding it.

Dave looked at his girls to make sure he had their attention. Nikki and Lauren were already riveted.

"Tamara, thank you for doing this for me," Dave began. "This is so difficult. Tell them,

Always remember I love you. Remember.
Remember they were conceived in love. Remember they were the most important things in my life.

Tell Nikki she is beautiful inside and out. Tell her not to be so hard on herself. Tell her life is about living and love, not about doing things perfectly. She doesn't have to have all the answers. She does not have to be in control. Nik, try not to be mad at me for leaving you so soon. I hope this doesn't make you grow up too fast. You are so much like Auntie Tami. Trust her. She will help you. Remember Nik. I love you. Always love yourself. You have nothing to prove. You are beautiful, talented, gifted and whole. Express yourself."

Dave paused to look up from the page for a second to catch Nikki's reaction. His daughter's eyes were watery, yet she was smiling.

"Loe,
You are like a bright shooting star whose light cannot be contained. Joy runs through you. Never let anyone take that away from you by making you feel inadequate or afraid. You have much to give people. Just your presence and energy enlivens a team or a room.

You are gifted, Lauren. Be strong in your body and your heart. Love life. Grab it moment by moment and share that joy. You are beautiful! I love you Lauren. You are my light.

John, my little buddy.
Oh John, I love you so much. Remember how I love you. You have a soft heart like me. You see into people's hearts. You're gentle, that's why you're so good with little kids, John. And you love the earth like I do—the forest, water and animals. John, think of me in those beautiful places and I will be there with you, in spirit. You will feel me as a soft breeze

against your cheek. Watch me wink at you from inside the stars and smile through the sunset.

I love you, John. You can be a tough football guy, but never lose that gentle heart. It is your great gift.

I know Dad, Grammy, Grampy, Gigi and Poppa, Auntie Tami and Auntie Lisa will take good care of you. They love you very much and promised me they would take good care of you. I'm sorry I have to leave you so soon. I wish it wasn't so. You know I am too ornery to give up.

Where I am going is beautiful, full of light and peace. And you know what? It is not far away. Very near actually. If you want me, take a few deep breaths and send me love with your heart and mind. I will come to you. Sometimes it will feel like a warm blanket of comfort, sometimes a soft voice in your mind, sometimes as a memory or an idea—and sometimes a kick in the butt!

I love you. I love you so much. Remember that whenever you remember me. There is a reason I am leaving now. It is part of a great master plan. I don't know what the reason is yet. Maybe I will soon. Maybe someday, you will discover it for yourself.

Just love yourselves. Love life. Love each other.

That's all that matters, guys. That's all I really want to tell you. When you're sad or scared or mad or lonely—reach inside and find the love. '

Love each other for me.

I love you forever!"

Dave turned his attention back to his daughters, who looked at him earnestly, with emotions beginning to overflow. The words from Teresa sounded like they had come straight from her mouth. They could imagine them spoken by her voice.

"Well, that's it, guys," Dave said softly.

Lauren began to cry, her tears a mix of joy and sadness.

Nikki, stoic as usual, put an arm around her sister.

Later that evening Dave explained the significance of the letter to Johnny, and read it to him.

Friday, August 10, 2001

Nine months had passed since Teresa's death by the time Dave finally went to select a permanent marker for the grave. "The last great act of defiance," Dave called it.

Dave finally stopped dragging his feet. He and Kellie had begun carving out a new future together. Approval from all sides—friends and family—was beginning to come around, even from the most disapproving critics.

On the way up the Columbia Gorge, Dave conducted an impromptu conversation with Teresa. With no one else in the truck, there was nothing to be embarrassed about.

"Well, things are good," Dave said aloud. "I'm sure you know. We miss you horribly and wish you were here. I hope you approve of all that's going on. The kids are doing well."

Dave could feel within every fiber that he had managed to keep the promise he made to Teresa. And he also felt sure that Teresa had laid some of the groundwork for it, though he couldn't even begin to speculate how.

Dave could imagine Teresa coming back, walking into the new five-acre horse farm he had bought with Kellie in Wilsonville. He could see her greeting Kellie, hugging her, and offering the first two words: "Thank you."

Dave pulled into the small parking lot at The Dalles Marble and Granite, and went inside the store to pick out a headstone.

He looked over a variety of granite markers. He wandered through the aisles, mulling all of the different color choices before settling on one that looked just right.

"I kind of like this one," Dave told the salesperson, pointing to a sample block. The stone was dark gray but there were flecks of color in it.

"Oh, we've just got some of those in, stacked in the back. They're 12-by-24s," the woman said.

"What do you call it?" Dave asked.

"Rainbow."

Monday, August 13, 2001

The veterinarian's face related the grim circumstances. The woman stood behind the horseshoe specialist as Sonny D's corrective aluminum shoes came off and was disappointed by what she saw.

After months of attempting to correct the damage done to the seven-year old quarter horse from the foundering of his hooves, Kellie, Dave and the experts were running out of hope that he could be saved.

"We're losing him," the vet said, rising up after inspecting the bottoms of Sonny D's hooves. The horse was drugged almost to the point of falling down. It was the only way to even get close to the painfully sensitive source of the horse's trouble.

"I'm afraid so," the farrier concurred.

Kellie's eyes reddened with emotion and became moist in the corners. She looked up to Dave and Wilma, her chin quivering.

Wilma held the lead rope attached to the horse's halter and as the medical experts said the words she leaned over and kissed Sonny D on the nose.

"Has the bone come through?" Dave asked. He had been fascinated by the whole process of caring for the horse since they had rescued him.

"Not yet," the vet said. "But it's about to."

"Oh my God, Dave, that's so awful," Kellie said, pleadingly. "I thought we could save him. This is so sad."

Kellie was disheartened. Over the past few days she thought the horse was getting better, not worse.

She stroked the horse's neck.

"I wanted him to get better so that he could at least walk me down the aisle at our wedding someday," Kellie said.

"We gave it a hell of a try," Dave said. He was discouraged as well, and he seldom admitted to defeat.

"The kids are going to be so sad to hear about this," Kellie said.

"What should we do?" Wilma asked.

"Well, he's not suffering too much yet," the vet said, reassuring all of them. "If it was me, I'd get an incredible cutting horse mare bought right away and breed him to her soon. Those bloodlines are too good to waste."

"Really?" Kellie asked, perking up a bit. "But how will we do it now? It's so late in the season. Will a mare still go into heat this late in the summer?"

"She will if we give a her the shot," the vet said, referring to a drug that acts like Viagra for horses.

"Wow, I didn't even know they had such a thing available," Kellie said.

"Just let me know, and I'll get out here as soon as possible to administer it," the vet said.

"Sure will," Dave said.

The vet and farrier finished up their work with Sonny D and left him to rest comfortably. Kellie, Dave and Wilma set out on a mission to find a registered quarter horse mare.

Monday, August 20, 2001

Kellie drove to Salem, and the Oregon State Fair, looking for a suitable mare for Sonny D. A flyer caught her eye in the equestrian pavilion. There was a chestnut-colored mare with beautiful features for sale in Canby.

Kellie made a call to the number on the flyer and then made a visit to the horse, and its owner, a struggling college student named Katie.

Everything about the horse was perfect. Kellie rode the horse, examined her, and inspected her registration papers.

Dave and Kellie decided to make the purchase.

They hauled the horse back to Frog Pond the next day.

The vet returned, and the breeding process began. Sonny D was a good stallion even though he had never bred a mare before. Dave joked that Sonny D practically pranced in his pen, as if he didn't feel a twinge of pain in his feet.

"Hurt hooves? What hurt hooves?" Dave joked.

The breeding worked and the mare became pregnant. It felt like another miracle.

Tuesday, September 11, 2001

Kellie heard the thump of feet hitting the floor above her and knew that it must be Nikki. But the footsteps were loud and quickly moving toward the stairs.

Nikki raced to the bottom of the stairs and turned toward her dad's bedroom, not hesitating to burst in with the news.

"Dad! Kellie! You've got to wake up," Nikki said.

The frantic shouting startled Dave awake, while Kellie, already awake, could sense the panic in Nikki's voice.

"The Pentagon has been bombed! I just heard it on the radio!" Nikki shrieked.

Dave calmly sat up, rubbing his eyes, and without a word reached for his own bedside radio. The cable hadn't been installed yet at the new house so clicking the TV on wasn't an option. All through the summer, they had eschewed the television and spent most of their time outside, riding horses and going to baseball and softball games.

Kellie put her arm around Nikki, who sat on the bed and told them of the news she had heard on her bedside radio..

Together, the three of them sat in astonishment and listened to a newscaster read reports of airplanes crashing into the Pentagon and the World Trade Center in New York.

With only the radio for a news source, Dave had the odd feeling that he was listening to a modern day Orson Welles-like "War of the Worlds" hoax. But with each passing minute, the science fiction quality of the unfolding story began to fade.

Lauren and Johnny joined them in the bedroom and the five of them sat and listened, and hugged, bewildered by the events transpiring on the East Coast. Lauren and Johnny, arriving late to the breaking story, asked repeated questions but Dave shushed them so he could hear the radio.

For the first time in several months, they needed to see a television.

Dave called his mom and dad at their condo in Charbonneau. Wilma answered the phone, horrified. She urged them to come immediately.

Kellie and the girls sat on the sofa and cried as they watched taped footage of the planes slamming into the skyscrapers, and later, as the buildings themselves collapsed like a house of cards. Gary, Dave and Johnny sat mesmerized as they watched.

Wilma made breakfast for them.

The kids asked Dave if they could stay home from school, but he said no. He wanted them to be with their classmates and teachers so that they could process the day's events at school.

"You guys are going to school," he said to them. "Terrorists want us to sit home and be afraid of them all day. If we do that, they win. We need to go about our normal lives."

Dave, Kellie and the kids rode back to the new home on Frog Pond Lane. The three kids finished getting ready for school. Dave drove them, and then went on to work.

Kellie rummaged through stacks of boxes and found the family's American flag and took it out front.

A few minutes later, the doorbell rang. It was Diane Reifert.

Kellie opened the door and saw Diane's tear-streaked cheeks.

Kellie walked out onto the porch to greet her friend.

"I've come to Rainbow Ranch where there is sunshine and happiness and love," Diane said, her voice shaking.

Kellie reached around Diane's shoulders and hugged her, and could feel a lump begin to resurface in her throat.

"My company, Morgan Stanley, lost over 30 floors in the first tower," Diane said. "They think all of the people we had there are buried in the rubble and probably dead."

Kellie gasped.

"Oh Diane, I'm so sorry," she said.

Diane's husband, Jim, was out of town taking part in a week-long bicycle tour.

"I'm alone," Diane said. "I can't reach Jim and he probably doesn't know any of this has happened. I'm so sickened by it all. I had to come over. I'm sorry I'm such a wreck."

"No, don't be," Kellie said. "It's fine. Come in. Come in."

Kellie led her to the living room and suggested that they sit down.

"I hope I haven't interrupted anything," Diane said.

"Not at all," Kellie said. "I was just starting to hang some pictures on the wall and trying to take my mind off all of this craziness."

Diane stayed about half an hour. Kellie showed her the rest of the house and the five acres and the horses.

Diane suggested they attend a church service honoring the victims of the tragedy on Thursday and Kellie agreed before giving her one more hug.

Diane left and Kellie went back to unpacking boxes. She turned the radio off.

Monday, September 24, 2001

Fearing she may get caught in the rain, Keely Jacobson grabbed her rain slicker and put it on before she left the house. Her two excited golden retrievers hustled outside in front of her, eager to begin their walk. It had become their ritual to walk in the early evening after she came home from teaching at West Linn High School.

Keely thought of Kellie as she started into a steady rhythm. She wanted to like her. She wanted to love her. But for some reason she couldn't. She had carefully watched Dave's close friends—even the mothers—as they interacted with Kellie at his birthday party over the weekend. It seemed as though almost everyone had come to terms with her presence now. They apparently accepted her.

But Keely still wasn't so sure. She couldn't get over her reservations. She had softened some. At the Susan G. Komen Race for the Cure, she had walked side by side with Kellie. And she could tell then that there was more to the loud redhead than her incessant talking.

Maybe it felt too much like betraying Teresa to fully accept this newcomer. However, it had become abundantly clear that Dave and his three kids loved her. They seemed happy and whole again. Wasn't that enough?

Keely thought about the Christmas party that she attended after Teresa died. It had been a somber and hollow experience. She remembered how Dave's eyes lacked their usual spark, and how the humor had drained out of him. She recalled the kids sitting on the couch, expressionless and withdrawn.

That certainly wasn't the case any more. The smiles were all back. And the reason was Kellie, much as she hated to admit it.

Keely wrestled with her feelings. Was she right about telling Dave he should have waited a year? Was Kellie really the right woman at the right time? Would the kids, in time, forget about their mother?

Keely picked up the pace and began to jog slowly as the long shadows began turning into dusk. The two dogs happily bounced along beside her.

Then she stopped.

"Teresa, I feel so confused," Keely said, whispering the words out loud through her heavy breathing. "I love you so much and I miss you terribly."

She started to cry.

"I want to accept Kellie. She is so nice and she has done so much for Dave and the kids. I do feel like she is very sincere and I know Dave is madly in love with her. And the kids adore her. It all seems so right, but why does it feel so wrong to me?"

By getting the words out, Keely seemed better able to process them.

"I don't know. It's just that I feel like if I love and accept her, then I'll be like everyone else who seems to be forgetting you. Well, not forgetting exactly, but just putting you aside. I don't ever want to put you aside. I love you. You're my best friend and I don't ever want to lose that. I know it's silly. I feel like if love her, then I can't love you as much. I know I should love and accept her, and maybe I already do . . . but . . ."

Keely noticed the sun begin to emerge beneath a wall of dark clouds. The sunlight shone across the clouds and filled the sky with brilliant hues of orange and pink and purple.

She stopped and stared into the sky, watching the brilliant sunset. She was awed by it in a way she had only ever felt once before: At Mt. Bachelor, after the day of skiing with the Grills.

It was a sign from Teresa, Keely thought.

She felt receptive to her friend's message, and interpreted its meaning.

Accept Kellie. Don't feel guilty. It's all OK.

Keely knelt down and wept briefly. The dogs came running to her side and began licking the tears from her cheeks. She smiled, and began to laugh at the sweet kisses—those that came from her dogs, and those that came in the form of a pink sunset from her best friend.

Wednesday, September 26, 2001

After a full week with the mare, Sonny D's health started to deteriorate once again. Kellie observed his temper become shorter. He tried to bite whenever Kellie or Dave tried to pick out the mud and manure from his tender hooves to relieve the pressure. His mood was perpetually sour.

Dave called the vet and she came out to appraise the situation. The stallion was practically shaking he was in so much pain. The Bute that the Grills mixed with his small ration of dry oats didn't seem to offer any relief.

The kids left for school knowing that the horse would be dead when they returned in the afternoon. They all went out to say their good-byes to him.

Kellie was in tears when the vet arrived.

"He's so moody and he's in so much pain," Kellie told the doctor. "He's just not himself."

The vet attempted to lift the horse's front hoof to check it more closely, and the weight distribution to the other side almost knocked the horse over.

"The coffin bone is about to break through," the vet said, regretfully. "His connective tissues just can't bear his weight any more."

Kellie cried harder as Dave and Wilma wrapped their arms around her.

"It's time we put him down," the vet advised. "I'm sorry. I wish I could have saved him."

"We do too," Dave said soothingly.

Kellie and Wilma walked up to Sonny D and opened his barn stall door. He pinned his ears back and then relaxed them, realizing they were friends. He leaned his face towards the women, accepting their love and attention. His chocolate brown eyes were sad and full of pain, yet they still showed some recognition for the family that fought for him and rescued him.

The vet returned from her van with a vial of drugs and began the procedure of euthanizing the horse.

Kellie walked away from the horse and approached Dave, hugging him and kissing him. She couldn't bear see Sonny D go down. The vet reached out and touched Kellie's arm as they passed one another.

Dave walked closer to the horse to offer a final good bye.

"Bye big guy," he said. "You've been quite a horse. Thanks for taking the kids' minds off of losing their mom and letting us try to heal you. You're a stud, Son. You can't say we didn't let you go out without a smile."

Dave put his hands on the animal's neck one final time. The vet took the lead rope and she used Dave's help to take the limping horse to the center of the field. She produced a syringe and injected the drug into the primary vein running through the horse's neck. Her eyes filled with tears too. She knew how much the horse had soothed the family's pain after Teresa's death.

CHAPTER ELEVEN

Full Acceptance

Monday, October 8, 2001

It seemed like old times back in Kenny Royster's Nashville studio. Kellie was in Tennessee to visit Kaysie for the first time since they had parted ways back in May. But she also had an agenda.

She wanted to have "These Boots and Me" recorded professionally and then give Dave a CD of the song for Christmas.

In the studio, Kellie caught up with friends. It felt good to be around the musicians again, and they laughed and joked together as if she'd never left.

Kellie had secured Buddy Jewell to perform the vocal track. He was one of her favorite singers, and a veteran of Nashville's club scene. She had introduced Dave to him on the Spring Break trip. Dave had quickly become a fan as well.

Kellie felt fortunate to know some of the best players that Nashville had to offer. She had been amazed by the talent she saw ever since she entered the studio for the first time many years ago.

But this song was special.

Kellie explained to them the significance of "Boots." It was a song about a true story. Dave, her new boyfriend, had lost his wife to breast cancer less than a year earlier. This, she told them, was to be his Christmas present.

The explanation brought a sense of emotion and concentration to the recording. Kellie could tell the story behind the song had affected them.

She walked out of the sound room into the engineer's room, shutting the sound-proof door behind her. She sat behind the control console and listened as the first notes of the song were played. As the musicians put down the track, Kellie's eyes watered. The emotion was palpable in the music, and it sounded better than she could have imagined. Kaysie noticed Kellie's reaction and she took her sister by the hand. She began to tear up as well.

The next day, Buddy came into the studio to record the vocals and harmonies. He, too, put his heart into the song. Kellie was thrilled with the results and couldn't wait to present it to Dave. She was unsure whether she could keep it under wraps until Christmas.

Tuesday October 30, 2001

Wilma and Kellie sat down for lunch together at the Tualatin Country Club, intent on making some arrangements for a wedding.

It had become a foregone conclusion that Dave and Kellie would wed, and that it would most likely happen in the spring.

Wilma wanted some dates set in stone before she and Gary left for Palm Desert, where they had made a habit of migrating to for the winter. She knew that by delaying they risked not being able to find the dates and venues that they wanted.

After lunch, the two women spoke with the program director at Tualatin Country Club to see what dates were still available for the rehearsal dinner. There were just three left in April and May of 2002.

Kellie and Wilma decided on Saturday, April 27 for the wedding, and booked the available evening of Friday, April 26 for the dinner. Next, they went to the Crowne Plaza Hotel and reserved the ballroom for the reception.

And they went to the Community of Hope Lutheran Church—just a half mile from Frog Pond Lane—to inquire about holding the ceremony there. In the span of a few hours, they had all three lined up.

The only thing left was for Dave to ask Kellie to marry him.

Wednesday, October 31, 2001

Kellie was practically bursting to tell Kathy Hart the good news about securing the church, the reception site and the rehearsal dinner location with Wilma.

Kathy was busily tending to two large pots on her stove—elk chili in one and chicken chili in the other. Johnny and Taylor were preparing their costumes to go trick-or-treating.

Kathy and Doug were expecting 30 guests, but Dave and Kellie were the first to arrive.

"You won't believe it," Kellie said, bounding into the kitchen. "We got all three!"

Kathy gave her a hug.

"That is great news. Kellie, your wedding is going to be amazing. I just know it."

In the other room, Doug gave Dave a puzzled look.

"Yeah," Dave said, noticing it. "My mom asked Kellie to marry me, she said yes, and so they set a date."

Dave chuckled as Doug shook his head.

Kellie overheard Dave's description of the events.

"That's exactly right!" Kellie said proudly. "If you want to get anything done around here you have to do it yourself!"

Kathy smiled.

"I agree," she said, stirring one of her pots.

"Well congratulations," Doug said. "That's great news."

"Thanks," Kellie said. "But we also have something we wanted to ask you guys, right Dave? It's partly why we wanted to come over a little early."

"Yes," Dave said. He stopped there because he knew Kellie was excited to continue.

"Well, we were wondering if you two would grace us with the honor of being in our wedding line?" Kellie asked.

Kathy was touched that Kellie thought so much of her after such a short period of time.

"Oh, Kellie," Kathy said. "That would be wonderful. I'd love to."

"How about it, Doug?" Dave asked.

"Does it mean I have to dress up and everything?" Doug asked, teasing. "I don't know. I've been in wedding lines before and it's not that fun."

"Well you haven't been in my wedding before," Dave said. "This one will be fun."

Doug nodded.

"Somehow I don't doubt that," he said. "OK. I guess I will . . . Hey, I just thought of something. Do you guys know where you're going on your honeymoon yet?"

Dave smirked.

"No, my mom and Kellie haven't planned that far ahead," he said, winking in Kellie's direction. "I'm sure I'll be told that next."

Kellie made a fist and thumped him in the shoulder of his denim jacket.

"Maybe I could see if I could get you the lodge in Eastern Oregon," Doug said, continuing his thought.

Dave knew it already. He had stayed there with Doug and their boys on hunting trips. It was a huge, seven-bedroom lodge in Kinzua. He had described it before to Kellie.

"Oh, Doug, that would be incredible!" Kellie exclaimed.

"Well, no guarantees yet, but I'll try," Doug said. "The date is April 27th?"

"Yes," Kellie said.

"Well I'll see what I can do for that following week," Doug said.

"Thank you," Dave said. "That would be a fun place to stay."

Kellie nodded her agreement. They both loved rugged outdoorsy places.

Dave and Doug soon left to walk with the boys as they went door to door soliciting candy in exchange for looking scary.

Back at the Harts' house, Kellie and Kathy told the remaining guests about the wedding news. The date was starting to sink in. It was official, Kellie thought: I'm going to marry Dave.

She felt like she needed to pinch herself to believe it.

Friday, November 2, 2001

Gold and red leaves littered the cold, wet lawn as Kellie returned from taking Johnny and Lauren to school. Dave had been in the shower when she left.

But all the way back from Tualatin, Kellie had been sure she couldn't contain her secret from Dave any longer.

As she walked in the door to the bedroom, she saw Dave sitting on the bed, pulling on his shoes. She walked over to him and gave him a hug.

"I don't want to let you go yet," she said.

"Why?" Dave asked, teasingly. "What do you have in mind?"

"I have something that I need to give to you," Kellie said. "I told myself I was going to wait, but it is just killing me to wait . . . and . . ."

"Well what is it?" Dave asked, curiously.

"Oh, I shouldn't," Kellie said hesitantly. "But I just want to do it. Do you need to get to the office right away or can you take a few minutes?"

"I'm fine for a while," Dave said. "What is it, Kell?"

"Well, you know when I went to Nashville?"

"Yeah."

"While I was there I bought your Christmas gift and you're never going to believe what it is!"

Dave was sure he had no idea.

"Just a minute and I'll be right back," Kellie said. And she turned and left the room.

Seconds later she reappeared, holding something in her hands behind her back.

"Guess what it is!" she said.

"Kellie," he said, chuckling. "I have got no clue."

"Well . . ." she said, drawing it out. "I went into the studio while I was in Nashville."

She brought her hands forward and handed Dave a CD. Written on the silver disc, in black ink, were the words "These Boots and Me."

"I had Buddy Jewell sing 'Boots' and it's done with a five-piece band," Kellie blurted.

"Wow!" Dave said, his eyes widened as he laughed. "That is so cool!"

"Merry Christmas!" Kellie said gleefully, leaning forward to give him a kiss.

"Thanks! Let's listen to it," Dave said.

They went up the stairs and Dave inserted the disc into the CD player.

"You're gonna love it!" Kellie said, squeezing the words in before the music began.

They sat down on the couch together and listened to it intently. Kellie studied the features of Dave's face as he listened, hanging on every word and note. When the song was finished playing, Dave got up to turn it off.

"That is the most incredible song I have ever heard," Dave said. "I absolutely love it. Thank you so much, Kell. I would have never known you were up to something like that in Nashville."

He shook his head, disbelieving that he had just heard the song he wrote for Teresa being performed by Nashville musicians.

"Wow! It is so good. Let's hear it again," Dave said. He hit play and sat down with Kellie again, holding her hand while they listened to it play once more.

When it was through, they played it again, and again.

Each time, Dave had something new to rave about.

"Kellie, there is nothing I can give you that will ever equal this," Dave said. "It is the best present ever."

He pulled her close and gave her a kiss.

"I'm so glad you like it," Kellie said. "I do too. And I love you."

"I love you," Dave said. "Thank you."

Dave took the CD with him as he left for work. Kellie could hear the song begin again from the front porch as he pulled out of the driveway.

Kellie called her accomplice, Kaysie, and told her how Dave's gift had been received. His reaction made her holiday complete even though it hadn't even begun.

Thursday, November 22, 2001: Thanksgiving

Tamara stood to offer the prayer as those seated around the table bowed their heads and held hands:

"Lord, we thank you today for our many blessings," she began.

"We thank you for the family that you have assembled here today and we thank you for the many blessings of health and happiness that you have offered to us.

"We thank you for this food that we are about to eat and for the hands that prepared it.

"And Lord, we thank you on this special day for the memories that we have of Teresa. Please help us continue to heal from the loss of her in our everyday lives, and thank you for the renewal you have seen fit to offer this family. Thank you for bringing us Kellie and working through her to help comfort Dave, Nikki, Lauren and Johnny.

In Christ's name we pray, Amen."

Tamara lifted her head and everyone else surrounding the table followed suit.

Kellie, seated next to Dave toward the far end of the table, sniffed back a surge of emotion and used her napkin to dab the corner of her eye.

Coming to San Francisco, to the new home of Teresa's sister, had brought some nervous tension with it. The Thanksgiving holiday fell close to the one-year anniversary of Teresa's death, and Tamara had convinced Dave to bring everyone down to her home so that they could be together.

Ron and Jean were there. Teresa's cousin Bobbi and her family were in town also. Kellie wondered if she would continue to receive a cold shoulder and whether it was a good idea for her to impose on their gathering at all.

Dave assured her it would be fine.

Tamara and Scott welcomed her with open arms. And during dinner, she felt graciously welcomed by Teresa's parents as well.

After the turkey dinner was finished, Kellie took several of the plates into the kitchen and took the opportunity to thank Tamara for her kind words during the prayer.

"It's the truth," Tamara said, hugging Kellie. "We're so grateful for you, and all you do."

Throughout the weekend, Kellie grew ever closer to the members of Teresa's family.

The CD that she made for Dave proved a big hit with all of them as well.

Of course, since the song was a tribute to Teresa, it provoked strong emotions. Kellie had made copies of the song to hand out to each family member.

"Dave, you did a beautiful job writing that song," Teresa's mother, Jean, said.

"Actually I didn't do very much," Dave said. "It was Kellie that wrote the song. All I did was give her the idea."

"Well, I know that she helped you put it into a song, but the words came from you, didn't they?" Jean asked.

"No, not really," Dave explained. "I told her over the phone that I had an idea about a song about that old pair of boots I had, and how I had married Teresa in them and then laid her to rest in them. That was it. After we hung up, Kellie wrote the song, and then next morning she faxed me a page with the lyrics."

Jean listened intently. She was a little surprised by that revelation. *Kellie* had written the song? How could that be?

The reaction by Teresa's family members was unanimous. They were deeply touched by the sentiment of the song, and the fact that Kellie had taken such a lead role in its production provoked warm feelings of love and acceptance. They were suddenly able to see the role that Kellie had carved out for herself within the family, and they were supportive. It made them feel at ease to know, for certain, that Kellie wasn't trying to replace Teresa. To the contrary, the song served as evidence that she was actually *honoring* her.

Kellie witnessed the song's power that weekend, and sensed it had healing properties for those still grieving Teresa's death a year later. She watched them cry and listen. It seemed cathartic.

Kellie had reached a new milestone with Teresa's family. She finally had their acceptance.

CHAPTER TWELVE

Closer to A Wedding

Sunday, November 25, 2001

After flying home from the Bay Area, the kids convinced Dave to take them up to Dufur so that they could see their mother's gravesite. They hadn't seen it since their father had picked out the tombstone.

And Kellie had never seen Teresa's final resting place.

Dave was impressed with the way his kids were handling the anniversary of their mother's death. They were reflective without moping. They sang along with the CDs that Kellie played for them in the Suburban. They laughed and talked and sang non-stop for nearly all of the 100 miles.

The kids made Dave proud. They were survivors. They understood the concept of making lemonade out of lemons. He knew that Kellie's continually upbeat and positive energy had something to do with it.

Yes, he thought to himself in a reflective moment as he gazed into the blue Columbia River, he and the kids are going to be fine. One year had passed and the Grill family was going strong.

The white Suburban rounded the last corner on the paved highway, and Dave pulled onto the gravel road that led to the cemetery, and then through the wrought iron gates.

"Oh my gosh!" Lauren said from the backseat. She was pointing at the clock on the dashboard.

"It's 3:33!" Nikki shouted.

Kellie felt a sudden shiver of goose bumps on her arm.

"Wow, Dave, what are the odds of that happening today right as we're pulling into the cemetery?" Kellie asked.

Dave shrugged, also amazed.

"Mom's saying 'Hi,'" Johnny said.

"You know John, I think you're right," Dave replied.

Dave pulled the Suburban up close to the O'Brien family plot and put the vehicle in park. Everyone hopped out, without saying a word. All of them contemplated the idea that Teresa was present with them, though they couldn't see or hear her.

Like Johnny said, maybe the coincidence of the 3:33 was her way of saying, "Hello."

Kellie absorbed the beauty of the scenery. The cemetery was solemn and beautiful, set between two rolling golden wheat fields.

She was also struck by another occurrence of 3:33. The numbers, like the songs and rainbows, had become strong symbols that Teresa used to communicate her love to them.

There was comfort in knowing that she was their guardian angel.

December 5, 2001

Kellie leaned over and put her hand on Dave's right arm as he drove.

"When you marry me I want a ring in the shape of a 'V,'" Kellie said, breaking the silence.

"How do you shape a ring into a V?" Dave asked.

"I don't know, but there's got to be a way," Kellie said. "It would come around your finger and then as I look at it there would be a notch in the shape of a V."

"Hmm," Dave said, beginning to think of what that might look like, and if there actually was a ring out there that would resemble something like that.

But the V pattern made perfect sense. "V" had been the nickname Kellie had chosen for Dave at their first weekend together in Lincoln City. It stood for Victory.

When they returned home, Dave sketched a picture of a ring pattern in the shape of a V. He showed it to Kellie.

"Kind of like this?" Dave asked.

"Yes!" Kellie said, enthusiastically. "That's it. I don't even care if it has a diamond. I'm more interested in the shape. I know it might be hard to find. Do you think you can find a ring like that?"

"Well, maybe I can find a jeweler who will make one like this," Dave said.

"No, don't," Kellie replied, momentarily surprising Dave. "My other rule is that you have to get it at a pawn shop. I don't need anything new or fancy, I just want a ring that I can wear everywhere and not worry about it getting beat up. And I want it to remind me of you."

"Well there's no way in the world you're ever going to find something like that in a pawn shop," Dave said. "I'll keep my eye out, but we may have to have one built."

Dave folded the sketch, and put it in his pocket.

The next day, Dave showed the drawing to a friend at Metro Metals. He pulled it out of his pocket and casually unfolded it, setting it down on a desk. He knew that John Lipp had a friend in the jewelry business.

Dave picked up a pen off John's desk and added a few more details to his drawing. He drew in little stars, to represent diamonds, along both spokes of the V. Then he drew a large diamond in the middle.

"John," Dave began. "Where do you think I could find a ring shaped like that? Any ideas?"

Dave's co-worker paused and picked up the scrap of paper, studying it.

"No where that I know of. You might have to get it custom designed."

"That's kind of what I figured," Dave said. "How long do you think something like that would take? Think I could get it done in a couple of weeks?"

"Why? You planning to use it as a stocking stuffer for Christmas?"

"Something like that," Dave said, smiling.

John shook his head slowly, still studying the drawing.

"I don't know, Mr. Grill," John said, trying not to sound too pessimistic. "I think you could be out of luck on that one. I can give you a couple of phone numbers of guys who could help you out."

Dave nodded.

"Let me kick it around a little while longer. But if I need those numbers I'll let you know. I think I might look around for a couple of days first."

Dave walked back to his desk, glanced at the sketch one more time and put it in his briefcase. He began to resign himself to the fact that he had procrastinated too long. The chances of finding a suitable ring by Christmas fit somewhere between slim and none.

Later that afternoon, Dave headed out of the office for an appointment in the Clackamas area southeast of Portland. Rather than take the I-205 freeway, Dave decided to meander south along 82nd Avenue, with its long strip of used car lots, Chinese restaurants and pawn shops.

He scanned both sides of the street for miles but didn't see any place worth pulling over for until he was out of the Portland city limits and approaching the Clackamas Town Center mall.

Dave came to a stop light, with three cars ahead of him. He swiveled his head to the left and saw a sign: "All That Glitters Jewelry." Dave didn't know if it was a retail store or second-hand. The left turn lane was empty and Dave checked his side mirror to see if anyone was coming.

He checked the clock on the dashboard to make sure he had enough time to stop.

It was 3:33 P.M.

Dave blinked, jolted alert by the numbers.

Now he had to stop. The decision had been made for him. Dave pulled hard on the steering wheel and moved into the turn lane. When the left arrow turned green, he pulled into the small parking lot.

Dave wasn't sure what to expect. He pushed open the door and walked in to find that the store was a combination of retail and consignment. He leaned over the first glass case and began to casually look at a group of rings.

He gave them a cursory glance and suddenly his eyes locked onto one ring near the middle.

A salesclerk approached the other side of the case.

"Anything I can help you with?" the woman asked.

Dave looked up to meet her.

"Are these new rings?" he asked.

"No. Most of them are either used or on consignment," she replied. "The new rings are over there." She pointed to the case behind Dave.

Dave glanced down one more time for a closer look at the ring that had caught his eye.

He looked up at the sales clerk again.

"Wait right here," he said. He wheeled and pushed the door open and walked out to the Suburban. He unlocked the door and grabbed his brief case, opening it in the driver's seat. He quickly grabbed the sketch, shut the case and walked back in the store.

The store clerk watched him come back in, perplexed.

Dave spread the piece of paper down on the top of the glass case and rotated it to face the clerk.

"See that ring there?" Dave asked, pointing downward into the case. "Does that ring look anything like this drawing?"

She reached under the glass to find the ring and pulled it out so that she could inspect it. She checked it against the crude sketch on the paper.

"Oh my God," the woman said. "That is the ring."

The woman's statement confirmed his initial thought. It was unbelievable.

The woman handed the ring to Dave and he studied it. It was shaped like a V, precisely like the drawing. The ring was 14 karat yellow gold with 15 miniature round diamonds in the channel that formed the V. In the center was a solitaire diamond with a yellow tint to it. Dave thought the center stone looked damaged.

"If I got this ring, could I take that center diamond out and replace it with one of my own?" Dave asked.

"Sure," she said.

Dave shook his head, still stunned at what he had stumbled across.

"I don't have anyone here now that can remove the setting, but we can do it for you if you want to come back tomorrow," she said. "Do you want to look at some loose diamonds?"

Dave just wanted the ring. He wasn't worried about the replacement diamond.

"I've got to get to an appointment, but I'll be back tomorrow," Dave said.

He discussed the terms of the sale with the clerk and walked back outside.

He hopped up into his driver's seat, shifted the briefcase over, and sat a moment. He couldn't believe the luck of what had just happened. Any more, luck didn't feel like the right word. It felt like another small piece of a grand scheme had come to pass.

Dave put the key into the ignition, shifted the Suburban into reverse, and the Lee Ann Womack song, "I Hope You Dance" started out of his radio speakers.

He smiled at the ticklish chills that raced up the back of his neck.

"Whoa," Dave said aloud.

Wednesday, Dec. 11, 2001

All three kids helped decorate the Christmas tree, and took the time to admire their handiwork as they added garland and ornaments.

Kellie, as usual, did most of the work. Her bottomless reservoir of energy had kept the household running smoothly and the three kids to their myriad of school functions on time. She had learned to master life as a full-time mom.

She was excited to be spending her first Christmas with the Grills and it was evident in the way she gleefully decorated the living room. With the final touches nearly completed on the tree, Kellie excused herself to the basement to find a box of decorative glasses.

Lauren met her halfway up the stairs, mustered a serious face, and said, "We need to talk to you."

They returned to the living room together. Johnny took Kellie by the hand. "You better sit down for this," he said. "This is serious."

Kellie's animated expression grew puzzled. She sat down, across the room from the Christmas tree.

The three kids knelt down in front of her, each on one knee. Lauren went first.

"Will you marry me?" she asked.

Then Johnny, pulling open a small jewelry box with a diamond ring, followed suit. "Will you marry us?"

And Nikki. "Will you marry me?"

Kellie was stunned. It seemed like a dream. Dave stood behind his kids, arms folded, smiling at the scene and chuckling under his breath.

"Yes!" Kellie said. "I'll marry you, I'll marry you, and I'll marry you!"

She looked up over the kneeling kids to see Dave's smug grin.

"Oh, and I guess I'll marry you too!" Kellie said, rising from her chair to hug Dave.

"Daddy, tell her about the ring!" Lauren squealed.

Dave went into the story about finding the ring, and how lucky he had felt stumbling across it. Of course, the story included a 3:33, and "I Hope You Dance" came on the radio. So maybe it wasn't luck after all.

Kellie could barely believe her ears, let alone believe the ring was actually on her finger. She made phone calls to each member of her family to tell them the news.

Meanwhile, Dave and the kids went back to hanging ornaments on the tree.

When Kellie came back into the living room, Lauren offered to paint Kellie's nails to better show off the ring.

Johnny paused from hanging an ornament.

"So Kellie," he began. "Does this mean that we have to call you 'Mom'?" It was a question that Nikki and Lauren were curious about too.

Kellie considered the question but had a quick response to it.

"No," she said. "Your mom is always going to be your mom. She is the one who gave birth to you and changed your diapers. I think you should just call me Kell. I think if you called me 'Mom' when my back was turned I wouldn't even know to turn around."

The kids seemed satisfied with the answer.

Three days later, the family hosted a lasagna dinner for 20 friends and family members. Afterward, they went to watch Nikki sing in the Wilsonville High School production of "Wizard of Oz."

As he watched his eldest daughter on the stage, Dave's mind floated back across the day, the week and the year. His three kids were flourishing, just as Teresa would have wanted. And he was in love again.

Dave turned in his seat to face Teresa's mother, Jean O'Brien, sitting in the row behind him.

He whispered to her. "Did you see the ring?"

"Yes," she said. "And it's beautiful."

Saturday, April 20, 2002

Kathy Hart's house had been meticulously cleaned and decorated, with swans and at least a dozen framed photos of Dave and Kellie, for the wedding shower.

Kathy had help—Wilma and Dave's sister, Lisa—in organizing the third of three wedding showers. Earlier, Kellie had flown back to Tennessee for a shower thrown by Kaysie and a couple of their closest friends. Another was thrown by her family in Salt Lake City in February during the Winter Olympics.

Kellie and Dave had reached an agreement that they didn't want anyone to give them gifts for their wedding. Instead, they asked their would-be gift-givers to donate money to the Susan G. Komen Breast Cancer Foundation in memory of Teresa.

However, most of the women had prevailed on Kellie to permit gifts for her bridal showers.

Kellie had the unsettled sense that a few of the women still had tentative feelings about the marriage. But she didn't let it upset her. Her spirits were high. In the past year, she had learned that everyone comes around to understanding in their own time. If Jean O'Brien could do it, then anyone could.

Some of the women, like Diane Riefert, had no qualms whatsoever about celebrating with Kellie. Diane had been an ally from the very start. She brought Kellie a porcelain, life-sized brown cowboy boot, filled with daffodils, daisies and Baby's breath.

And Kathy Hart offered Kellie her wedding dress. It was a perfect fit.

Saturday, April 27, 2002

Kellie followed closely behind Kathy Hart's black Ford Expedition as it wound through the curving Lake Oswego streets. The wedding day had arrived and they were going to Kathy's regular salon to get their hair done.

Kathy was in the chair first and Kellie watched the stylist fix her blonde hair and artfully apply her makeup.

As Kellie watched, she thought about how much Kathy and Doug had been supportive since the first day she met them. The first time Kellie and Kathy had gone out for lunch together, Kathy said something that had struck a chord: "We love Dave and the kids. Whatever, or whomever, makes them happy, makes us happy. All we want is to see that family heal and be whole again. If you are the one who does that for them, then count us in all the way."

Kellie imagined that, at some level, everyone at Teresa's memorial service must have felt the same way. Acceptance had been more difficult to come by from some than others. Eventually, she had earned their respect.

When Kathy's hair and makeup were done, Kellie took her turn in the chair.

Kathy needed to run a few errands before the photo shoot in the front yard of Dave and Kellie's house.

"OK, well I'll see you later for photos," Kathy said, getting ready to walk out to the parking lot. "Do you know how to get back home from here?"

"Yeah, I should be fine," Kellie answered as her strawberry blonde hair was being tied into a knot on the top of her head. "You look great."

"Oh, thanks," Kathy said, coyly. "I have on so much makeup, but I guess it will be good for photos. Do you want them to do your makeup too?"

Kellie started to shake her head but decided she better keep it still.

"That's OK," she said. "I can do it when I get home."

"I'd be happy to pay for that too, as part of my gift to you," Kathy said, beginning to open her purse again.

"No! You don't have to do that too!" Kellie protested.

"I'd love to do it for you," the makeup artist said. "I could make you look beautiful for your wedding day and I've done lots of makeup for photography."

"Well . . . if you want . . ." Kellie said. She was warming up to the idea. It would be one less thing to do when she got home.

"Good!" Kathy said. She handed cash to the makeup artist.

"Thank you so much," Kellie said. "You spoil me!"

"Everyone should be spoiled on their wedding day," Kathy said. "See ya later."

Kellie was pleased with the results of her hair and makeup. She checked the time and decided she needed to hustle back to the house to start getting dressed. She needed to meet the photographers and the rest of the wedding party when they arrived.

Kellie left the salon and drove through the downtown Lake Oswego streets, confident that she could retrace her steps back home.

But in a matter of eight blocks, she was confused. Is it a right here? That doesn't look familiar, she thought. She knew that she needed to go south, so she determined to find streets that pointed in that direction. But she missed the turn off for Wilsonville, and as she drove deeper and deeper into West Linn, she began to feel a wave of panic.

She was lost, and making matters worse, she wasn't carrying her cell phone.

She was too embarrassed to stop and call for directions, for pride's sake, and decided to keep going until she saw something familiar. It didn't work. She turned around and tried to relocate the salon again. She couldn't find that either.

Suddenly, her wedding day seemed on the brink of disaster.

She was near tears, which would sure ruin her fresh makeup job, when she pulled over.

"Oh please, Teresa, help me get home," Kellie said aloud. "It's getting so late and I've got to still get in my wedding dress and take photos and greet everybody who comes to the house . . . and . . ."

She stopped her rambling prayer for a moment.

She saw a sign—an actual address sign—on the side of the road. It was next to a strip mall and a Taco Bell. The digits were 333.

She pulled into the parking lot and turned around, and then re-entered the street and drove in the opposite direction. She saw a green sign, partly obscured by the branch of a tree. It read "Wilsonville" and pointed to the road she had missed.

Kellie made a right turn onto Stafford Road and found her way home again.

"Thank you," she whispered with relief.

∞

While Kellie had been frantically praying for a clue how to find her way home, Dave had spent the morning fishing in a boat on the Willamette River.

If there was any better way to illustrate their contrasting energies it must be that, Kellie concluded.

Once home, Kellie hurriedly dressed. The white dress had a sequined bodice with a peak-a-boo front and lace arms. It was a form-fitting gown with no train.

Once she had the dress on, she came upstairs and began trying to manage the chaos brewing in the front yard. Not only was the photographer busily preparing his equipment, guests and friends—in addition to those being photographed—were spilling into the yard for hugs and best wishes because the church was just a few blocks away and they had time to kill.

Kellie, still settling down from her frantic drive home, was beginning to feel a new wave of anxiety as she tried to meet and greet all of the people stopping by. Her nervous hands couldn't get the fragile clasp of the antique pearl necklace to latch right so she enlisted the help of a friend.

Dave, on the other hand, remained cool as a cucumber.

He wore black Wrangler jeans and put on a long black suit jacket over his white shirt. He wore a gray Stetson, black boots and a bolo tie to accessorize his chic cowboy look.

Kellie saw him calmly smiling and greeting friends and family in the front yard and wished some of his calm would rub off on her.

Kellie's father, Brent, sought out Teresa's dad. The two of them had met at the rehearsal dinner the night before.

Brent spotted Ron standing alone in the front yard.

"It's sure going to be a beautiful setting for these photos with these flowering trees, won't it?" Brent said, referring to the pink cherry blossoms hanging like cotton candy in the limbs above them. He extended a hand.

"Sure will," Ron agreed, accepting the handshake. "I can't believe it was raining so hard this morning and now it's perfect."

"Yeah," Brent said. "You'd think God knew there was a wedding or something going on today."

He paused briefly, and then continued.

"Hey, I wanted to say something and I was going to tell you last night and I didn't get around to it," Brent said. "I just wanted to tell you how awful sorry I am that you lost your daughter, and I just wanted to thank you and your wife for being so good to Kellie. This has all got to be so hard for both of you. I get to walk Kellie down the aisle in about an hour, and it got me to thinking—you don't get to walk with Teresa again. That's just gotta hurt like hell, and I'm so sorry for your pain."

Ron, dignified as ever, resisted the tears that had so frequently flowed in the past year.

He liked Brent, a big burly guy who reminded him so much of Brett.

"Well thank you," Ron said graciously. "I appreciate your telling me that."

"I'm just damn impressed with you and Jean," Brent said. "You are very strong. It's got to be the hardest damn thing in the world."

"It is," Ron agreed.

"Dad! Come on!" Kellie yelled from across the yard. "We need you over here for a photo with me and Kaysie!"

"Well, the princess calls," Brent said. "I'll see you a bit later."

"OK," Ron said, smiling. "Thanks again for your concern."

"You betcha," Brent said, turning to walk toward his twin daughters, one in white and the other in black. His mind was still stuck with Ron and Jean. To bury a child, he thought, must be the most unimaginable thing he could think of.

Over by the front patio, Jean O'Brien chatted amiably with Kay Davis, Kellie's mom. They floated from one topic to the next—all related to the busy day.

Kay had been on the verge of joyful tears all day and was so excited that her baby girl Kellie—one minute younger than Kaysie—was getting married. The sight of Kellie in her white wedding gown had put her over the edge. She used her handkerchief to dab the corners of her eyes.

"It almost seems like a dream," Kay told Jean. "I would never have believed that my Kellie would end up with Dave Grill. I guess it just goes to show you that you never do know in life, do you?"

Kay tried to be careful with her words. She knew this wasn't an easy day for the O'Briens.

"Now that's true," Jean agreed. "You never do know. It seems like just yesterday we were at Teresa and Dave's wedding. Time does fly."

"I know," Kay said. She quietly reached out and put her hand on Jean's arm. "This must be so hard for you guys. I'm sorry that you have had to go through all you've been through. I can't even imagine burying one of my children. It's not right and I'm so sorry."

"Well thank you," Jean said. "Yes. Even now, sometimes Ron and I can't believe she's really gone."

"I'm sure," Kay said, nodding. "Are you doing OK?"

"Oh yes," Jean said. "We keep on and stay strong. We have to. We have too much to live for."

Jean nodded toward the three Grill kids and their cousins, laughing and joking with Tamara and Ron.

"Yes, you do," Kay said. "They are incredible kids. Teresa did a wonderful job in raising them."

"Yes, she did," Jean said proudly. "She and Dave were great parents. And Dave and Kellie will continue doing a great job."

"I think so too," Kay said. She admired Jean, tall and strong like a pillar. She could scarcely comprehend Jean's suffering but loved her for the way she had warmed to Kellie.

They were united by one thing.

They both raised daughters that fell in love with Dave Grill.

∞

Nikki sang to the seated guests at Community of Hope Lutheran Church while they waited for the service to begin.

Seventeen months had passed since she last sang to a sanctuary full of people. This time it was a much happier occasion. She sang "Could Not Ask For More" by Sara Evans. Kaysie's husband, Mark, accompanied Nikki with his guitar.

The church was bright and modern with upholstered chairs that hooked together instead of pews. More than 200 people filled the room.

Nikki finished her song to a rousing applause, which also served to cue the beginning of the ceremony.

A flower girl wandered down the aisle, delicately picking rose petals out of a small basket and dropping them by her feet.

Brent Poulsen, with his twin daughters linked on either elbow, came in next. Kellie, in white, was on his right. Kaysie, in a black gown, was on the left.

Two by two, members of the wedding party entered the room, followed by Dave.

Pastor Doug Adams, a bespectacled man with a friendly voice and a mustache, wore a white robe.

He offered words of welcome and then an opening prayer.

Kellie wrapped her right arm around Dave's elbow. She was living her dream, savoring every second.

"Now we'll do your vows," the pastor advised.

"Dave, I ask you these questions: Do you take this woman to be your wedded wife, to live together in God's holy ordinance of marriage? Do you promise to love her, honor her, comfort her and keep her, in sickness and in health, forsaking all others, and keep only unto her as long as you both shall live?"

Dave's answer was firm and confident.

"I will," he said.

The pastor turned to ask the same of Kellie.

"Do you take this man to be your wedded husband, to live together in God's holy ordinance of marriage? Do you promise to love him, honor him, comfort him and keep him, in sickness and in health, forsaking all others, and keep only unto him as long as you both shall live?"

"I will," Kellie said, grinning.

"You've made it clear," the pastor said. "It's your intention to share with each other your laughter and tears. Bind your hearts and minds to each other."

Kellie, on cue, handed her wedding bouquet to Kaysie before turning to face Dave and taking his hands in hers.

Dave lifted his chin as he prepared to speak.

"Is this where I go?" he asked aloud, making sure. Dave hadn't prepared his vows ahead of time. He preferred to shoot from the hip.

"Umm," he began. "When the idea of us doing our own vows was brought up, I started brainstorming, and let the pen and mind ramble, and got quite a bit down. As I read it back I reflected on how you came into our lives and made us laugh again. And how you let us cry. And how your absolute unselfishness not only allowed Teresa's memory to come into our home, but your home."

Kellie let go of Dave's hand briefly to wipe the tears from her eyes.

"But you insist that she come there and be with us, and that to me was a remarkable gift to both the kids and me. Your passion, compassion . . . I could go on and on . . ." Dave continued.

Kellie interjected.

"Please don't!" she said, causing the attentive gathering a moment of laughter.

"These are all attributes of which you have many that I love," Dave said. "What kind of vow could I possibly give you? There are so many things we don't have control over in this life. What can I say to you that I have absolute control over? I'm going to steal a line that Tamara wrote in a letter to me in December of 2000. Whether it was intended or not, it's one of the most gratifying compliments I've ever had. She said it about my marriage with Teresa. And I want to share it with you now. No matter what happens in our lives, I will love you well."

Kellie had tears streaming down her face. "Thank you," she said, raising a tissue up to dab the moisture before it caused her makeup to run.

"Amen," the pastor said.

"Amen," Kellie added.

It was Kellie's turn, and for one of the rare times in her life, she struggled to get the words out. She had to concentrate to suppress the emotion.

"Twenty-five years ago," she said, "You came into my life, or at least that big guy's life."

She pointed over Dave's shoulder at Brett.

"I was a little teenage girl hiding behind doors to watch you. You were magnificent then and you are magnificent now. And I can't believe you've reappeared in my life when I was at my darkest of darks, and the light at the end of the tunnel was an oncoming train. I told God I surrendered because there was no one for me.

"And then there you were and God showed me His plan. You and the kids are my destiny. I absolutely couldn't live without you because you are my life. All four of you—the fabulous four. I didn't have a choice. I moved to Portland and I've been led here by a guardian angel, and we all in this room know who that was, and is.

"I have a rainbow everyday. In a city famous for rain the sun always shines on us, and I'm so happy. You are the most incredible man that was ever made. I know that sounds corny but it's true. And everybody in this room knows what I'm talking about. I love you. You are my victory."

"Amen."

The pastor asked for the rings, and Dave and Kellie slid them onto one another's fingers.

After a blessing from the pastor, he invited Dave and Kellie forward to sign the marriage license that would legally unite them.

A pianist began playing "The Rose" as Dave and Kellie moved from signing their names to lighting a unity candle. Then they retuned to their original places on the stage and resumed holding hands. Kaysie and Brett stepped forward to sign as the official witnesses.

The pastor spoke.

"Kellie and Dave have asked a few of their friends to write a few words and I'm going to share some of those with you now," he said.

He held several pieces of paper in his hand.

"This is from Kellie's mom: What I can say about this whole situation is, Wow. For so long, Kellie's waited for this day. We're excited for her happiness and our newly extended family. We're thankful that our prayers have been answered."

The pastor read two more before coming to Lauren's page.

"To dad: For the past year and a half you have been the most supportive, loving father any child could ask for. I admire everything about you, especially the fact people thought it was too soon—and you went with what you thought was right and everything worked out perfectly. That's why we're here today. Kellie's wonderful and we're so glad you chose her. To Kellie: From the first moment I met you I knew you were the one that our family needed. You are the strongest, most loving person I know, and I look forward to our future together. Welcome to our family. I love you."

The final words came from a page written by Brett.

"Last night I went to bed and asked the Lord and Teresa to please give me the words to explain to hundreds of people the concept of love after tragedy. This morning at 5:30 I was awakened, a 300-pound sobbing mess, with these thoughts that so overwhelmed me.

"I believe the power that has placed my bright, bubbly, beautiful sister with my big, bad, but brokenhearted best friend is the miracle of divine love. This unseen and unstoppable love from God slammed Kellie and Dave together like a train wreck right at the time of all our darkest tragedy; not because we were tacky, but because that was exactly when we needed to start to heal.

"I believe Kellie and Dave's love is so remarkable because it has helped to heal kids, parents, friends and family as quickly as possible. I have witnessed the miracle of God's power through Kellie's and Dave's love. I've seen it heal and unite three wonderful families, and I know that having been a small part of it has changed me forever."

When the pastor was done reading, Wilma came forward and read a poem that she wrote, and then introduced Nikki to sing a song that she had written for the occasion, called "I Wish You A Rainbow." Once again, Nikki sang with nerves of steel.

When Nikki's song was through, the pastor led the congregation to one more emotional twist.

"It may seem strange to sing a patriotic song at a wedding, but as we sing these words it will remind us the hands of God are upon us," the pastor said.

On the back of the wedding program were the words to "America the Beautiful."

The pastor closed the ceremony with a final prayer.

Dave planted two kisses on Kellie's mouth, then took her by the hand and led her back up the aisle.

Emptied cans of Hamm's beer, tied with string to the tailgate and bumper of the white Chevy diesel pickup, scraped across the pavement as Dave and Kellie waved out the windows in the church parking lot.

Lauren and Makenna had decorated the truck, scrawling "Dave & Kellie," "Just Hitched" and "The Love Shack" on the windows with white shoe polish.

Dave gave Kellie a long kiss before he pulled onto Stafford Road, heading north to Interstate 5 and toward the reception.

"Well, we did it," Dave said happily.

"Yes, we certainly did," Kellie said. She sat as close to Dave as she could, hugging him as he drove. It was the first time all day that they were alone together for a few minutes of relative quiet.

"Wow, for a minute there I didn't think I was going to get through it. I was crying so much," Kellie said. "Is my makeup all smeared?"

As she asked, Kellie glanced up into the rearview mirror.

"Nope, you look beautiful," Dave said.

"That church was packed," Kellie said, recalling her view from the front of the sanctuary. "I think all 200 people showed. And I don't think there was a dry eye in the house, except of course, yours."

Dave's demeanor had remained confident and upbeat all day.

"Well, you cried enough for both of us," Dave said teasingly. Kellie playfully made a fist and slugged him in the arm.

"I was emotional," Kellie said. "It was my first wedding. You're just a pro because you've done it before."

"Maybe," he agreed.

On the radio, all they heard were commercials. Kellie grew annoyed by them.

"Hey, I want to do something weird, OK?"

"Sure, what is it?" Dave asked.

"I want to hear 'These Boots and Me,'" Kellie said. "Do you have that CD here?"

"Sure," Dave said, a little surprised. "It's right in that case, in the first sleeve. Pop it in."

"I know it's a little weird to want to hear a song about Teresa on my wedding day," Kellie said. "It's just that . . . I felt her presence at the wedding so strongly tonight. I just really want to hear it."

She got no argument from Dave.

"Fine by me," he said. "You know I love that song."

Dave appreciated Kellie's openness and respect for his former wife. It had been there ever since their trip to the coast 15 months earlier.

As the song began, Kellie closed her eyes and tilted her head back, smiling as she enjoyed each word and note.

"She's here, Dave," Kellie said. "And she's always with us. Do you feel it?"

Dave nodded.

"I do," he said. "She's our co-pilot."

"And one of my best friends," Kellie added. "You know, Dave, I couldn't do all of this without her. She guides me all the time. Whenever I feel discouraged she picks me up. She's my biggest fan."

Kellie felt a rush of emotion begin rise up in her throat. She wanted to continue with her thought.

"I know she is," Dave said tenderly. "She appreciates all you do for us. She knows I'd probably screw the kids up without you here."

Kellie knew Dave was joking a bit about that, but he was serious too.

"You're sweet," Kellie said. "You're wrong though. You'd do a great job without me. I'm just glad that I'm here and get to share in all of this with you."

"Me too," Dave said. "We're a great team. All three of us."

Teresa's words in life had been loud and clear. Dave thought about how he had come full circle by adhering to her wishes.

"You can choose to be a victim," she would say. "Or you can choose to move on. And if you choose to move on and make something better of your situation, I will help you."

Dave smiled as he pulled the truck into the parking lot of the Crowne Plaza.

He spotted a prime parking spot near the front doors and circled around the lot to take it.

"That was perfect timing," Dave said, satisfied as he turned off the ignition.

He opened the door and hopped down. Kellie, in her tight-fitting wedding dress, followed him out the driver's side door and he held her waist and hand as she carefully slid out of the seat and landed on her high heels.

"Thanks, babe," Kellie said. They started to walk towards the entrance of the hotel, holding hands, and Kellie suddenly stopped.

"Dave, look," she said, pointing toward an old sedan parked next to the truck.

It was an Oregon plate. The digits were 333.

"Huh!" Dave said, amazed. "Would you look at that? What are the odds?"

"Yeah, and that we would find a parking spot right next to it on our wedding day when we had just been talking about Teresa and listening to 'Boots,'" Kellie said.

They agreed it must be more than a coincidence.

"We've got to find a camera and take a photo of this," Kellie said. "I know. We'll use your mom's when she gets here. They should be arriving soon."

Jim and Diane Reifert came walking up to Dave and Kellie in the parking lot, greeting them with congratulations.

"Hi guys!" Diane said. "Great wedding!"

"Thanks," Kellie said, beaming. She hugged her friend and Dave shook Jim's hand.

"I'll bet you're glad that's over with," Jim said. "Now the fun can begin."

"You better believe it," Dave said. "We're ready to party."

Kellie noticed Wilma's car enter the parking lot.

"Oh, good, Dave," Kellie said. "There's your mom. We have to flag her down to take a picture of this for us."

Kellie paused to point out the license plate to Diane.

"You don't happen to have a camera, do you?" Kellie asked.

"We have a thing with the number three and we can't believe this license plate is here on our wedding day," Dave explained.

"Yeah, that is weird," Diane agreed. "We're going to head inside. See you in there, OK?"

Kellie and Diane exchanged another hug.

Gary and Wilma joined Dave and Kellie and remarked on the surprising timing and location of the number.

Wilma snapped several photos of it before they all went inside to join the party.

Monday, April 29, 2002

Brett parked his truck and got out to follow Dave and Kellie into The Char Burger, a popular cafeteria-style diner in the picturesque Columbia Gorge town of Cascade Locks. The towering steel structure of the Bridge of the Gods rose just a stone's throw from the parking lot. The bridge links Oregon and Washington and spans one of the most scenic stretches of the Gorge.

The small restaurant had become a traditional stop over the years for the Grills and O'Briens when they traveled between Dufur and the Willamette Valley.

Dave and Kellie were on their way to their honeymoon destination at Kinzua. Brett was going with them—much like he did on Dave's first honeymoon. He wanted to see Teresa's marker and planned to spend some time at the lodge before moving on toward Utah.

After lunch, they moved further east on Interstate 84, to the Dufur exit. They turned south and headed up the hill past sprawling apple and cherry orchards. As they crested the hill, they continued another nine miles through rolling hills and vast expanses of contoured wheat fields. They rounded a final curve before the cemetery, and Dave saw the familiar outcropping of trees that stood next to where Teresa had been laid to rest.

Dave's mind flashed back to the December day 17 months earlier, when he had come to this place to say good-bye to Teresa. This time, he and Kellie were here to leave their wedding bouquet next to her grave. It was a symbol of Dave's fulfilled promise.

Dave admired the silhouette of Mt. Hood rising into the western horizon as Brett pulled up next to his pickup.

"It's beautiful up here," Brett said. "I don't think I've ever seen anything quite like it."

Dave smiled.

"I know, isn't it gorgeous?" Kellie replied.

"It might not be for everybody, but this is an important place for Teresa and her family," Dave said. "She loved it here and so this is where we thought she'd like to be."

Brett nodded.

Dave took Kellie by her left hand and they walked together toward Teresa's headstone, maybe a dozen steps away. She held the flowers with her other hand. Brett followed them, hands in his coat pockets.

"Here she is," Dave said, stepping to the side so that Brett could see Teresa's name etched in the marble.

Brett kneeled down to get a closer look at the marker, and he read it out loud, barely over a whisper.

"Wife, mother, daughter, sister, teacher, friend—Our Angel," Brett said, reading the inscription. Then he added. "Hello there, friend. They've got you in a pretty neat place."

Brett stood up, and backed away.

Kellie handed Dave the flowers and he moved forward to set them down in front of the headstone.

For a moment, all were silent.

Then Dave, with his head bowed, spoke. Kellie and Brett stood on either side of him.

"Well, as you know, we're doing great," Dave began. "We tied the knot. It was a beautiful ceremony and you were a huge part of it, so it seemed like a good idea to bring you these flowers and to let you know how much we still think of you. You'll always be a part of us."

Dave paused again.

"Do you guys mind if I have a few words with her?" Brett asked.

"No," Dave said. He and Kellie wandered back in the direction of the truck.

Brett removed his glasses. They were beginning to fog up as the moisture began to seep from his eyes.

He stepped closer and kneeled down once again.

"T," Brett said. "Can you believe we pulled it off? It was very fast and it sure ruffled some feathers. But you told me it had to be done and now it is. You and I both know that this fixes a lot of things. Thank you for showing me God's power and choosing me to help do this for you. I love you, T."

Brett put his hand on his knee and pressed on it as he straightened his legs to stand up. He wiped his face on the flannel sleeve of his shirt and put his glasses back on.

Back at Brighton High School, it had been Brett's job, as center, to protect Dave, the star quarterback. Brett felt a certain pride in the fact that 20-some years later he had worked to protect Dave, and his kids, again.

Kellie came up behind him and put a hand on Brett's shoulder.

"I want a minute with her too, and then we can go," Kellie said. Brett nodded. He turned and walked over to Dave, and they walked over to the edge of the barbed wire fence and looked out over the expansive green fields.

Kellie stood in front of the marker and held her hands together as if to pray.

"I can't believe it," Kellie said. "Dave Grill is mine. It still hasn't sunk in yet. Thank you for that. Thank you for the gift of him and thank you for the gift of the kids too. I love them like they are my own. And thanks for guiding me. I know how much you help and support me. And I love you. You're our guardian angel."

Kellie sniffed back her tears and turned to go. When she reached the truck, she reached out for Dave and hugged him.

"Are we ready to go now?" Dave asked. Kellie and Brett nodded, solemnly.

Dave turned the truck around and prepared to accelerate onto the highway. Kellie, meanwhile, ejected a CD they had been listening to. The radio snapped on. It was KWJJ, a Portland station that Dave had never known to come in so far away from the city.

His head snapped to the right to catch Kellie's reaction to the song on the radio.

"Oh my God, Dave," Kellie said, emphatically. "Call Brett on his cell."

Dave dialed Brett.

"Turn your radio to 99.5," Dave instructed. Brett told him he already had it and was in the middle of reaching for his phone.

Dave set the phone down and slowed the truck to a crawl, fearing that he would lose the signal. The words coming through the speakers seemed to be intended for him.

It was "The Dance," by Garth Brooks, coming through crisp and clear on a radio station that by all rights shouldn't have been able to reach them.

Dave sat staring at the radio, frozen. Kellie reached out to grab his hand.

Brett watched through his windshield and pressed on the brake pedal. He could feel a surge of emotion starting to rise up in his throat and took a deep breath to head it off.

Static began to overtake the signal, and by the time the last of Brooks' words had been sung and the instrumental began to fade, the clarity of the station was gone.

There was no questioning the clarity of Teresa's communication. "I'm here," she seemed to say. "And thank you for the flowers."

All three of them felt it, knew it, and trusted it.

Dave pulled back onto the road and continued on.

The boots.

DAVE

KELLIE

THE KIDS (PAST)

THE KIDS (PRESENT)

TERESA & DAVE

KELLIE & DAVE

Wedding day: August 4, 1984

Wedding day: April 27, 2002

Kellie and a rainbow in Depoe Bay, Oregon on January 26, 2001.

Dave in Depoe Bay.

Kellie and Dave pose with the rainbow in Depoe Bay.

ABOUT THE AUTHORS

Doug Binder, a sports reporter for *The Oregonian* in Portland, has written about sports and sports figures for the past 12 years. Before returning to his native Portland he worked for the Corvallis (Ore.) *Gazette-Times* and the Bozeman (Mont.) *Daily Chronicle*. His list of writing awards date back to high school. *Send Me A Sign* is his first book.

∞

Dave Grill and Kellie Poulsen-Grill live in Wilsonville, Oregon where they are the parents of three teenagers. Nicole attends the University of Oregon, and Lauren and John are both students at Tualatin High School. Dave continues to be active in youth sports and works for Metro Metals in Portland. Kellie is a proud twin who manages a busy household and enjoys traveling. They also continue to dabble in song writing. *Send Me A Sign* is their story.